COMPANY LAW Made Simple

The Made Simple series
has been created
primarily for self-education
but can equally well
be used as
an aid to group study.
However complex the subject,
the reader is taken
step by step,
clearly and methodically,
through the course. Each volume
has been prepared by experts,
using throughout the
Made Simple technique of teaching.
Consequently the gaining
of knowledge now becomes
an experience to be enjoyed.

Accounting
Acting and Stagecraft
Additional Mathematics
Advertising
Anthropology
Applied Economics
Applied Mathematics
Applied Mechanics
Art Appreciation
Art of Speaking
Art of Writing
Biology
Book-keeping
British Constitution
Business and Administrative
  Organisation
Calculus
Chemistry
Childcare
Commerce
Company Administration
Company Law
Computer Programming
Cookery
Cost and Management
  Accounting
Data Processing
Dressmaking
Economic History
Economic and Social
  Geography
Economics
Electricity
Electronic Computers
Electronics
English
English Literature

Export
Financial Management
French
Geology
German
Human Anatomy
Italian
Journalism
Latin
Law
Management
Marketing
Mathematics
Modern Electronics
Modern European History
New Mathematics
Office Practice
Organic Chemistry
Philosophy
Photography
Physical Geography
Physics
Pottery
Psychology
Rapid Reading
Retailing
Russian
Salesmanship
Secretarial Practice
Social Services
Soft Furnishing
Spanish
Statistics
Transport and Distribution
Typing
Woodwork

COMPANY LAW Made Simple

Ronald R. Pitfield, ACIS, MInstAM, AMBIM

Made Simple Books
W. H. ALLEN London
A Howard & Wyndham Company

Printed and bound in Great Britain
by Richard Clay (The Chaucer Press), Ltd.,
Bungay, Suffolk
for the publishers W. H. Allen & Company Ltd,
44 Hill Street, London W1X 8LB

ISBN 0 491 02076 7 casebound
ISBN 0 491 02086 4 paperbound

Preface

The three Companies Acts now in operation contain no less than 620 extant sections and 24 schedules. Additionally, there are other statutes which are applicable to companies. In elaboration of this mass of legislation there is a very large collection of law reports. The student of company law is therefore faced with an extensive range of often complex legal precepts.

The aim of this book is to provide a reasoned and logical description of the purposes of the law and the mechanics by which its objectives are attained. Showing the *reasoning* giving rise to various legal strictures should make it easier to grasp the technicalities of the law. The aim, therefore, is not to present an 'outline' version (the subject is, in fact, dealt with completely and in adequate detail), but to promote an understanding of how and why the law operates as it does. With a basis of understanding it is much easier to acquire that degree of knowledge demanded of students and required by those interested in the subject.

Learning can also be facilitated by the style of presenting information to the reader. This principle is followed in the book by the method of grouping the subject areas and the use of headed and subheaded sections. The aim is to provide a structured treatment to try to make it easier to assimilate what is essentially a complicated subject. An easier understanding is further promoted by the provision of extensive cross-referencing in the text, thereby avoiding constant 'back-tracking' through the index.

Detailed repetitions of the often abstruse wording of sections of the Acts are not given except where it is vital to do so, but the basic material is presented always. The sections of the Acts are referred to throughout and the reader should therefore have the Acts immediately available for reference. All the relevant sections and cases are indexed at the end of the book.

It is hoped that this method of presenting the law will be of practical benefit to the businessman who wishes to have a better understanding of the subject. Particular attention is given to the requirements of those who have to study the subject with a view to passing examinations, and in this respect emphasis is given to clarifying those matters which one knows from experience present particular difficulty.

As a further aid to students there is, at the end of the book, a list of revision questions which indicate areas from which examination questions could well derive. Where appropriate, brief guidance to the answers is included. Some of the questions are designed to lead the student to 'search', so that a particular legal aspect is more clearly understood and remembered. It is considered that this method is more valuable to the student than providing him with examination-style questions in the hope that some of them will appear in an actual paper!

R.R.P.

References to the Companies Acts

All references to sections are to the *Companies Act, 1948,* unless otherwise indicated. References to sections of the *Companies Act, 1967,* and the *Companies Act, 1976,* are shown thus: S.33(1967) and S.12 (1976).

The Registrar of Companies

The Registrar of Companies is usually referred to as 'the Registrar'.

To Ena
for her understanding and encouragement

Contents

1

THE NATURE OF LIMITED COMPANIES

Historical Background

The Oldest Form of Companies

The history of companies extends back several centuries, the earliest companies being those formed by Royal Charter and known as Chartered Companies or sometimes as Common Law Corporations. The Bank of England, for example, was formed as a Chartered Company in 1694; the Hudson's Bay Company was established in 1670; and the formation of the East India Company was as long ago as 1600. The granting of a Charter was a royal prerogative which was further facilitated by the *Chartered Companies Act* of 1837, enabling the Crown to bestow the advantages of incorporation by Letters Patent on groups associated together for trade. The extent of the members' liability for company debts is as determined by the terms of the Charter or Letters Patent, as the case may be.

Royal Charters are today granted to non-trading bodies such as learned societies. Charters granted in the past hundred years include those for the Institute of Chartered Accountants, the Institute of Chartered Secretaries and Administrators and the Law Society.

A chartered company *may* (but need not) register under the Companies Act (S. 382), in which case the provisions of the Act will apply unless exempted by the Department of Trade (S. 435 and the Fourteenth Schedule).

Later Developments

In the period of industrial development in the early nineteenth century, many companies were formed. Because there were no legal provisions specific to companies, such concerns were treated as partnerships in law. This carried the serious disadvantage of unlimited liability on the members, which resulted in the ruin of many investors following the not infrequent collapse of companies.

Exceptions were those companies formed by special Acts of Parliament, known as 'statutory companies'. These were created to promote public utility enterprises, such as the owning of railways, docks, gas and water undertakings, etc. Developments in those areas was possible only if the compulsory purchase of land was permitted and the only available

1

means was to bestow the necessary powers by individual Acts of Parliament. The members of such companies enjoyed the advantage of limited liability for company debts. (Most public utility companies have since been nationalised.)

In 1844 the *Joint Stock Companies Act* gave facilities for creating companies by registration without the need for a Royal Charter or special Act of Parliament. This, unlike the old partnerships, carried the benefits of the company being recognised as a legal entity with contractual rights but still did not bestow limited liability. However, in 1855 the *Limited Liability Act* provided this valuable advantage and thus started the rapid growth in the number of companies which has continued ever since.

The previous legislation was repealed and consolidated by the *Companies Act* of 1862, which with amending Acts was consolidated by the Act of 1908, followed by the Act of 1929. The latter Act was amended by the *Companies Act* of 1947 and followed by the *Companies Act* of 1948, which made far-reaching changes and is now the principal Act.

The 1948 Act

Besides including all such previous legislation as was not amended or repealed, this Act introduced a considerable amount of new law, including that relevant to prospectuses, disclosures concerning directors and the form and content of the accounts.

The 1967 Act

This Act added to the 1948 Act (that is, it is not a consolidating Act), besides making important amendments. The main aim was to ensure wider disclosure of information to members and investors generally. It also stipulates that *all* limited companies must file accounts with the Registrar. (The 1948 Act had not placed this requirement on certain companies, which were referred to as 'exempt private companies'. Such of those companies as wished to avoid publication of their accounts were given the opportunity in the 1967 Act to re-register as unlimited companies—see page 9.)

The 1976 Act

This Act introduced, *inter alia*, important regulations concerning the laying and delivery of accounts. Substantial changes were made relevant to auditors, and the requirements for disclosure of interests in shares were made more demanding.

Citation of the Acts

The following Acts may be cited together as the '*Companies Acts 1948 to 1976*': the *Companies Act, 1948*, Parts I and III of the *Companies Act, 1967*, the *Companies (Floating Charges and Receivers) (Scotland) Act*,

1972, section 9 of the *European Communities Act, 1972*, sections 1 to 4 of the *Stock Exchange* (*Completion of Bargains*) *Act, 1976*, section 9 of the *Insolvency Act, 1976*, and the *Companies Act, 1976*.

Limited Companies as Legal Entities

A company is a legal entity; that is, it is a 'person' in law and is quite separate from those persons who constitute the company. Thus, if a company has two shareholders there exist three legal persons: the two members and the company. A company is a form of 'corporation aggregate'; that is, one consisting of persons contemporaneously associated so as to be regarded as one legal person.

The principle was firmly established in *Saloman v. Saloman & Co., Ltd* (1897). In that case, most of the shares were held by Saloman, who was also owed £10,000 in the form of a secured loan. The company was wound up as insolvent, the assets realising only £6,000. The unsecured creditors contended that to all intents and purposes Saloman *was* the company and therefore could not owe money to himself. The House of Lords decided against the creditors, stating that in law Saloman and the company were two different persons. Saloman was therefore entitled to the available assets in his preferred position of secured creditor.

The *Interpretation Act, 1889*, states that the word 'person' in any Act of Parliament includes an *incorporated* firm unless the context shows that only a natural person is intended.

In *Lee v. Lee's Air Farming Ltd* (1960), Lee held 2,999 of the company's 3,000 shares and was the governing director and chief pilot at a salary. Whilst working for the company he was killed in an air crash and his widow claimed compensation from the company on the ground that he had been an employee under a contract of service. It was held that the company and Lee were separate persons in law and therefore the claim was upheld.

This basic and very important principle is, however, subject to exceptions where otherwise it would be abused. Thus, in *Jones and Another v. Lipman and Another* (1962) it was decided that a person may not avoid a decree of specific performance by forming a company and transferring the object of the decree outside his personal responsibility.

The application of the principle of separate personality can, where the law so decides, be tempered. This is known as 'lifting the veil of incorporation'. Thus, the Acts contain instances enabling identification of the persons who in fact control the company and providing for personal liability to attach to members in respect of transactions in the name of the company.

The Advantages of Incorporation

Capitalisation of Goodwill

If the owner of a business converts it into a company he may capitalise the goodwill he has built up in that he could sell the business to the new company at a price based on its profitability potential. If the purchase price was in the form of shares, his interest in the company would continue and if he held sufficient shares he could have a controlling interest. Alternatively, he could accept cash instead of shares and sever his connection with the business. Whichever course he adopted, profit would accrue from his ability to sell the business at the market price as a consequence of the large amount of money which would be available from the investing public.

Perpetual Succession

A company will continue in existence, unaffected by any changes in its ownership. The membership could be altered completely by the transferring of shares; unlike a partnership, the business would not come to an end because a member wished to leave or because of the bankruptcy or death of a member.

The property of a company belongs to the company, whereas assets of a partnership firm are in the joint ownership of the partners. The withdrawal of a partner may cause an upheaval in the firm because of the requirement to repay his share of the business.

Contractual Capacity

A company may incur contractual obligations, but a contract by a partnership is the joint and several responsibility of the partners. Also, a company may sue and be sued by a shareholder.

Separation of the Management Function

Management of a company is in the hands of elected directors. Accordingly, shareholders who are not directors may not bind the company by their acts. Partners, however, may involve the other partners in obligations entered into by them for the firm.

A further advantage is that management of a company is a specialised function. The directors would be chosen for their apparent ability to manage and a non-director shareholder, no matter how large his investment, would have no rights in that respect. A partnership business may well be ruined by the inexperience of a partner with a large financial stake who insists on making important decisions.

Transferability of Shares

Shares listed on the Stock Exchange are freely transferable. A shareholder may therefore withdraw his interest at any time, subject to his finding a buyer for his shares. The advantage of such liquidity is therefore an attraction to investors.

Limited Liability

The prime advantage is, of course, the fact that at the worst a shareholder can lose only what he has paid or agreed to pay for his shares. A partner in an insolvent firm is liable to contribute to the firm's debts from his personal estate.

The Appeal to Investors

In addition to the obvious advantage of limited liability, investment in companies has other attractions.

A variety of securities can be offered to meet the particular requirements of investors. As explained later, specific characteristics attach to different types of security, so that an investor may choose between a comparatively safe share at a fixed rate of return and one with a greater risk carrying the possibility of high returns; he may decide on a safe investment in the form of a secured debenture; or he may take other securities which offer various options exercisable at a later date.

Investors in companies also have the protection afforded by the Companies Acts and other relevant legislation. If the shares are 'listed' on the Stock Exchange, advantages accrue to the investors in the form of marketing facilities, the sundry measures of protection available, the daily quotation of prices, etc.

A prospective investor as well as a present investor has available to him the considerable amount of information which a company must disclose and which is open to inspection by anyone.

There are also the rules and regulations specific to any one company which can be examined. These are considered in detail later in the book but at this stage it may be useful to mention them briefly. The **Memorandum of Association** contains such important information as the objects of the company—that is, its purposes and any limitations to them. The **Articles of Association** list the internal rules of the company. (In this book they are usually referred to, as a matter of convenience, as the 'Memorandum' and the 'Articles'. Where reference is made to 'Table A', this refers to a model set of Articles provided by the First Schedule to the 1948 Act, which a company may or may not adopt, as it wishes.)

Thus, before investing, an investor has a wealth of information available to him. After he has invested, information continues to be offered. And at all stages he has safeguards in the form of legislation and, where relevant, in the form of rules imposed by the Stock Exchange.

2

TYPES OF REGISTERED COMPANIES

Classification of Companies

There are two broad methods of classifying companies incorporated under the Companies Acts (known as **registered companies**). One refers to **status**; that is, whether a company is a public company or a private company. The other relates to the **possible liabilities of the members**; that is, if it is limited by shares, limited by guarantee or unlimited.

Public Companies and Private Companies

Distinction by the Articles

Every registered company is a public company unless its Articles contain the provisions necessary to constitute it as a private company. By S. 28 a company will be classified as a **private company** if its Articles:

(*a*) *Restrict the right to transfer shares.* (A public company *may* restrict the right to transfer shares if its Articles so permit—see page 68.)

(*b*) *Limit the number of members to fifty*, exclusive of employees and past employees who have continued to be members since they were employed. (There is no maximum membership for a public company.)

(*c*) *Prohibit any invitation to the public to subscribe for its shares or debentures.* (Thus, only a *public* company may go to the public for finance.) Under S. 4 of the *Protection of Depositors Act, 1963*, a private company which advertises for **deposits** is deemed to be *not* a private company for specified purposes under the Companies Acts.

Thus, the status of private company is established by the **terms of its Articles.**

Privileges and Exemptions of Private Companies

Private companies are privileged in relation to public companies in the following respects:

(*a*) The minimum membership is two, whereas a public company must have at least seven members (S. 1). A private company may continue with *one* member for six months before that member assumes unlimited liability (S. 31).

(*b*) Shares may be allotted immediately the certificate of incorporation

6

is received; a public company may not do so until it has received the minimum subscription (S. 47) (see page 54).

(*c*) It does not have to file a statement in lieu of prospectus before allotment (S. 48).

(*d*) It may commence business immediately upon incorporation without the formalities required of a public company (S. 109) (see page 56).

(*e*) There is no requirement to hold a Statutory Meeting or file a Statutory Report (S. 130) (see page 143).

(*f*) It need have only one director (S. 176), but that director may not also be the secretary (S. 177).

(*g*) Separate resolutions are not demanded if more than one director is to be appointed at the same time (S. 183).

(*h*) The age limit regarding directors imposed by S. 185 (see page 81) is not applicable.

(*i*) A proxy may speak at a general meeting (S. 136).

(*j*) Its directors are not subject to S. 181 concerning restrictions on the appointment of directors (see page 78).

(*k*) Subject to the articles, a quorum at a meeting is two (S. 134).

It is a common procedure for a company to be formed as a private company when it is intended that it will later become a public company, in order that it may obtain the privilege (*d*) above. It may thus enter into contracts and then convert to a public company immediately before a public issue is made.

Default by a Private Company

If a private company does not comply with those of its Articles which constitute it as a private company, it ceases to be entitled to the privileges conferred on private companies. If, however, as a result of an application by the company or any interested person, the Court is satisfied that the default was accidental or due to inadvertence or to some other sufficient cause, or on the ground that it is just and equitable to grant relief, it may order that the company be relieved of the consequences of the default (S. 29).

Requirements Specific to Private Companies

Subject to the privileges and exemptions mentioned above a private company must comply with those provisions of the Act which apply to public companies, but with the following additional requirements as prescribed by S. 128:

(*a*) With the Annual Return must be filed a certificate, signed by a director and the secretary, stating that since the previous Return (or since incorporation in the case of a first Return), the conditions of S. 28 have been complied with; that is, the company has continued to be eligible for the status of private company.

(*b*) If the number of members exceed fifty, a certificate similarly signed must state that the excess comprises employees and past employees.

Conversion of a Private Company to a Public Company

If a private company alters its Articles so that they no longer include the S. 28 provisions, the company becomes a public company from the date of the alteration. Within fourteen days it must file with the Registrar, either:

(*a*) A prospectus complying with the Fourth Schedule as required by S. 41 *if it makes an invitation to the public* to subscribe; or

(*b*) *If no invitation is made*, a statement in lieu of prospectus, containing the particulars prescribed in Part I of the Third Schedule. Such a statement must, where relevant, contain reports as specified in Part II of the Third Schedule regarding (*i*) the profits or losses, assets and liabilities, of any business to be acquired from unissued shares or debentures of the company, and (*ii*) any company or group of companies which will become a subsidiary by reason of a purchase of shares out of unissued shares or debentures of the registering company (S. 30).

Conversion of a Public Company to a Private Company

This can be achieved by altering the Articles so that they contain the provisions relevant to private companies.

Companies Limited by Shares

By far the commonest form of registered company is that where the liability of the members to contribute to the assets of the company is limited to any amount unpaid on their shares.

Companies Limited by Guarantee

These companies may or may not have a share capital. The guarantee consists of an undertaking by members to contribute up to a stated amount in the event of winding up (S. 1 (2)(*b*)), such a guarantee being incorporated in the Memorandum (S. 2 (3)).

Most guarantee companies do not have profit-making as an objective and therefore are mainly professional bodies, trade organisations, educational establishments, charities, etc.

The following provisions apply:

(*a*) The guarantee may be enforced at the time of winding up on those who were then members, and on those who ceased to be members within one year prior to winding up, for liabilities of the company contracted before membership ceased (S. 2 (3)).

(*b*) Special Articles of Association must be registered (S. 6) and these must state the number of members with which the company proposes to be registered (S. 7 (2)).

(*c*) A guarantee company *without a share capital* must set out its Memorandum and Articles in the form required in the First Schedule, Table C. If it *has* a share capital, the documents must conform with Table D of the First Schedule.

(*d*) If the company has no share capital, no person other than the members may participate in any division of profits (S. 21).

(*e*) If the company has a share capital, it must file the Annual Return required by S. 124.

(*f*) If the company has *no* share capital, it: (*i*) can commence business on incorporation, no statement in lieu of prospectus or certificate to commence business being required (Ss. 48 and 109); (*ii*) is not required to hold a Statutory Meeting (S. 130); (*iii*) must file a special form of Annual Return (S. 125).

(*g*) If the company has a share capital, a member is liable to contribute in a winding up any amount unpaid on his shares *as well as* the amount of his guarantee (S. 212(3)).

(*h*) If the company increases either its membership or capital, or both, notice of the increase must be given to the Registrar within fifteen days (Ss. 7(3) and 63(1)).

Unlimited Companies

Members of unlimited companies derive all the benefits of incorporation except that their liability is unlimited. Any liability ceases after a year from the date of ceasing to be a member. Such companies are useful for managing family estates, for example.

(*a*) An unlimited company without a share capital must file an Annual Return in the form prescribed by S. 125. If it has a share capital the Return must be in the form required by S. 124.

(*b*) Special Articles must be filed with the Memorandum (S. 6). These must state the proposed number of members and the amount of the share capital (if any) (S. 7(1)).

(*c*) The Memorandum and Articles of an unlimited company with a share capital must in the form set out in Table E of the First Schedule (S. 11).

Re-registration of a Limited Company as an Unlimited Company

Prior to the 1967 Act, 'exempt private companies' were not required to file accounts, but this type of company was abolished under the Act and now all private companies must publish accounts. A company wishing to continue to enjoy confidentiality of its accounts may, under S. 43 of the 1967 Act, re-register as an unlimited company.

(*a*) Application in the prescribed form, signed by a director or the secretary, must be lodged with the Registrar, setting out the alterations to the Memorandum and Articles so as to conform with the requirements relevant to unlimited companies; accompanied by:

(*i*) an assent to the change to unlimited liability, signed by or on behalf of *all* the members;

(*ii*) a statutory declaration by *all* the directors that the persons by whom or for whom the assent was submitted constitute the whole membership of the company;

(These conditions are obviously necessary to ensure that no member assumes unlimited liability without his agreement.)

(*iii*) printed copies of the Memorandum and the Articles incorporating the alterations and additions.

(*b*) The Registrar will issue a Certificate of Incorporation as evidence that the requirements have been met and that the amended Memorandum and Articles have become effective.

Re-registration of an Unlimited Company as a Limited Company

Where a company was previously known to be an unlimited company and the members now wish to limit their possible liability, it is obviously necessary to ensure that the rights of creditors are not thereby endangered. The legal provisions are outlined at (*e*) below. S.44(1967) prescribes the procedure (replacing that of S.16 of the 1948 Act) whereby an unlimited company may assume the status of a limited company, provided it had not previously changed to an unlimited company under S.43(1967).

(*a*) The procedure requires a special resolution to be passed, specifying the manner of the limitation (i.e. by shares or by guarantee) and what, if any, the share capital is to be. (The resolution must provide for alterations to the Memorandum and alterations and additions to the Articles such as are necessary for them to be in a form appropriate to a limited company.)

(*b*) An application in the prescribed form, signed by a director or the secretary, must be lodged with the Registrar.

(*c*) Printed copies of the Memorandum and Articles as altered must be submitted.

(*d*) The Registrar will issue a Certificate of Incorporation appropriate to the new status of the company.

(*e*) In the event of subsequent winding up of the company:

(*i*) present members who were members at the time of re-registration have *unlimited* liability to contribute to debts contracted *before re-registration*;

(*ii*) past members who were members at the time of re-registration are liable as contributories if the winding up commences within three years of re-registration;

(*iii*) if none of the members at the time of winding up were members at the time of re-registration, both present and past members at the time of re-registration are liable to contribute without limit, notwithstanding that the existing members have already satisfied the contribution required of them.

Overseas Companies

An overseas company is one incorporated outside Great Britain which has a place of business within Great Britain (S. 406).

(*a*) Within one month of establishing a place of business, it must deliver to the Registrar:

(*i*) a certified copy of its Charter, Statutes or Memorandum or Articles, or other statement of its constitution, together with an English translation if necessary;

(*ii*) particulars (similar to those required under S. 200) of its directors and secretary;

(*iii*) names and addresses of one or more persons resident in Great Britain authorised to accept service of legal processes and notices on behalf of the company (S. 407).

(*b*) Any alteration to the above information or of the corporate name must be notified to the Registrar within twenty-one days (S. 409 as amended by the 1976 Act).

(*c*) A balance sheet, profit and loss account and, where relevant, group accounts must be filed in respect of each accounting reference period of the company, the accounts being in such a form and having annexed such documents as would have been required if it had been a company within the meaning of the 1948 Act (S. 9(1976)). Penalties for non-compliance are prescribed in S. 11(1976). With certain modifications, Ss. 2 and 3 (1976) regarding the accounting reference period are applicable (S. 10(1976))—(see Chapter 12).

(*d*) In the event of a prospectus being issued inviting subscriptions in Great Britain for its shares or debentures, it must state the company's date and country of incorporation. It must also give particulars of the instrument establishing the constitution of the company; the provisions under which its incorporation was effected; an address in Great Britain where these documents (or copies thereof) can be inspected; and the address of its principal office in Great Britain if it has established a place of business in Great Britain.

The contents of the prospectus must, subject to certain provisions, conform with the Fourth Schedule (S. 417).

(*e*) It must exhibit in every place in Great Britain at which it carries on business, the company's name and country of incorporation, and a statement (where appropriate) that the liability of its members is limited. Similar information must be given on all letters, bill-heads, etc. (S. 411).

(*f*) The provisions of Ss. 95 and 105 relevant to the registration of charges on property in England (see pages 109 and 111) also apply to overseas companies (S. 106).

(*g*) The Registrar has authority to refuse registration of the corporate name of the company if it is thought to be undesirable (S. 31 (1976)).

Associations not for Profit

This term refers to companies (usually limited by guarantee) formed to promote commerce, art, science, religion, charity or any other useful objects, which intend to apply their profits in the promotion of such objects and which prohibit payment of dividends to their members.

Under S. 19 such a company may, by special resolution, apply for a licence to omit the word 'Limited' from its name. Alternatively, it may apply for it to be omitted when it registers as a company. Where such a licence is granted, the company is excepted from the provisions of S. 108 concerning publication of its name (see page 22) and the requirement of S. 124 to send a list of its members to the Registrar with its Annual Return. But the *European Communities Act* S. 9 (7) requires there to be mentioned in business letters and order forms that it is a limited company.

3

FORMATION AND INCORPORATION

As mentioned in the previous chapter, if it is intended that a company should operate as a public company it is common practice first to form it as a private company and immediately thereafter to convert it into a public company. Thus, the legal entity provided by company status would first be achieved so that as a private company it may enter into contracts. Later, the public would be invited to subscribe to what would then be a public company.

It may be useful to give an outline of the complete process so as to provide an easier understanding of the stages involved and their positions in the sequence of events:

(1) The procedure for **registration**—in this case as a private company —would be adopted (see page 16).

(2) The company would then receive its **Certificate of Incorporation,** confirming it as a body corporate. As a private company it could then enter into contracts.

(3) **The Articles would be altered** to remove S. 28 provisions relevant to private companies (see page 8).

(4) **A prospectus would be published** (or an Offer for Sale made) and shares issued to the public (see Chapter 5).

(5) On meeting the requirements of S. 109, the company would receive its **Trading Certificate** entitling it to commence business (see page 56).

If it was intended that the shares of the company were to be dealt in on the Stock Exchange, application for the shares to be 'admitted to listing' would have been made at a prior stage. If this was so stated in the prospectus, any allotment of shares would be void if application had not in fact been made or if the necessary permission of the Stock Exchange was not forthcoming (see page 55).

Activities prior to Incorporation

Before a company can be legally established, some person or persons must carry out the preliminary work. This would include all the arrangements incidental to setting up any business, such as agreeing contracts, arranging for capital and credit facilities, planning in respect of premises, machinery and equipment, staff, etc. At this stage, of course, the persons

13

concerned would be acting as individuals, but they must also be planning to set up a body with a constitution. They would therefore attend to such matters as the drafting of the Memorandum and the Articles; nominating directors, auditors, solicitors, bankers and the secretary; preparing a prospectus if a public issue was planned; and the registration of the company.

Promoters

The above functions would be carried out by persons generally referred to as 'promoters'. The promoter may be the vendor of the business which it is intended the company will purchase or it may be another person or persons. Frequently, the promoter is a company.

No precise definition of 'promoter' exists and it is a question of fact in any particular instance as to whether or not a person is a promoter, although the Act does say that for the purpose of S.43 (misstatements in a prospectus) the term does *not* include persons acting in a professional capacity (such as a solicitor or accountant). In *Twycross v. Grant* (1877) a promoter was described as 'one who undertakes to form a company with reference to a given project and to set it going, and who takes the necessary steps to accomplish that purpose'. A further description was 'the term "promoter" is a term not of law but of business, usefully summing up in a single word a number of business operations familiar to the commercial world by which a company is brought into existence' (*Whaley Bridge Calico Printing Co. v. Green* (1880)).

Liabilities of Promoters

A promoter is entitled to make a profit but he may not make a *secret* profit. As soon as a promoter begins to act with the proposed company in mind, even though at that time he may not be actively promoting it, he has a fiduciary relationship with the company and must disclose any profit he is making (*Gluckstein v. Barnes* (1900)). The disclosure of profits from the promotion must be made to an independent board of directors (that is, one of which he is not a member or has any influence on) or to subscribers for shares in the company by way of prospectus or otherwise (*Re Leeds and Hanley Theatre of Varieties Ltd* (1902)). The latter method is the most usual practice and many of the regulations concerning prospectuses are designed to ensure full disclosure of the interests of promoters.

Disclosure must be full and explicit. Failure to do so may have the following consequences:

(*a*) The company may rescind the contract by which the profit was made, unless it has become impossible to restore the parties to their former positions (e.g. if innocent third parties have acquired rights under the contract).

(*b*) The company may recover the profit made. In *Jubilee Cotton Mills Ltd v. Lewis* (1924) a vendor was allotted shares before the statement in lieu of prospectus was filed, thereby constituting an irregular allotment. The vendor then sold the shares at a profit and was held liable to account for such profit.

(*c*) A claim may be made by the company for damages for breach of fiduciary duty.

A person convicted on indictment of an offence in connection with the promotion or formation of a company may have a Court order made against him, prohibiting him, without leave of the Court, from acting as a director or taking part in the management of a company for a period not exceeding five years (S. 188). (The legal position of a promoter in connection with a prospectus is discussed in Chapter 5.)

Promotion Services and Preliminary Expenses

A promoter has no automatic right to payment for 'promotion services'. A company obviously cannot, before it is formed, contract to pay, and after formation such services would constitute a past consideration.

'Preliminary expenses' include such items as those relating to the registration of the company; preparing and printing the necessary documents; stamp duties; professional fees, etc. These would be the liability of the promoter unless the company agreed to pay them. The company could make itself liable for them by agreement after it has been registered, and the usual practice is to include the power to do so in the Articles.

A commonly adopted practice is for the preliminary expenses and the cost of promotion services to be added to the assets to be acquired by the company and for the amount to be passed on by the vendor to the promoter.

Pre-incorporation Contracts

As mentioned earlier in the chapter, sundry contracts would normally require to be made before the company is incorporated. Obviously, however, they could not be made by the company because it would not then be in existence. The contracts must therefore be made by another party. Such contracts could not be ratified by the company after its registration, however, because the ostensible principal would not have existed at the time of making the contract (*Kelner v. Baxter* (1866)).

The *European Communities Act, 1972*, now provides that if a contract purports to be made by a company or by a person as agent for a company before its incorporation, it is the *person or agent* making the contract who is personally liable on it, subject to any agreement to the contrary.

A person acting for a company yet to be formed would therefore be unprotected against personal liability unless measures such as follows were adopted:

(*a*) The contract would be prepared in draft form only, expressed as being between the company and the other party, on the understanding it be executed by the company after incorporation. Until that time, neither party would incur any liability. The company would be empowered by its Memorandum to enter into the contract and the Articles would authorise the directors to sign it.

(*b*) The contract would contain a clause stating that it would cease to have effect and would not bind any party to it if the company was not formed within a stipulated time or did not execute the contract within a stated period after formation.

Registration of a Company

A preliminary stage before formal application for registration of a company is made, would be to ask the Registrar if the proposed name of the company would be acceptable (see page 20). First getting 'clearance' of the name would allow the promoters to proceed with the documentation with some confidence, but submission of the documents must follow without delay because a name, even if informally approved, cannot be 'reserved' for a company.

The following documents must be lodged with the Registrar.

(1) **The Memorandum of Association.** The requirement to deliver is contained in S. 12 as amended. It must be signed by at least seven persons in the case of a public company and by two in the case of a private company (S. 1). The signatures must be attested (S. 3). If the company is to have a share capital, each subscriber must write opposite his name the number of shares he is taking up (S. 2).

(2) **The Articles of Association.** These must be filed with the Memorandum (S. 6). They must be signed by the signatories to the Memorandum and the signatures attested (S. 9). If no Articles are filed, Table A will apply (S. 8). In this case, the Memorandum must be endorsed 'Registered without Articles of Association'.

(3) **A form for assessment of capital duty.** Duty is payable *ad valorem* on the nominal value of the shares to be issued.

(4) **A statutory declaration of compliance.** This is a sworn statement by a solicitor engaged in the promotion of the company or by a person named as a director or secretary in the statement delivered under S. 21 (1976) (see below), that the requirements of the Act relevant to registration and the matters precedent and incidental thereto have been complied with (S. 15(2) as amended).

(5) **Particulars of directors and secretaries and consents to act.** S. 21 (1976) provides that with the Memorandum there must be delivered a statement containing the names and other particulars as prescribed by

S. 200 (see page 96) of the persons who are to be the first directors and the person(s) who is(are) to be the first secretary or joint secretaries. The statement must be signed by or on behalf of the subscribers to the Memorandum and must contain a consent to act signed by each person named as a director or secretary. If the Memorandum is delivered by a person acting as agent for the subscribers, the statement must specify that fact and give the name and address of the agent.

(6) **Undertakings concerning qualification shares** (if any) (see page 81). A person may not be named in a prospectus or a statement in lieu of prospectus as a director or proposed director of a company to be formed unless he or his agent authorised in writing has signed the Memorandum for a number of shares not less than his qualification, or has taken from the company and paid or agreed to pay for such shares, or has delivered to the Registrar a statutory declaration that such shares are registered in his name (S. 181 as amended by the 1976 Act).

(As these provisions relate to prospectuses and statements in lieu of prospectus, they do not, of course, apply in respect of private companies.)

(7) **Notice concerning the registered office.** The statement required by S. 21 (1976) at (5) above, must also specify the intended situation of the registered office of the company (S. 23 (1976)).

The Certificate of Incorporation

After approval of the above documents and payment of the fee, the Registrar will issue a certificate to the effect that the company is incorporated and, in the case of a limited company, that the company is limited (S. 13 (1)). Such a certificate is:

(*i*) Conclusive evidence that the company is authorised to be and is duly registered and that the requirements of the Act in respect of registration have been complied with as at the date of the certificate (S. 15 (1)). In *Jubilee Cotton Mills Ltd v. Lewis* (1924) the Registrar accepted the Memorandum and Articles on 6th January and so dated them, but they were not signed until 8th January. On 6th January, before filing a statement in lieu of prospectus, the company made an allotment to Lewis. It was held that the certificate was conclusive evidence that the company was incorporated on 6th January and that the allotment could not be declared void on the ground that it was made before incorporation.

(*ii*) *Not* conclusive evidence that the company is one which could lawfully be registered and that the objects of the company are legal (*Bowman v. Secular Society Ltd* (1917)).

There is no provision under the Companies Acts whereby the Registrar can cancel a Certificate of Incorporation because of an irregularity in registration, although the Attorney-General may do so if the company was shown to have been formed for an illegal purpose.

The Effect of Registration

From the date of incorporation, the subscribers to the Memorandum, together with such persons as may from time to time become members, constitute a body corporate under the name contained in the Memorandum, having perpetual succession and a common seal, but with such liability to contribute to the assets of the company in the event of winding up as is mentioned in the Act (S. 13(2)).

A **private company** and a company with no share capital may commence trading upon receipt of its Certificate of Incorporation, but a **public company** must first meet the requirements of S. 109 (see page 56).

Contracts of a Company

As a body corporate, a company may enter into contracts in the same ways and subject to the same conditions as a private individual—that is, orally, in writing and under seal (S. 32). Similarly, the rules of agency also apply, so that a duly authorised agent (such as a director) may bind the company when contracting within the scope of his authority. S. 33 states that bills of exchange and promissory notes made, accepted or endorsed on behalf of a company by a person authorised to do so become binding upon the company.

The Seal

Every company must have a **common seal**, upon which its name is engraved in legible characters (S. 108).

A company wishing to execute deeds outside the United Kingdom may, by writing under its common seal, empower any person, generally or specifically, to act as its attorney in a specified place outside the United Kingdom. A deed signed by such an attorney is binding on a company as if it were under its common seal (S. 34).

Also, a company may, if authorised by its Articles, have for its use in any place outside the United Kingdom an **official seal**. This must be a facsimile of its common seal with the addition of the name of the place in which it may be used. The company may, by writing under its common seal, authorise any specified person to affix the official seal on any document to which the company is party in that place (S. 35).

Authentication of Documents

A document requiring authentication by a company may be signed by a director, secretary or other authorised officer of the company and need not be under its common seal (S. 36).

4

THE MEMORANDUM AND THE
ARTICLES OF ASSOCIATION

The Nature of the Memorandum

The Memorandum is, in effect, the charter of the company, in that it identifies the company and defines its objectives and powers. In fact, it was stated to be 'the charter, and defines the limitation of the powers of a company to be established under the Act' (*Ashbury Railway Carriage and Iron Co. v. Riche* (1875)). It enables any person (such as a prospective creditor or investor) who examines it, to be satisfied as to the scope of its permitted activities. This is possible because the Memorandum is one of the documents lodged with the Registrar and is capable of examination by any person.

Contents of the Memorandum

S. 2 prescribes that the Memorandum must state:

(*a*) **The name** of the company. The word 'Limited' must be the last word of the name if the liability of the members is limited by shares and/or guarantee, unless a licence has been granted under S.19(1) to dispense with the word 'Limited' (see page 23). The name of a company whose registered office is to be situated in Wales may be stated with 'cyfyngedig' as the last word in its name, but the fact that the company is a limited company must be stated in English on all prospectuses, letter paper, etc. (S. 30(1976)).

(*b*) **The domicile of the registered office**; that is, whether it is in England (including Wales) or Scotland. Under the 1976 Act a company may state that its registered office is situated in Wales.

(*c*) **The objects** of the company.

(*d*) **That the liability of the members is limited**, if such is the case.

(*e*) **The amount of the nominal share capital and its division into shares of fixed amounts** (if it is to have a share capital).

(*f*) In the case of a company limited by guarantee, a statement that each member undertakes to contribute to the assets of the company in the event of winding up and to the extent as prescribed by law but not exceeding a specified amount.

At the end of the Memorandum will appear the **subscription clause**, (known as a Declaration of Association), to the effect that the subscribers are desirous of being formed into a company. There must be at least two subscribers in the case of a private company and seven in the case of a public company (S. 1). Each must sign his name and have it attested by a witness (S. 3). Opposite each name must appear the subscriber's address and description, and the number of shares he agrees to take (S. 2).

The forms of Memorandum contained in the First Schedule are rarely adopted because of the restrictive nature of the objects clauses. They are Tables B to E, as listed below:

Table B—Form of Memorandum of Association of a company limited by shares.

Table C—Form of Memorandum and Articles of Association of a company limited by guarantee and not having a share capital.

Table D—Form of Memorandum and Articles of Association of a company limited by guarantee and having a share capital.

Table E—Form of Memorandum and Articles of Association of an unlimited company having a share capital.

(It will be seen that with the exception of Table B, the above Tables include the Articles of Association.)

The Name of the Company

No company may be registered in a name regarded by the Department of Trade as being undesirable (S. 17). The Department's discretion to refuse is absolute. Guidelines on this subject have been issued and the following principles have been established:

(*a*) No name will be registered if it is identical to or closely resembles one already registered.

(*b*) A name will not be accepted if it is considered to be misleading, e.g. if it suggests it is a large company when it is not.

(*c*) A name will be rejected if it suggests association with the Crown; an overseas country (unless circumstances justify it); a Government department or other official authority.

(*d*) Such words as 'Bank', 'Building Society', 'Co-operative', etc., would be rejected unless the choice was justified.

(*e*) A name suggesting or including a registered trademark would not be permitted without the owner's consent.

(*f*) A surname may not be included which is not the surname of a director or proposed director unless circumstances justified it.

(*g*) Certain names are protected by special Acts of Parliament—e.g. 'Red Cross', 'British Legion'.

Regulation of Names used by Overseas Companies

If the Secretary of State is of the opinion that it is or would be undesirable for an overseas company to carry on business in the United

Kingdom under its corporate name, he may cause a notice to that effect to be served on the company by the Registrar of Companies. Such a notice may not be served later than six months after the relevant date. (The 'relevant date' is the date of registering documents by an overseas company when establishing a place of business in Great Britain, as required by S.407, or on making a return under S.409(2) upon change of name.)

In the event of a notice being served, the company may deliver to the Registrar a statement specifying a name approved by the Secretary of State, other than its corporate name, under which it proposes to carry on business in the United Kingdom. Upon registration, such a name shall be deemed to be the corporate name of the company for all purposes of the law applying in Great Britain.

A company on which a notice has been served may not at any time after the expiration of two months from service of the notice, carry on business in the United Kingdom under its corporate name. Contravention would make the company and every officer or agent guilty of an offence and liable to fines. Any transaction entered into by the company would not, however, be thereby invalidated (S.31(1976)).

Change of Name

There are four circumstances in which the name of a company may be changed:

(1) *The Department of Trade may direct* a company to change its name if the Department considers that the company's registered name gives *so misleading an impression of its activities as to be likely to cause harm to the public*. The company must comply with the direction within six weeks (or such longer period as the Department may grant), but the company has the right of appeal to the Court within three weeks of the direction. If the Court confirms the direction, it will specify the period within which it must be complied with (S.46(1967)).

(2) *The Department of Trade may direct* a company to change its name if, through inadvertence or otherwise, the company has been registered with a name *too similar to an existing one*. Such a direction must be made within six months of registration of the name or registration of a change of name. The company must comply within six weeks of the direction or such extended period as the Department may allow (S.18 (2)).

(3) Under similar circumstances, *a company* may change its name with the sanction of the Department (S.18(2)).

(4) *A company* may change its name by passing a special resolution and obtaining the written consent of the Department of Trade (S.18(1))

Any change of name is not effective until the new name is entered by the Registrar and a new Certificate of Incorporation is issued (S.18(3)).

Thus, in (4) above, the change is *not* effected when the resolution is passed.

A change of name does not affect rights and obligations of the company nor any legal procedures brought by or against the company under its prior name (S. 18(4)).

The Department of Trade will not sanction a change of name if it implies a variation in the principal objects of the company.

'Passing off'

Any person, firm or corporation trading under an established name (which may or may not be registered) has a right under general law to obtain an injunction to restrain the registration by a company of a certain name or to prevent a company from carrying on business or selling goods of that name, if, because of a similarity between the names and the types of business, the company may possibly be 'passing off' its business or products as those of the other. The mere fact of registering a company name under the Act, therefore, will afford no protection against such a claim.

To be successful, the claimant must show there is a similarity between the types of business. If no possibility of confusion exists because of the differing natures of the businesses, the action will fail (*McCulloch v. Lewes A. May Ltd* (1947)). It must also be shown that the choice of name by a new company is calculated to deceive the public into thinking the company is the one which is aggrieved. Thus, a new company's name may be so similar to that of another company or product in the same commercial activity so as to give an impression which would be damaging 'to the credit and prosperity of the plaintiff'. In *Ewing v. Buttercup Margarine Co. Ltd* (1917) Ewing was trading as the Buttercup Dairy Company, retailing butter, margarine, eggs, tea and condensed milk. He secured an injunction restraining the defendant company from trading under a name which had been registered the previous year.

However, a company may not complain if a word or term relevant to its name or product is in common use in the English language. In *Aerators Ltd v. Tollett* (1902) a claim failed because the word 'aerator' was in common use and was not exclusive to the plaintiff.

Publication of Name

By Section 108, every company must:

(*a*) Print or affix its name on the outside of every office or place of business.

(*b*) Have it engraved on its seal.

(*c*) Have it printed on all business letters, bills of exchange, promissory notes and cheques; on all notices and other official publications; and on all orders for money or goods, invoices, receipts and letters of credit.

Penalties for not doing so may be imposed on the *company*. An *officer* of the company or any person acting on its behalf who (*a*) uses or authorises the use of a seal on which the company's name is not engraved, or (*b*) issues or authorises the issue of any document mentioned above whereon the company's name is not mentioned, is liable to a fine not exceeding £50 and is further *personally* liable to the holder of the bill of exchange, promissory note, cheque or order, unless the liability is met by the company.

Misquoting the name can make the signatories personally liable (*Atkins and Co. v. Wardle and others* (1889), but personal liability may not be incurred if the word 'Limited' is abbreviated to 'Ltd' (*F. Stacey & Co. Ltd v. Wallis* (1912)).

A company incorporated outside Great Britain which operates in this country, must exhibit its name and include it in documents as set out in S. 411 (see page 11).

The *European Communities Act* requires to be shown in all business letters and forms the place of registration of the company and the number with which it is registered, the address of its registered office and, in the case of a company exempt from using 'limited' in its name, the fact that it is a limited company.

Use of the Word 'Limited'

A person trading under a name of which the last word is 'Limited' or any contraction or imitation thereof without being incorporated with limited liability, is liable to a fine of £5 for every day upon which that name or title had been used (S. 439).

Dispensation from using 'Limited'

Under S. 19, the Department of Trade may grant a licence to 'an association not for profit' (see page 12) to dispense with the word 'Limited' in its name, subject to its being satisfied that the company intends to apply its profits to the promotion of its objects and to prohibit the payment of dividends. The Department may also permit such a company already registered to delete the word 'Limited', following the passing of a special resolution. The licence may at any time be revoked upon giving written notice to the company of the Department's intention to do so.

These provisions do not exempt compliance with the requirement of the *European Communities Act* for a statement that it is a limited company to appear on all 'business letters and orders forms'.

The Registration of Business Names Act, *1916*

S. 1 of the above Act requires all individuals and firms carrying on business under a name which does not consist of their true names to register under that Act. S. 58 of the *Companies Act, 1947*, states that every company registered under the Companies Acts carrying on business under a name which does not consist of its *corporate* name without any additions, must register the business name with the Registrar of Business Names within fourteen days after commencing the business. The Registrar has authority to reject any name which he considers to be undesirable (S. 116(1947)).

In addition to filing particulars of the business name and the corporate name, the company must state the general nature of the business, the registered office or principal place of business, the date of commencement of the business, and any other business names under which its business is carried on. The statement must be in the form of a statutory declaration by a director or the secretary.

(Ss. 58 and 116 above are two sections of the 1947 Act not repealed by the 1948 Act.) S. 32(1976) extends these provisions to overseas companies having a place of business in the United Kingdom.

The Registered Office

The Memorandum must state the **country** in which the registered office is situated. This is known as the 'domicile' of the company and will be either England (which, for this purpose, includes Wales) or Scotland. Under the 1976 Act a company may state that its registered office is situated in Wales. The domicile of the company cannot be changed, but changes of address within the domicile are permissible.

S. 23(1976) (which supersedes S. 107 of the 1948 Act) states that the intended situation of the registered office must be set out in the statement delivered prior to incorporation, as required by S. 21(1976) (see page 16). Notice of any change must be given to the Registrar within fourteen days.

Documents (including writs, etc.) may be served on a company by leaving them at or sending by post to the registered office of the company (S. 437). Such an office need not be one at which the company's business is carried on; for example, the registered office of a small company could be the office of its accountant or a secretarial services company.

An overseas company must register the names and addresses of one or more persons resident in the United Kingdom who are authorised to accept any legal documents required to be served on the company (S. 407).

The Objects Clause

This clause is of vital importance because it establishes what the purposes of the company are and what it may do to achieve its objectives. Thus, prospective investors are made aware of the types of activity in which the company is involved and those other activities into which it may venture in the future; those contemplating dealing with the company as its creditors can discover what activities the company may engage in, what powers it has to carry out those activities and any limitations on those powers.

The 'Substratum'

In drafting the Companies Act it was the intention that the objects clause would consist of a short statement of the 'main objects'. Those incidental powers deemed reasonably to be necessary to the achievement of the main objects were to be implied. The attitude of the business community, however, was to be wary of the vagueness of such implied powers and thus it became the normal practice to draft extensive clauses to include all the powers which the company could possibly wish to use. Accordingly, they included activities which the company would be unlikely to engage in but which it might *possibly* enter into.

In an endeavour to make the application of the law more closely resemble the intention of the law, the Court introduced its own interpretation of the 'main objects rule'. This was to the effect that the main objects would be identified and the other powers would be regarded as ancillary ones, available only so far as being necessary or incidental to the attainment of the main objects. By following this concept it could be decreed that if a main object failed a company could not continue in business by regarding one of its subsidiary powers as a main object.

In *Re German Date Coffee Co.* (1882) a company was formed to acquire and exploit a German patent for making coffee from dates. The company was forced to obtain a Swedish patent for the same process because the German patent became unavailable. It was held that the main object (also known as the **substratum**) had failed and the company was ordered to be wound up. Similarly, in *Re Amalgamated Syndicate* (1897) a company used a subsidiary object to operate as house agents, although the main purpose of the company was to erect and let stands for Queen Victoria's Diamond Jubilee procession. The company was ordered to be wound up.

The aims of the Act can still be avoided, however, it is expressly stated in the Memorandum that each subsection may be regarded as an independent clause, not limited by any reference to any other clause (*Cotman v. Brougham* (1918)). Thus, in these circumstances, if what is obviously the main object fails, a company could continue in business by operating under one of the other clauses, which would then be regarded as a main object (*Re Kitson & Co. Ltd* (1946)).

However, this ability to convert what is effectively a subsidiary clause into a major one may be limited. In *Introductions Ltd v. National Provincial Bank* (1969), the power to borrow by issuing debentures was bestowed as a subclause and it was expressly stated that each subclause should be construed independently. The company attempted to use this clause to borrow money to finance a pig-breeding business, whereas the sole activity of the company was stated to be the provision of facilities to visitors to the 1951 Festival of Britain. The court decided that the sub-clause could not be used to enable the company to engage in activities which were *ultra vires*. This would no doubt be decided differently today in view of S.9(1) of the *European Communities Act, 1972* (see page 34).

Implied Powers

As mentioned above, it was intended that powers necessary and incidental to the main objects were to be implied. Sundry interpretations of what would be recognised as implied powers have been made, including the following:

Every *trading* company has implied power to borrow money for the purpose of trading.

There is implied power in respect of preliminary expenses, payment of dividends from profits and the sale of land (*Re Kingsbury Collieries Ltd and Moore's Contract* (1907)).

It has been held that the power to employ persons includes the power to pay pensions to ex-employees and their dependants (*Hampson v. Price's Patent Candle Co.* (1876)). Any such payments, however, must be for the benefit of and in the interests of the company and reasonably incidental to the company's business. Thus, in *Re Lee, Behrens & Co. Ltd* (1932), the proposed payment of a pension to the widow of the managing director was not allowed to be proved in a winding up because it was not reasonably incidental to the business of the company.

Contractual Ability

The broad principle is that any transaction not within the powers of a company as set out in the objects clause of the Memorandum is *ultra vires* and therefore void. It follows that such a transaction cannot be validated by the members in general meeting. The leading example of this principle was the decision in *Ashbury Railway Carriage and Iron Co. v. Riche* (1875). It was held that a company whose objects included making and selling railway equipment, engineering and general contracting, and buying and selling property, could not validly purchase a concession to build a railway in Belgium.

Consideration of the effectiveness of this doctrine in any one circumstance is, however, complicated by other possible factors. One relates to the extent to which an outside party may be cognisant of the company's powers. Another is that a contracting party would normally be unaware that any internal regulations of the company necessary to authorise the making of the contract may not, in fact, have been complied with. Protection for a contracting party may therefore be dependent not only on the capacity of the company to contract but also on the internal machinery of the company. Establishment of the former would depend upon an interpretation of the objects clause in the *Memorandum*; for the latter, reference would have to be made to legal provisions and decisions relevant to the *Articles*. (*As a study of the effects of both those documents may be necessary to determine an issue, a comprehensive view of the 'ultra vires doctrine' is given on page* 33.)

Alteration of the Objects Clause

The purposes for which the objects may be altered are set out in S.5 and are as follows:

(*a*) To carry on the business more economically or more efficiently.

(*b*) To attain the main purpose by new or improved methods.

(*c*) To enlarge or change the local area of operation.

(*d*) To carry on some other business which under existing circumstances may conveniently or advantageously be combined with the present business.

(*e*) To restrict or abandon any of the objects.

(*f*) To sell or dispose of the whole or part of the undertaking.

(*g*) To amalgamate with another company or body of persons.

Some of the interpretations of S.5 are as follows:

(*a*) New power completely incompatible with the original powers would not be permitted. A cycling association could not alter its objects to admit motorists because the purpose of the company was specific to cyclists (*Re Cyclists' Touring Club Ltd* (1907)).

(*b*) A fundamental change in the objects may be permitted, however, if it makes possible the carrying on of the business more economically or efficiently (*Re Scientific Poultry Breeders Association* (1933)).

(*c*) The Court may make the changing of the company's name a condition before permitting alteration of the objects, so that the new name is more indicative of the changed objects (*Re Indian Mechanical Gold Extracting Co.* (1891)).

(*d*) A new kind of business may be taken on if it can be done so as to carry on the original business more advantageously (*Re Parent Tyre Co. Ltd* (1923)).

The decision to alter the clause must be by special resolution in general meeting.

Objections to an Alteration

An alteration to the objects clause may have far-reaching consequences for its members and, consequently, S.5 contains provisions whereby objectors may apply for the alteration to be cancelled. Any such objection must be made to the Court within twenty-one days of passing the resolution and if no objection has been made within that time the resolution becomes effective from the date it was passed. This rule applies even if objection could have been made that the alteration was not one of the seven prescribed in the Act.

Those who may apply to the Court for cancellation of the resolution are the holders of not less than, in the aggregate, 15 per cent in nominal value of the company's issued share capital or any class thereof, or, if the company is not limited by shares, by not less than 15 per cent of the company's members. Thus, a small minority of shareholders or even of a class of shareholder may effect a reversal of a decision made in general meeting, even if such objectors have no voting rights under the Articles.

The application to the Court may be made by one or more applicants appointed in writing for that purpose. No application may be made by a person who consented to or voted in favour of the resolution to alter the clause.

If an application for cancellation is made, the company must notify the Registrar immediately. Meanwhile, the special resolution would be ineffective.

A Court order confirming the alteration, wholly or in part, may include such terms and conditions as the Court thinks fit. It may adjourn the proceedings so that arrangements can be made for purchase of the interests of dissentient members. A copy of the Court order, either cancelling or confirming the alteration, must be filed with the Registrar within fifteen days.

If no application for cancellation is made within the prescribed twenty-one days, a printed copy of the Memorandum as altered must be filed with the Registrar within fifteen days from the end of that period (i.e. not later than thirty-six days from the passing of the resolution). If the Court confirms the alteration following objections, a printed copy of the Memorandum as altered must be lodged with the Court order.

Limited Liability

The limitation of liability clause states that liability of the members is limited by shares and/or by guarantee. Such liability would become operative upon the winding up of the company (see page 191). The only circumstances whereby the effect of this clause could be altered would be:

(*a*) Upon the winding up of an unlimited company which had re-registered as a limited company (S. 44(1967)) (see page 10).

(*b*) If the company carried on buisness for a period of more than six months with its membership below the statutory minimum. If members were aware of that fact they could be severally liable for debts incurred after the period of six months (S. 31).

(*c*) Where the liability of directors was made unlimited in the Memorandum or by an alteration thereto by special resolution, provided it was so authorised by the Articles (Ss. 202, 203).

(*d*) In the case of winding up, as regards persons who had been party to fraudulent trading (S. 332) (see page 195).

S. 22 states that no member, as a consequence of an alteration in the Memorandum or Articles, may be required to take or subscribe for more shares than he held at the time of the alteration, nor may his liability to contribute to the share capital be increased, unless he so agrees in writing.

The Capital Clause

This clause may set out the rights attaching to each class of share, but it is usual to provide this in the Articles. (Alterations and reduction of capital are dealt with in Chapter 9.)

Alterations to the Memorandum

A company may not alter its Memorandum except in the cases, in the mode and to the extent as provided in the Act (S. 4). Where a Memorandum has been altered it is an offence to issue copies which are not in accordance with the alteration (S. 25).

The *European Communities Act, 1972,* provides as follows:

(*a*) A printed copy of the Memorandum or Articles as altered must be filed with the Registrar, other than an amendment to the objects clause.

(*b*) Following the filing of a resolution to amend the Memorandum or the Articles, the amendment does not become effective until the Registrar has notified receipt in the *Official Gazette*. A company may not rely on the effectiveness of its resolution, as against any other person who cannot be shown to have knowledge of the facts or events of which the document is evidence, until the fifteenth day after publication in the *Official Gazette*.

Apart from the provisions relevant to alterations of specific clauses in the Memorandum, there is *general* power under S. 23 to alter by special resolution any condition contained in the Memorandum which could lawfully have been contained in the Articles. The power does not apply, however, (*i*) if the Memorandum provides for alterations or prohibits them; (*ii*) to permit alteration of the rights attaching to different classes of shares if those rights are prescribed in the Memorandum (see page 172).

The Nature of the Articles

Whereas the Memorandum is concerned with the identification of a company and its external relationships, the Articles relate to the *internal* affairs of a company. They set out the regulations as they affect members of the company in the same way as do rules of a club. Similarly, a person applying for membership of a company accepts and agrees to be bound by those rules as they then obtain but with the right subsequently to amend them within the prescribed procedure.

The Articles are subordinate to the Memorandum because incorporation of a company is granted on the fundamentals established in the Memorandum, whereas members have the right to alter the Articles within the scope of the Memorandum. Articles must be filed with the Memorandum when the company is registered (S.6). They must be:

(a) Printed.

(b) Divided into paragraphs, numbered consecutively.

(c) Signed by each signatory to the Memorandum, with at least one witness who must attest the signatures (S.9).

Table A and Special Articles

Table A is a model set of Articles, which may be adopted wholly or in part by a company limited by shares. Part I of Table A, in the First Schedule of the 1948 Act, sets out Articles suitable for a public company; Part II includes additional clauses relevant to private companies. A company adopting Table A, completely or in part, is regulated by the Table A appearing in the Companies Act under which the company is registered.

Most companies either exclude or modify Table A and register **Special Articles** drafted to suit the particular company. S.8 states that a company limited by shares may:

(a) Register a complete set of Articles and exclude Table A entirely; or

(b) Register its own Articles and allow Table A to apply so far as it is not excluded or modified by the Articles filed; or

(c) Adopt Table A in its entirety (in which case the Memorandum must be endorsed 'Registered without Articles of Association').

Tables C, D and E are forms of Articles for, respectively, a company limited by guarantee without a share capital; a company limited by guarantee with a share capital; and an unlimited company. These do not have the possibility of automatic application as does Table A; they are merely guides. Such companies must always file Special Articles, even if they exactly resemble the models.

Alteration of Articles

A company may, by special resolution, alter or add to its Articles (S.10). This is a fundamental right bestowed on a company and there can be no regulation forbidding the right to alter, even if the restriction was designed to protect the rights of members or third parties (*Walker v. London Tramways Co.* (1879)). Such power to alter Articles is, however, subject to certain conditions:

(a) No alteration may be made which exceeds or conflicts with the Memorandum.

(b) Any alteration may not result in contravention of any Statute.

Thus, an alteration could not give a company power to purchase its own shares (*Trevor v. Whitworth* (1887)).

(*c*) An alteration may not excuse a breach of contract. In *Southern Foundries* (*1926*) *Ltd v. Shirlaw* (1940), Shirlaw had been appointed as managing director by a contract outside the Articles. The company was taken over by another company, whereupon the acquiring company altered the Articles to give it power to remove any director from office. Shirlaw was dismissed as a director and it was held that the company was liable for damages for breach of contract.

(*d*) Any alteration must be for the benefit of the company as a whole. Whether an alteration meets that requirement is, in general, for the members to decide and the Court will interfere only on suspicion of illegality or unfairness. An alteration must not be such as to cause hardship to a minority unless it can be shown to be for the benefit of the members as a whole. Thus, an alteration may be valid even if it adversely affects a minority provided it is for the general good. This was illustrated in *Shuttleworth v. Cox Brothers & Co.* (*Maidenhead*) *Ltd* (1927), where a director could not be removed from office because an offence of which he was guilty did not constitute one of the specified events which the Articles prescribed as ground for dismissal. The Articles were altered to make it possible for a director to be removed by a written demand signed by all the other directors. The Court of Appeal decided the alteration was valid because it had been made for the benefit of the company as a whole.

It has been held that an alteration in the Articles to vary the rights of one class of shareholder whereby some shareholders lose an advantage, is not necessarily invalid if it can be shown that it was for the benefit of the company (*Rights and Issues Investment Trust Ltd v. Stylo Shoes Ltd* (1964)).

An alteration would be invalid, however, if it resulted in oppression or unfairness by a majority on a minority. In *Brown v. British Abrasive Wheel Co.* (1919), the majority shareholders, in order to help the company in its financial difficulties, offered to provide additional capital if the minority shareholders sold them their shares. Upon the refusal of the minority, the majority passed a resolution altering the Articles so as to be able to acquire the minority shares compulsorily. The company was not permitted to make the alteration because it constituted an oppression on the minority whereby the majority would have benefited financially. (Further comments on minority rights are given in Chapter 17.)

Recording Alterations

A copy of the special resolution altering the Articles must be filed with the Registrar within fifteen days of it being passed. Where Special Articles have been registered, a copy of any resolution or agreement for the time being in force affecting the Articles must be embodied in or annexed to every copy of the Articles issued after the passing of the resolution. If Special Articles have not been registered, a copy of any such resolution or agreement must be sent to any member at his request (S. 143).

The provisions of the *European Communities Act, 1972*, relevant to alteration of the Memorandum also apply to alterations of the Articles (see page 29).

The Consequences of Registration of the Memorandum and the Articles

When registered, the Memorandum and the Articles bind the company and the members as if they had been signed and sealed by each member and contained covenants on the part of each member to observe all the provisions of the documents (S. 20). The consequences of this are as follows:

(*a*) *Each individual member is bound to the company*. This was illustrated in *Hickman v. Kent and Romney Marsh Sheep Breeders' Association* (1915). The Articles contained a clause that any dispute between a member or members and the company should be referred to arbitration. A member in dispute with the company insisted on bringing an action against the company, but the company applied for a stay of proceedings on the ground that recourse to law was not open to the member. The company's contention was upheld.

This relationship between a member and the company exists only in the member's capacity as a *member*, however. In *Beattie v. E. & F. Beattie Ltd* (1938) it was held that a dispute between a member in his capacity as *director* and the company could not be referred to arbitration when the Articles prescribed arbitration for disputes between *members* and the company.

(*b*) *The company is bound to each individual member*. Thus, a member may enforce his rights against the company by legal action—e.g. his right as a member to vote at a meeting of the company (*Pender v. Lushington* (1877)). Again, action can be taken only in the plaintiff's capacity as a *member* and in respect of his rights as a member. In *Eley v. Positive Government Security Life Assurance Co. Ltd* (1876), a clause in the Articles provided that Eley be employed for life as the company's solicitor. Subsequently, Eley became a shareholder. At a later stage the company dispensed with his services and, relying on the clause in the Articles, Eley sued the company for breach of contract. It was held that the Articles bound the company to its members in their capacity as *members* and that, accordingly, Eley's claim could not succeed on the basis of the Articles.

(*c*) *The members are bound to each other*. For many years it was uncertain as to whether the Articles constituted a contract between the members themselves. It had been held in *Welton v. Saffery* (1897) that members could enforce rights between themselves only through the company. However, in *Rayfield v. Hands* (1960) it was held that where the Articles of a private company gave a personal right to a member it was enforceable directly against another member.

(*d*) *A contract with non-members may be implied.* As stated above, the Articles cannot constitute a contract between the company and another person other than in his capacity as a member. A clause in the Articles may, however, form the basis of a contract or may be quoted as implying the existence of a contract. Thus, if the Articles set out the terms as to remuneration to be paid to directors and a director takes office on that basis, the Court will infer that the terms are part of his contract with the company (*Re New British Iron Co., ex parte Beckwith* (1898)).

The *ultra vires* Doctrine

The basic principle that a contract beyond the powers of a company is void is stated earlier in this chapter. As regards a party contracting with a company, matters which may have to be determined are:

(*a*) To what extent the party was or should have been aware of the company's powers.

(*b*) The degree of reliance he may reasonably have that the persons acting for the company have the necessary authority and that any requisite internal regulations of the company have been complied with.

The influencing factors would include the effectiveness of public documents; the implications which may reasonably be made from the prevailing circumstances; the principles of agency; and the provisions of the *European Communities Act*

'Constructive Notice' and 'Public Documents'

Any person dealing with a company is deemed to have notice ('fixed with notice') of the terms contained in the Memorandum and the Articles, because these and other documents are available for inspection by anyone at the office of the Registrar of Companies. This is known as the **doctrine of constructive notice**. Such persons are therefore presumed to be aware of the powers of the company and the limitations on those powers, and those of the directors. The general principle is that a person cannot obtain any rights against the company in respect of a contract which could have been seen to be beyond the powers of the company.

There are, however, two important modifications of this principle.

1. The Rule in Royal British Bank v. Turquand

The relevant part of the findings was as follows: 'Persons dealing with the company are bound to read the public documents and to see that the proposed dealing is not inconsistent therewith. But they are not bound to do more; *they need not enquire into the regularity of the internal proceedings.*' Thus, a contracting party is entitled to assume that the company's internal regulations which are necessary to implement a contract which is within the powers of the company have been complied with.

A person may not necessarily always be able to rely upon the Rule, however, as the following instances indicate:

(*a*) *Where he knew, or ought to have known, of the irregularity.* A director contracting with his company must, obviously, be aware of the regulations and of any irregularity (*Howard v. Patent Ivory Co.* (1888)).

(*b*) *Where he relies upon a forged document.* No rights can be obtained on a document which is a forgery. Such a document could be one on which the seal is affixed without authority and the signatures are counterfeit (*Ruben v. Great Fingall Consolidated* (1906)).

(*c*) *Where he failed to make investigation when put upon enquiry.* For example, it has been held that a person should have been put upon enquiry when a bill of exchange, purporting to be on behalf of a company, was drawn by a branch manager of the company, on the ground that such authority would normally be beyond the scope of such an official (*Kreditbank Cassel v. Schenkers Ltd* (1927)). Again, the type of contract may be reasonable ground for suspicion. In *Houghton & Co. v. Nothard, Lowe and Wills* (1928) an unusual contract was made by a director without authority, and the secretary purported to confirm it. In both these cases, it was held that the company was not liable.

A company may be liable, however, where it has held out that an official had the powers he claimed and such powers could have been conferred by the Articles. Thus, one could assume the existence of authority if a director had acted, to the knowledge of the other directors, as if he were the managing director and his actions were within the usual powers of a managing director though not of an ordinary director (*Freeman and Lockyer v. Buckhurst Park Properties* (*Mangal*) *Ltd* (1964)).

Certainly, then, the 'Rule in Turquand' provides much protection for parties contracting with companies. It has been described as 'one of the most efficacious rules of company law for ensuring that persons who deal with companies in good faith are treated fairly, and the essentially commonsense solutions it produces contrast notably with the unjustices worked by the *ultra vires* rule' (*Pennington's Company Law*).

2. The European Communities Act, 1972 (S. 9)

The introduction of this legislation may possibly be regarded as an extension of the Turquand rule. It states that in favour of a person dealing with the company *in good faith*, a transaction *decided upon by the directors* shall be deemed to be *within the capacity of the company* and that the powers of the directors to bind the company shall be deemed to be *free of any limitation* under the company's Memorandum or Articles.

A claimant must prove good faith in entering into the contract; that is, that he had no knowledge or reasonable suspicion to the contrary about the ability of the company and the directors. The Act states that good faith must be presumed unless the contrary can be proved. No protection is available to the company and the directors since, obviously, they cannot claim they were misled as to the powers of the company or themselves.

The basic principle is to give protection to a contracting party when the contract is based upon decisions made by the directors; that is, the directors may be assumed to 'hold out' (*a*) that the contract is within the company's powers, and (*b*) that they have authority to bind the company.

The result of this legislation is that the decision in *Re Jon Beauforte* (*London*) *Ltd* (1953) would no doubt be different today. This held that a creditor had notice that a transaction into which he had entered was *ultra vires* the company since he had constructive notice of the provisions of the Memorandum concerning limitations on the company's powers. The precise extent to which the Act modifies the 'doctrine of constructive notice', however, remains to be determined by the Courts.

Right to Inspect and obtain Copies of the Memorandum and the Articles

Any member may require the company to provide him with a copy of the Memorandum and the Articles for a fee not exceeding 5p (S. 24). The documents are among those which may be inspected by any person at the office of the Registrar of Companies, and the Registrar will also supply copies certified by him upon payment of a fee (S. 426).

5

THE PROSPECTUS AND STATEMENT IN LIEU OF PROSPECTUS

A fundamental characteristic of public companies is that they may invite the public to subscribe for their shares and debentures. It is common practice for a public company to obtain some of its finance privately (by bank loans, for example), but the major part of its share capital will normally be forthcoming from the public (unless it is a wholly-owned subsidiary). Some of its shares may be issued privately, however, for a consideration other than cash, such as when a company formed to take over an existing business issues shares to the vendor as the purchase consideration.

There are three methods of issuing shares to the public. These are considered in detail in this chapter but the circumstances in which each method is employed may firstly be summarised as follows:

A **prospectus** is used when a company makes a *direct* invitation to the public to subscribe.

An **offer for sale** is used by an issuing house in offering to the public newly issued shares it has purchased from the company for that purpose.

A **placing** relates to small issues whereby an issuing house or broker offers the shares to its clients and the public.

The Nature of a Prospectus

A prospectus is an advertisement inviting the public to buy securities in the company. It is therefore an 'invitation to treat'. When an investor applies for shares or debentures in response to the publication of a prospectus he is **offering** to buy the securities. Accordingly, the directors (to whom the offers are addressed) may reject the offers or accept them as they think fit. (This may be compared with a **transfer** of listed fully-paid shares which directors may not reject.)

The offer signed by the applicant is to subscribe for a stated number of shares or any less number the directors decide to allot. Therefore, if the issue is **oversubscribed** (that is, more shares in total are applied for than are to be issued) the directors may allot any applicant a smaller number than applied for; the acceptance by the directors would coincide with the terms of the offer.

36

Definition of 'Prospectus'

A prospectus is defined in S.455 as 'any prospectus, notice, circular, advertisement or other invitation offering to the public for subscription or purchase any shares or debentures of the company'. Thus, any document, by whatever name it is called, complying with the above description, is a prospectus as recognised by law and must be registered as such.

Defining 'the Public'

It may be a question of fact as to whether a particular document is a prospectus, and one of the questions to be answered may be 'is it issued to the *public*?' The term goes beyond the public in general because, for this purpose, 'the public' includes 'any section of the public, whether selected as members or debenture-holders of the company or as clients of the person issuing the prospectus or in any other manner' (S.55(1)).

The general rule is that if it is intended that only the persons receiving a restricted invitation can take it up then it is not an issue to the public. Also, an invitation is deemed not to have been made to the public if it can be regarded, in all circumstances, as being a 'domestic' concern of the persons making and receiving it. An example would be where a promoter offers the shares to a few friends, customers or relations (*Sherwell v. Combined Incandescent Mantles Syndicate* (1907)). But in *Re South of England Gas Co. Ltd* (1911), where 3,000 copies of a document entitled 'For private circulation only' were issued by a promoter to shareholders in certain gas companies, it was decided it was an offer to the public although no advertisement had been issued.

A **rights issue** is an offer to subscribe made to existing members and it would not be regarded as being an offer to the public if only those members could take it up. Almost invariably, however, the recipients of such an offer may 'renounce'; that is, they may sell the *right* to subscribe. Accordingly, as the shares would thereby possibly be available to the public, the document would be regarded as being a prospectus. Such an offer, however, would not be one 'issued generally' which, under S.39(1)(*a*), means one issued to persons who are not existing members or debenture-holders. The legal requirements as to the content of a prospectus not issued generally are less demanding (see page 45).

In the case of a **takeover bid**, in which the scheme was for an exchange of shares, it was decided that the offer was not made to the public since it could be accepted only by the shareholders of the company concerned (*Governments Stock and Other Securities Investment Co. Ltd v. Christopher* (1956)). (In the same case it was also decided that the circumstances did not entail 'subscription or purchase' as stated in the definition, because the shares were unissued shares and, also, to 'subscribe' must imply the payment of cash.)

Contents of the Prospectus

The principle underlying the legal requirements as to the contents of a prospectus is that sufficient information must be given to enable a reasonable person to make a fair assessment in deciding whether or not to invest. Because the public is being invited to provide money for a company, it is obviously essential that full disclosure is made, and, accordingly, the demands of the law are stated in positive terms. The contents may be categorised as follows.

(*a*) Those prescribed by S. 38 as specified in the Fourth Schedule.

(*b*) Additional particulars demanded by the Stock Exchange in respect of a company whose shares are to be admitted to listing.

(*c*) Further information voluntarily supplied.

The Fourth Schedule

S. 38 states that every prospectus must contain the matters specified in Part I of the Fourth Schedule and the reports required by Part II of the Schedule. No issue of an application form for shares or debentures may be made unless it is accompanied by a prospectus fully complying with the Fourth Schedule, *unless*

(*a*) A Certificate of Exemption has been obtained under the provisions of S. 39 (see page 46); or

(*b*) The invitation is to some person to underwrite the issue (see page 58); or

(*c*) The offer is not made to the public; or

(*d*) The issue is made to existing members or debenture-holders, with or without the right to renounce; or

(*e*) The shares or debentures to be issued are in all respects uniform with shares or debentures previously issued and listed on the Stock Exchange.

The provisions of S. 38 also relate to prospectuses issued by overseas companies (S. 417).

Because of the importance of the detailed provisions, the Fourth Schedule (as amended by S. 33 (1976)), is given in full as follows:

PART I

Matters to be specified

1. *The number of founders' or management or deferred shares*, if any, and the nature and extent of the interest of the holders in the property and profits of the company.

2. *The number of shares, if any, fixed by the articles as the qualification of a director, and any provision in the articles as to the remuneration of the directors.*

3. *The names, descriptions and addresses of the directors or proposed directors.*

4. Where *shares* are offered to the public for subscription, particulars as to:

   (*a*) the *minimum subscription*, i.e. the amount which, in the opinion of the directors, must be raised by the issue of those shares in order to provide the sums, or, if any part thereof is to be defrayed in any other manner, the balance of the sums, required to be provided in respect of each of the following matters:

      (i) the *purchase price of any property* purchased or to be purchased which is to be defrayed in whole or in part out of the proceeds of the issue;

      (ii) any *preliminary expenses* payable by the company, and any *commission* so payable to any person in consideration of his agreeing to subscribe for, or of his procuring or agreeing to procure subscriptions for, any shares in the company;

      (iii) the repayment of any moneys borrowed by the company in respect of any of the foregoing matters;

      (iv) *working* Capital; and

   (*b*) the amounts to be provided in respect of the matters aforesaid otherwise than out of the proceeds of the issue and the sources out of which those amounts are to be provided.

5. *The time of the opening of the subscription lists.*

6. *The amount payable on application and allotment* on each share, including the amount, if any, payable by way of premium and, in the case of a second or subsequent offer of shares, *the amount offered for subscription on each previous allotment made within the two preceding years, the amount actually allotted, and the amount, if any, paid on the shares so allotted* including the amount, if any, paid by way of premium.

7. *The number, description and amount of any shares in or debentures* of the company which any person has, or is entitled to be given, *an option to subscribe for*, together with the following *particulars of the option*, that is to say:

   (*a*) *the period* during which it is exercisable;

   (*b*) *the price* to be paid for shares or debentures subscribed for under it;

   (*c*) *the consideration* (if any) given or to be given for it or for the right to it;

   (*d*) *the names and addresses* of the persons to whom it or the right to it was given or, if given to existing shareholders or debenture holders as such, the relevant shares or debentures.

8. *The number and amount of shares and debentures* which within the two preceding years have been issued, or agreed to be *issued, as fully or partly paid up otherwise than in cash*, and in the latter case the extent to which they are so paid up, and in either case *the consideration* for which those shares or debentures have been issued or are proposed or intended to be issued.

9. (1) As respects any property to which this paragraph applies:

   (*a*) *the names and addresses of the vendors*;

   (*b*) *the amount payable in cash, shares or debentures* to the vendor and, where there is more than one separate vendor, or the company is a sub-purchaser, the amount so payable *to each vendor*;

(c) *short particulars of any transaction relating to the property completed within the two preceding years* in which any *vendor* of the property to the company or any person who is, or was at the time of the transaction, a *promoter* or a *director* or *proposed director* of the company had any interest direct or indirect.

(2) The property to which this paragraph applies is *property* purchased or acquired by the company or proposed so to be purchased or acquired, which is *to be paid for wholly or partly out of the proceeds of the issue* offered for subscription by the prospectus or the purchase or acquisition of which has not been completed at the date of the issue of the prospectus, *other than* property:

(a) the contract for the purchase or acquisition whereof was entered into *in the ordinary course of the company's business,* the contract not being made in contemplation of the issue nor the issue in consequence of the contract; or

(b) as respects which the amount of the purchase money is *not material.*

10. *The amount, if any, paid or payable as purchase money* in cash, shares, or debentures for any property to which the last foregoing paragraph applies, *specifying the amount, if any, payable for goodwill.*

11. The amount, if any, paid within the two preceding years, or payable, as *commission* (but not including commission to sub-underwriters) for *subscribing* or agreeing to subscribe, or procuring or agreeing to procure subscriptions, for any shares in or debentures of the company, or the rate of any such commission.

12. The *amount* or estimated amount of *preliminary expenses* and the *persons by whom any of those expenses have been paid or are payable,* and the amount or estimated amount of the *expenses of the issue* and the *persons by whom any of those expenses have been paid or are payable.*

13. *Any amount or benefit paid or given within the two preceding years or intended to be paid or given to any promoter, and the consideration for the payment or the giving of the benefit.*

14. *The dates of, parties to and general nature of every material contract,* not being a contract entered into in the ordinary course of the business carried on or intended to be carried on by the company or a contract entered into more than two years before the date of issue of the prospectus.

15. The names and addresses of the auditors, if any, of the company.

16. Full particulars of the nature and extent of *the interest, if any, of every director in the promotion of, or in the property proposed to be acquired by, the company,* or, where the interest of such a director consists in being a partner in a firm, the nature and extent of the interest of the firm, with a statement of all sums paid or agreed to be paid to him or to the firm in cash or shares, or otherwise by any person either to induce him to become, or to qualify him as, a director, or otherwise for services rendered by him or by the firm in connection with the promotion or formation of the company.

17. If the prospectus invites the public to subscribe for shares in the company and the *share capital* of the company is divided into different classes of shares, *the right of voting* at meetings of the company conferred by, *and the rights in respect of capital and dividends* attached to, the several classes of shares respectively.

18. In the case of a company which has been *carrying on business*, or of a business which has been carried on for *less than three years, the length of time during which the business* of the company or the business to be acquired, as the case may be, *has been carried on.*

PART II

Reports to be set out

19. (1) A report *by the auditors of the company* with respect to:

   (*a*) *profits and losses and assets and liabilities*, in accordance with sub-paragraph (2) or (3) of this paragraph, as the case requires; and

   (*b*) *the rates of the dividends*, if any, paid by the company in respect of each class of shares in the company in respect of each of the *five financial years* immediately preceding the issue of the prospectus, giving particulars of each class of shares on which such dividends have been paid and particulars of the cases in which no dividends have been paid in respect of any class of shares in respect of any of those years;

   and, if no accounts have been made up in respect of any part of the period of five years ending on a date three months before the issue of the prospectus, containing a statement of that fact.

   (2) *If the company has no subsidiaries*, the report shall:

   (*a*) so far as regards *profits and losses*, deal with the profits or losses of the company in respect of each of the *five financial years* immediately preceding the issue of the prospectus; and

   (*b*) so far as regards *assets and liabilities*, deal with the assets and liabilities of the company *at the last date to which the accounts of the company were made up.*

   (3) *If the company has subsidiaries*, the report shall:

   (*a*) so far as regards *profits and losses*, deal *separately with the company's profits or losses* as provided by the last foregoing sub-paragraph, *and* in addition, deal *either*:

   (i) as a whole with the combined profits or losses of its subsidiaries, so far as they concern members of the company; *or*

   (ii) individually with the profits or losses of each subsidiary, so far as they concern members of the company; *or*, instead of dealing separately with the company's profits or losses, deal *as a whole with the profits or losses of the company and*, so far as they concern members of the company, *with the combined profits or losses of its subsidiaries*; and

   (*b*) so far as regards *assets and liabilities*, deal *separately with the com-*

pany's assets and liabilities as provided by the last foregoing sub-paragraph *and*, in addition, deal *either*:

- (i) as a whole with the combined assets and liabilities of its subsidiaries, with or without the company's assets and liabilities; *or*
- (ii) individually with the assets and liabilities of each subsidiary; and shall indicate as respects the assets and liabilities of the subsidiaries the allowance to be made for persons other than members of the company.

20. *If the proceeds*, or any part of the proceeds, of the issue of the shares or debentures *are* or is *to be applied* directly or indirectly *in the purchase of any business*, *a report made by accountants* (*who shall be named in the prospectus*) upon:

- (*a*) the *profits or losses of the business* in respect of each of the *five financial years* immediately preceding the issue of the prospectus; and
- (*b*) the *assets and liabilities* of the business *at the last date to which the accounts of the business were made up.*

21. (1) *If*:

- (*a*) *the proceeds*, or any part of the proceeds, of the issue of the shares or debentures *are* or is *to be applied* directly or indirectly *in any manner resulting in the acquisition* by the company of *shares in any other body corporate*; and
- (*b*) *by reason of that acquisition* or anything to be done in consequence thereof or in connection therewith *that body corporate will become a subsidiary of the company*;

a report made by accountants (*who shall be named in the prospectus*) upon:

- (i) the *profits or losses of the other body corporate* in respect of each of the *five financial years* immediately preceding the issue of the prospectus; and
- (ii) the *assets and liabilities of the other body corporate at the last date to which the accounts of the body corporate were made up.*

(2) The said report shall:

- (*a*) indicate how the profits or losses of the other body corporate dealt with by the report would, in respect of the shares to be acquired, have concerned members of the company and what allowance would have fallen to be made, in relation to assets and liabilities so dealt with, for holders of other shares, if the company had at all material times held the shares to be acquired; and
- (*b*) where the other body corporate has subsidiaries, deal with the profits or losses and the assets and liabilities of the body corporate and its subsidiaries in the manner provided by sub-paragraph (3) of paragraph 19 of this Schedule in relation to the company and its subsidiaries.

PART III

Provisions applying to Parts I and II of Schedule

22. Paragraphs 2, 3, 12 (so far as it relates to preliminary expenses) and 16 of this Schedule shall not apply in the case of a prospectus issued more than two years after the date at which the company is entitled to commence business.

23. Every person shall for the purposes of this Schedule, be deemed to be *a vendor* who has entered into any contract, absolute or conditional, for the sale or purchase, or for any option of purchase, of any property to be acquired by the company, in any case where:

    (a) the purchase money is not fully paid at the date of the issue of the prospectus;

    (b) the purchase money is to be paid or satisfied wholly or in part out of the proceeds of the issue offered for subscription by the prospectus;

    (c) the contract depends for its validity or fulfilment on the result of that issue.

24. Where any property to be acquired by the company is to be taken on lease, this Schedule shall have effect as if the expression 'vendor' included the lessor, and the expression 'purchase money' included the consideration for the lease, and the expression 'sub-purchaser' included a sub-lessee.

25. References in paragraph 7 of this Schedule to subscribing for shares or debentures shall include acquiring them from a person to whom they have been allotted or agreed to be allotted with a view to his offering them for sale.

26. For the purposes of paragraph 9 of this Schedule where the vendors or any of them are a firm, the members of the firm shall not be treated as separate vendors.

27. If in the case of a company which has been carrying on business, or of a business which has been carried on for less than five years, the accounts of the company or business have only been made up in respect of four years, three years, two years or one year, Part II of the Schedule shall have effect as if references to four years, three years, two years or one year, as the case may be, were substituted for references to five years.

28. The expression 'financial year' in Part II of this Schedule means the year in respect of which the accounts of the company or of the business, as the case may be, are made up, and where by reason of any alteration of the date on which the financial year of the company or business terminates the accounts of the company or business have been made up for a period greater or less than a year, that greater or less period shall for the purpose of that Part of this Schedule be deemed to be a financial year.

29. Any report required by Part II of this Schedule shall either indicate by way of note any *adjustments* as respects the figures of any profits or losses or assets and liabilities dealt with by the report which appear to the persons making the report necessary or shall make those adjustments and indicate that adjustments have been made.

30. Any report by accountants required by Part II of this Schedule shall be made by *accountants qualified* under this Act for appointment *as auditors* of a company and shall *not* be made by any accountant who is *an officer or servant*, or a partner of or in the employment of an officer or servant, of the company or of the company's subsidiary or holding company or of a subsidiary of the company's holding company; and for the purposes of this paragraph the expression 'officer' shall include a proposed director but not an auditor.

Additionally, a prospectus must include, where relevant, particulars of

(*a*) Commission paid for subscribing or procuring subscription for shares (S. 53) (see page 59).

(*b*) Discounts on issued shares (S. 57) (see page 57).

Notes on the Fourth Schedule, Part I

The following comments are in explanation of certain provisions of the Fourth Schedule.

(*a*) *Founders', management or deferred shares* (para 1). These are shares which could carry rights specific to certain persons, such as the vendor of the business acquired by the company. Such shares are now very rare, but in the past some were issued to provide disproportionate (and unfair) advantages to the holders. Prospective investors must therefore be made aware of the special rights attached to any such shares.

(*b*) *The minimum subscription* (para 4). This is an estimate made by the directors of the costs covered by items (*a*)(i) to (*a*)(iv). Additionally, there must be shown the amount of such costs to be provided *other* than from the issue. The significance of the issue not producing sufficient funds to cover the minimum subscription is stated on page 54.

(*c*) *The subscription lists* (para 5). This relates to the time limits concerning allotment and revocation of applications (see page 53).

(*d*) *Special rights to acquire shares* (paras 7 and 8). There must be disclosure of any arrangement whereby a person *may* acquire shares or *has* acquired shares, other than on the terms applicable to subscribers on the prospectus.

(*e*) *Property acquired* (paras 9, 10 and 20). The opportunity for abuse exists where the proceeds or part of the proceeds of an issue are to be used to purchase property, in that the vendor of the property may have an interest in the company. Similarly, any transaction to purchase property may include a deliberately inflated price.

(*f*) *Material contracts* (para 14). This has been defined as any contract which would be likely to influence the judgment of a prospective investor (*Sullivan v. Mitcalfe* (1880)). A material contract need not be in writing (*Arkwright v. Newbold* (1881)). Note that the clause does not refer to contracts made in the ordinary course of business or those entered into two years or more before the date of the prospectus.

(g) *Directors' interests* (para 16). The possible interests are in the promotion of the company and any property to be acquired, and include any financial inducements to be a director.

Paragraphs 2, 3, 12 (so far as it relates to preliminary expenses), and 16 do not apply to a prospectus issued more than two years after the company became entitled to commence business.

Reports required by the Fourth Schedule, Part II

These may be summarised as follows:

(a) **Auditors' reports** concerning the company (para 19).

(b) **Accountants' reports** on any business to be purchased (para 20); and on any business in which shares are to be purchased so that the acquired company becomes a subsidiary (para 21).

Registration of a Prospectus

On or before a prospectus is issued by or on behalf of a company or by a promoter of an intended company, a copy of the prospectus must be lodged with the Registrar for registration (S. 41 (1)). The copy must:

(a) **be dated** (That date, unless the contrary is proved, is deemed to be the date of publication (S. 37));

(b) **be signed** by every person named therein as a director or prospective director, or by his agent authorised in writing (S. 41 (1));

(c) have endorsed thereon or attached, **the written consent of any expert** to the inclusion in the prospectus of any statement made by him in the form and context in which it is given. There must also be a statement that there has been no withdrawal of such consent (S. 40 (1)). The same provisions apply to any statement in a prospectus issued by an overseas company (S. 419)—see also page 51.

If the prospectus is **issued generally** (i.e. it is issued to persons who are not present members or debenture-holders (S. 39)), the following must be endorsed on or attached to the filed copy:

(a) A copy of every material contract mentioned in the prospectus as required by paragraph 14 of the Fourth Schedule.

(b) A signed statement by persons making any financial reports in the prospectus, specifying any adjustments they have made to the figures and giving reasons.

Every prospectus must state on the face of it that a copy has been delivered for registration and must specify the documents required to be endorsed on or attached thereto (S. 41 (2)).

The issue of a prospectus without delivery of a copy and the documents to be endorsed or attached is punishable by a fine not exceeding £5 a day from the date of issue to the date of delivery, imposed on the company and on every person knowingly a party to the issue (S.41(4)).

Shares to be 'Admitted to Listing'

If it is intended that the securities are to be dealt in on the Stock Exchange, application must first be made to the Stock Exchange for the securities to be 'admitted to listing' (see page 217). In addition to the requirements of the law on the contents of the prospectus, the demands for disclosure made by the Stock Exchange must also be met. The proposed prospectus is one of the documents which must be produced to the Stock Exchange when Permission to Deal is sought and it cannot be issued until it has been approved. When the Stock Exchange is satisfied, it will signify its 'preliminary agreement' and the fact that application has been made must be clearly and prominently displayed in the prospectus.

That the permission will be granted after issue of the prospectus is a fundamental condition of any application for shares or debentures. The consequences of failure to obtain permission would mean that the condition had not been complied with and any allotment would be void (see page 55).

Certificate of Exemption

If the securities offered are to be dealt in on the Stock Exchange, S.39 gives the Council of the Stock Exchange authority to grant the company exemption from full compliance with the Fourth Schedule. The decision rests with the Stock Exchange and relief would be given only if full compliance would be 'unduly burdensome'. Thus, a company may be relieved of the expense of full disclosure if the Stock Exchange considered it to be unnecessary because the issue was a small one or there was a limitation on the number of persons to whom the offer was to be made. A prospectus issued on the terms agreed by the Stock Exchange is deemed to comply with the requirements of the Fourth Schedule. The securities offered must be by a prospectus 'issued generally'. Such a prospectus is known as an **abridged prospectus.**

Offer for Sale

Most shares offered to the public are by offer for sale. The principle is that the company allots the whole of the issue to an issuing house which in turn offers them to the public. As the public applies for the shares, the house renounces its rights so that the purchasers become allottees of the *company*, thereby incurring no liability for stamp duty on transfer.

The requirements of S.38 applicable to prospectuses cannot be avoided by issuing an offer for sale instead of a prospectus. S.45 states that where a company allots shares or debentures *with a view to their being offered for sale to the public*, the document by which the offer is made to the public *shall be deemed to be a prospectus issued by the company*. Thus, not only is an offer for sale treated as though it is a prospectus but, also, it is regarded as having been issued by the company. Consequently, all the rules of law relevant to an issue of a prospectus will apply to issues of securities to the public, whether it is by means of a prospectus or an offer for sale. In the latter case, therefore, any misstatements in the document will be the responsibility of the directors of the company or the promoters and of the issuing house.

Where an offer of sale is made, the following information, *additional* to the requirements of S. 38, must be stated:

(*a*) The net amount of the consideration received by the company in respect of the securities issued. (The house issues to the public at a price above that paid to the company.)

(*b*) The time and place at which the contract between the company and the issuing house can be inspected.

Copies of the offer for sale must be lodged with the Registrar under the same conditions as set out in S. 41 for prospectuses. It must be signed by those making the offer (two directors if a company or not less than half of the partners) as though they were named in the documents as directors of the company (S. 45(4)).

Placings

If the number of shares or debentures to be issued is small, they can be 'placed' instead of a prospectus or offer for sale being issued. The usual procedure is for the securities to be purchased by an issuing house which then invites its clients to take up some of them. If the shares are to be listed, the Stock Exchange will require that a proportion be made available to sections of the public in order to create a market. The balance not taken up by clients of the issuing house will become available to the public through their brokers.

The provisions of S. 45 will apply but exemptions will be available under S. 39 if all or part of the existing share capital has been admitted to listing.

Misstatements in the Prospectus

Penalties for making a misstatement in a prospectus may take the form of civil liability or criminal liability. In the latter category, the provisions of the Companies Acts apply but it could include provisions in the *Prevention of Fraud (Investments) Act, 1958*, the *Protection of Depositors Act, 1963*, and the *Theft Act, 1968* (see Chapter 23).

There is no general requirement placed upon persons concerned with issuing a prospectus to reveal every material factor. Thus, if there had been a failure to disclose information required by the Fourth Schedule and the omission did not amount to a misstatement, an allottee would have no right of action against the company, nor could he repudiate the shares (*McKeown v. Boudard, Peveril Gear Co.* (1896)). If, however, disclosure would materially have altered the facts, the failure to disclose may be construed as a misstatement. In such an instance, those responsible for issuing the prospectus may be liable to those who suffered loss. S.46 states that a statement would be deemed to be untrue if it was misleading in the form and context in which it was included.

The remedies available to a person who was induced to apply for shares by a misstatement, innocent or otherwise, or by an omission amounting to a misstatement, are set out below. There is, however, a general provision that no liability would be incurred by a person responsible for issuing a prospectus if he could prove that:

(*a*) He was not cognisant of the omission; or

(*b*) There was an innocent mistake of fact on his part; or

(*c*) The non-compliance or contravention was in respect of matters which in the opinion of the Court were immaterial and ought reasonably to be excused (S.38(4)).

Remedies against the Company for Misrepresentation

Rescission of the Contract to take Shares

This right enables the allottee to repudiate the contract, to have his name removed from the Register of Members and to claim repayment of the amount paid with interest at 4 per cent (*Re Scottish Petroleum Co.* (1883)). To succeed, he must prove:

(*a*) There was a *material* misrepresentation of fact; i.e. it was one likely to influence a reasonable person in his decision to apply for the shares. Also, the statement must be one of *fact* and not merely an *opinion* (although a false statement of opinion may possibly amount to a misstatement). The determining principle is whether all the stated facts taken as a whole present a substantially true picture. It may be impossible to show any one statement as being untrue, yet if the facts generally give a false impression the prospectus must be regarded as false (*Greenwood v. Leather Shod Wheel Co.* (1900)).

(*b*) That he entered into the contract relying on the statements in the prospectus. He would not be required to look beyond those statements or to satisfy himself they were true. Thus, it would be no defence to say that the true facts would have been found in a contract referred to in the prospectus and that the facts could have been learned by reading the contract (*Aaron's Reefs Ltd v. Twiss* (1896)).

(*c*) That he took immediate steps to rescind the contract on discovering the misrepresentation. Mere notice to the company is insufficient; he must take effective steps without delay (*First National Reinsurance*

Co. v. Greenfield (1921)). A delay of two weeks has been construed as unreasonable (*Re Scottish Petroleum Co.* (1883)). The right of rescission may also be lost if the allottee does anything to affirm the contract after discovering the misrepresentation—e.g. by endeavouring to sell the shares (*Re Hop & Malt Exchange and Warehouse Co., Ex parte Briggs* (1866)); by accepting a dividend (*Scholey v. Central Railway Co. of Venezuela* (1868)); or by voting at a general meeting (*Sharpley v. Louth & East Coast Railway* (1876)).

Any proceedings to rescind must be commenced before the commencement of winding up (*Oakes v. Turquand* (1867)).

Under the *Misrepresentation Act, 1967* (S.2(2)), the court may refuse rescission and declare any contract still subsisting in the case of innocent misrepresentation and award damages in lieu. This power would be exercised by the Court if it was of the opinion that it would be equitable to do so having regard to the nature of the misrepresentation and the loss which would be incurred if the contract was upheld and the loss which rescission would impose on the other party.

Action for Damages

The company may be sued for damages *in tort for deceit* where the misrepresentation was made fraudulently. There can be no claim for rescission *and* damages (*Houldsworth v. City of Glasgow Bank* (1880)).

Under Section 2(1) of the *Misrepresentation Act, 1967*, a company may be liable for damages where the other party has entered into a contract after an *innocent* misrepresentation, unless it can be proved there was reasonable ground to believe the facts represented were true.

Remedies against those Responsible for Issuing the Prospectus

Action for Damages

An action for damages in tort for deceit may be brought against directors, promoters or others who signed or authorised the issue of a prospectus, if the representation was *material and fraudulent*.

'Fraud is proved when it is shown that a false representation has been made knowingly; or without belief in its truth; or recklessly, careless whether it be true or false.' (*Derry v. Peek* (1889).) In that case it was held that the directors were not liable because they had an honest belief in the truth of the statement.

This right to damages is open only to the allottee. It would not accrue to a person who took the shares from the allottee by purchase (*Peek v. Gurney* (1873)).

Compensation under the Companies Act

Because of the inadequate protection under Common Law as evidenced in *Derry v. Peek* (above), the *Directors' Liability Act, 1890*, was passed to give the right of compensation for misrepresentation, *irrespective* of fraudulent intent. The current legislation is S. 43 of the *Companies Act, 1948*, whereby any person who has subscribed for shares or debentures on the strength of a prospectus containing untrue statements may claim compensation for any loss or damage sustained against every director, promoter and person who has authorised issue of the prospectus. Although the claimant does not have to prove fraud, he must prove:

(*a*) That a material misstatement was made;

(*b*) That he was thereby deceived; and

(*c*) That he suffered loss or damage as a consequence.

Compensation may be claimed even though the contract to take up the shares has not been rescinded and even if winding up has commenced.

The rules of S. 43 also apply in respect of overseas companies (S. 422).

A defence to a claim under S. 43 will be available if the party can prove any of the following:

(*a*) That having consented to become a director, he withdrew his consent before issue of the prospectus and that the prospectus was issued without his authority or consent.

(*b*) That the prospectus was issued without his knowledge or consent, and that on becoming aware of its issue he forthwith gave reasonable public notice that it was so issued.

(*c*) That after issue of the prospectus and before allotment thereunder, he, on becoming aware of any untrue statement therein, withdrew his consent and gave reasonable public notice of his withdrawal and the reason therefor.

(*d*) That

(*i*) as regards every untrue statement (not purporting to be made on the authority of an expert or of a public official document or statement) he had reasonable grounds to believe, and did, up to the time of allotment, believe the statement to be true; and

(*ii*) as regards every untrue statement which did purport to be a statement by an expert or contained in a report or valuation by an expert, it fairly represented the statement or was a correct copy of or extract from the report or valuation, and he had reasonable grounds to believe and did believe up to the time of the issue that the person making it was competent to make it and had not withdrawn his consent before registration of the prospectus or before allotment; and

(*iii*) as regards every untrue statement which did purport to be made by an official person or contained in what purported to be a copy of or extract from a public official document, it was a correct representation of the statement or copy or extract from the document (S. 43(2)).

Under the *Limitation Act, 1939* (S. 2), legal action must be brought within six years from the date of allotment; but if there has been fraud, the period runs from when the fraud was or ought to have been discovered.

Remedies against Experts

A claim against an expert can be made only for untrue statements made by him *as* an expert; but if he was also one of the persons who authorised issue of the prospectus, he will be liable in respect of any misstatements, innocent or fraudulent. (An expert does not 'authorise the issue' by giving his consent for a statement by him to be included in the prospectus.) He will not be liable as an expert if he proves:

(*a*) That having given his consent under S. 40 to the issue of the prospectus, he withdrew in writing *before registration of the prospectus*; or

(*b*) That *after registration and before allotment*, on becoming aware of the untrue statement, he withdrew his consent in writing and gave reasonable public notice of his withdrawal and the reasons therefore; or

(*c*) That he was competent to make the statement and had reasonable ground to believe (and did believe up to the time of allotment) that the statement was true (S. 43(3)).

Criminal Liability for Misrepresentation

The rights of aggrieved parties as given in the preceding pages are relevant to *civil* proceedings. S. 44 states that any person authorising the issue of a prospectus containing an untrue statement is liable to imprisonment for up to two years and/or a fine not exceeding £500, unless he can prove:

(*a*) That the statement was immaterial; or

(*b*) That he believed the statement to be true and had reasonable ground for doing so.

Under S. 15 of the *Theft Act, 1968*, a director would be liable to prosecution if he published in a prospectus a statement which he knew to be false with the intention of inducing persons to take shares in the company and money was received from them in reliance on the false statement.

Statement in lieu of Prospectus

Where securities are not offered to the public, no prospectus, obviously, will be issued. A prospectus serves not only as an advertisement, however; it also provides a record in that a copy must be filed with the Registrar. The purpose of requiring a statement in lieu of prospectus to be filed, therefore, is to ensure that the necessary information about the company is available as a public record even though no prospectus has been issued.

The statement must be filed when *a private company converts into a public company* (S. 30). The particulars to be filed are prescribed in the *Third Schedule* (see page 8).

It must also be filed by a *public company* at least three days *before issuing shares or debentures* if it did not issue a prospectus upon formation or it did not allot on a prospectus issued at that time (see page 55). S. 48 requires that the statement be signed by every person named therein as a director or proposed director. The statement must be in the form set out in Part I of the *Fifth Schedule*. Where relevant, Part II will apply, giving reports on any business to be purchased or on any body corporate whose shares are to be purchased with the result that that body would become a subsidiary of the company. In general, the requirements of the Fifth Schedule correspond with those of the Fourth Schedule, except that the following are omitted:

(*a*) Particulars of founders' or deferred shares.

(*b*) The share qualification of the directors and any Articles dealing with their remuneration.

(*c*) Particulars of the minimum subscription.

(*d*) The time of opening the subscription lists.

(*e*) The amount payable on application and allotment, and details of allotments in the two preceding years.

(*f*) The length of time the company has been carrying on business where less than three years.

(*g*) A report by the auditors on profits and losses, assets and liabilities.

Criminal Liability for False Statements

A person authorising the delivery of a statement in lieu of prospectus containing an untrue statement is liable to imprisonment for up to two years and/or a fine not exceeding £500 (Ss. 30(4), 48(5)). The defences contained in S. 44 relevant to prospectuses are available.

S. 438 is also relevant in that it states that any person wilfully making a statement false in some material particular in a statement in lieu of prospectus is guilty of a misdemeanour.

The provisions of the *Theft Act, 1968,* relevant to prospectuses also apply.

Right of Rescission

An allottee who was induced to apply for shares upon the faith of a filed statement in lieu of prospectus which contained an untrue statement may claim rescission of the contract to take up the shares, provided he inspected the document and was influenced thereby (*Re Blair Open Hearth Furnace Co.* (1914)).

Right of Compensation

There is no right of compensation as is provided by S. 43 in respect of prospectuses, although the right to sue in deceit will exist.

6

APPLICATION AND ALLOTMENT

The Subscription Lists

The Companies Acts contain regulations concerning application for and allotment of securities. To appreciate the significance of the time limits in the Act it is necessary to understand 'the time of the opening of the subscription lists'. This is defined in S.50 as the beginning of the third day after that on which the prospectus was first issued *generally* (or such later time as may be specified in the prospectus), and must be quoted in the prospectus. The provisions concerning the date of the subscription lists are therefore applicable only in respect of those prospectuses issued to persons other than existing members and debentureholders. The date of issue is generally deemed to be the date of the newspaper advertisement.

The Application

As explained in the previous chapter, a request to be allotted shares is an **offer**, made in response to an invitation to apply. The allotting of shares by the directors in reply to an offer constitutes an **acceptance** of that offer.

Revocation of Application

The general rule of offer and acceptance is that an offer can be revoked at any time before acceptance is made. The Act, however, makes an exception to this rule, as it relates to application for and allotment of securities, as follows:

(*a*) S.50 prescribes that an application based on a prospectus issued generally may not be revoked until the expiration of the *third day after the time of the opening of the subscription lists*. This is aimed at preventing the activities of 'stags'. (These are people who apply for shares in the hope of selling them almost immediately at a profit.) If it were not for this legal restriction, such speculators could cancel their applications if the shares fell in value instead of rising as they had hoped. This could result in a fully subscribed issue being converted into an undersubscribed one.

(*b*) But S.50 also states that, within the same period, an application *may* be revoked if any person has given notice of withdrawal of his consent in respect of matters published in a prospectus issued generally, as provided in S.43 (see page 50). Obviously, the serving of such a notice must give rise to doubt about the truth of the contents of the prospectus, and revocation is permitted because the application would have been made in the belief that the statements were true.

The above provisions do not apply where a Certificate of Exemption has been granted.

Conditional Applications

If an application is conditional, then an acceptance which does not include the condition is void. Thus, if an application was conditional upon the applicant being given a position in the company and this did not happen (*Rogers' Case, 1868*), or if the applicant was not given a certain contract, contrary to the condition forming part of the application (*Woods' Case, 1858*), the allotment would be void.

The Act of Allotment

An application for shares or debentures is addressed to the *directors* and, consequently, an allotment of securities (being the acceptance of the offer) must be made by the directors. This consists of a resolution passed by the directors but the contract is not complete until the acceptance, in the form of an **Allotment Letter**, has been communicated to the applicant. Ordinarily, the post is the accepted method of communication and the allotment is completed when the Letter is posted, even if it is never received (*Household Fire Insurance Co. v. Grant* (1879)) or it is delayed (*Dunlop v. Higgins* (1848)).

Prohibitions on Allotment

The prohibitions listed below apply only to public companies; private companies may allot immediately upon incorporation.

(a) Relevant to the minimum subscription (S.47)

In the case of the *first* occasion on which *shares* are offered to the public, no allotment may be made unless

(*i*) The amount stated in the prospectus as the minimum subscription (see page 44) has been subscribed; and

(*ii*) The sum due on application (which must be at least 5 per cent of the nominal value of the shares) for the amount so stated has actually been received by the company.

In the event of the above conditions not being met within forty days of issuing the prospectus, the application moneys must be repaid forthwith without interest. If they are not repaid within forty-eight days of the issue of the prospectus, the directors are jointly and severally liable to repay with interest at 5 per cent after the forty-eighth day.

The provisions of S.47 apply only to the *first* public offer because the purpose of stating the minimum subscription in the prospectus is to ensure companies do not collapse as a result of commencing trading with insufficient capital.

(b) Relevant to a statement in lieu of prospectus (S. 48)

A public company (*i*) which *does not issue a prospectus* on or with reference to its formation (i.e. the share capital was provided privately), or (*ii*) which *has* issued a prospectus but *did not allot* any shares thereby offered (i.e. the public offer was a failure but finance was obtained from another source), may not allot shares or debentures until, at least three days before allotment, it has filed a statement in lieu of prospectus (see page 52).

(c) Relevant to the time of the opening of the subscription lists (S. 50)

No allotment may be made on a prospectus issued generally until the opening of the subscription lists. The purpose of this ruling is to allow time for investors to study the documents and for applications to reach the company. An allotment made before that time *is not invalid*, but the company and every officer in default would be liable to a fine not exceeding £500.

(d) Relevant to securities to be admitted to listing (S. 51)

An investor will be much influenced if he understands that the securities offered in a prospectus will be dealt in on the Stock Exchange, and failure to get the necessary permission would probably be regarded by him as breach of a fundamental condition upon which he had relied. If a prospectus, issued generally or not, states that application for permission for the shares to be dealt in on the Stock Exchange has been made, then any allotment thereunder *will be void* (*i*) if permission *has not been applied for* before the third day after issue of the prospectus, or (*ii*) if permission *has been refused* before the expiration of three weeks from the date of closing the subscription lists (or such longer period, not exceeding six weeks, as may be granted by the Stock Exchange). The company would be required forthwith to repay all moneys received, and any money not repaid within eight days of the company's liability to repay it would become the joint and several liability of the directors to repay with interest at 5 per cent.

All money received by the company, pending the granting or refusal of permission to deal, must be kept in a separate bank account and would not be regarded as the company's property (*Re Nanwa Gold Mines Ltd* (1955)).

Irregular Allotments

S. 49 states that an allotment in contravention of S. 47 (minimum subscription) or of S. 48 (statement in lieu of prospectus) is *voidable* at the instance of the applicant, (*a*) within one month after the statutory meeting, or (*b*) within one month of the date of allotment where the holding of a statutory meeting is not necessary or the allotment is made after the statutory meeting, even if the company is in the course of winding up. This remedy is not available to an allottee who, after discovering the irregularity, acquiesces to it in any way (*Finance and Issue Ltd v. Canadian Produce Co.* (1905)).

A director who knowingly permits contravention of the section is liable, for a period of two years after the allotment, to compensate the company and the allottee for any loss sustained thereby.

As stated above, an allotment in contravention of S.50 (opening of the subscription lists) *is not void*; an allotment in contravention of S.51 (admission to listing) *is void*.

Return of Allotments

S.52, as amended by the 1976 Act, requires that a company must, within one month of an allotment of shares, file with the Registrar:

(*a*) A *return*, giving
   (*i*) the number and nominal amount of the shares allotted;
   (*ii*) the names, addresses and descriptions of the allottees;
   (*iii*) the amount (if any) paid or payable on each share, including any amount payable by way of premium.
(*b*) In respect of any shares issued *for a consideration other than cash*
   (*i*) a contract in writing, constituting the title of the allottee to the allotment;
   (*ii*) any contract for sale or for services or other consideration in respect of which the allotment was made;
   (*iii*) a return stating the number and nominal amount of the shares so allotted, the extent to which they are to be treated as paid up and the consideration for the allotment.

The allotting of shares for a consideration other than cash is most frequently used when shares are part or all of the price paid to a vendor, particularly when a business is converted into a company.

If shares have been allotted to promoters for services which have enhanced the value of property acquired, this is regarded as part of the purchase price of the property. If shares are issued in satisfaction of a debt due, they are regarded as being for consideration other than cash and a contract must be filed (*Re Johannesburg Hotel Co.* (1891)).

Commencement of Business

A private company and any company without a share capital may commence business immediately upon incorporation.

A public company may not commence business or exercise any borrowing power until it has been issued with a **certificate to commence**

business (known as a **Trading Certificate**). Such a certificate is conclusive evidence that a company is entitled to commence trading (S. 109). It will not be issued unless:

(*a*) *In the case of a company which has issued a prospectus:*
  (*i*) shares payable in cash have been allotted for an amount not less than the minimum subscription;
  (*ii*) every director has paid on the shares taken or to be taken by him and payable in cash, a proportion equal to the proportion payable on application and allotment on the shares offered for public subscription;
  (*iii*) no money is liable to be repaid to applicants because of failure to apply for or to obtain permission for the shares or debentures to be dealt in on the Stock Exchange;
  (*iv*) a statutory declaration by a director or the secretary has been delivered to the Registrar stating that the above conditions have been complied with.
(*b*) *In the case of a company which has not issued a prospectus:*
  (*i*) a statement in lieu of prospectus has been delivered to the Registrar;
  (*ii*) every director has paid an amount as stated in (*a*)(*ii*) above;
  (*iii*) a statutory declaration has been made as in (*a*)(*iv*) above.

Any contract made by a company before its Trading Certificate is received is provisional, but becomes binding on the day it is received. Accordingly, if a company is wound up before its Trading Certificate is received, it is not liable on any contracts it has made (*Re Otto Electrical Manufacturing Co.* (1906)).

If a company commences business or exercises borrowing power before it is entitled to do so, every person responsible is liable to a fine not exceeding £50 for every day the contravention continues.

If a company does not commence trading within a year of its incorporation, ground exists for petitioning the Court for a winding-up order (S. 222).

Issue of Shares at a Discount

A fundamental rule is that the share capital must be maintained. It also follows that a company must have or can receive the full amount of the nominal value of its issued shares. Accordingly, shares may be issued at a discount only under conditions which comply with the Act. S. 57 prescribes as follows:

(*a*) The shares must be of a class already in issue.
(*b*) At least one year must have elapsed since the company was entitled to commence business.
(*c*) The issue must be authorised by a resolution passed in general meeting, and the resolution must specify the maximum rate of discount.

(*d*) The issue must be sanctioned by the Court and it must be made within one month of that sanction or within any extended period allowed by the Court.

Every prospectus must give particulars of the discount allowed on the issue of shares or of so much of any discount as has not been written off at the date of the issue of the prospectus. The amount of any discount so far as not written off must also be shown as a separate entry in the balance sheet and in the Annual Return.

Debentures may be issued at a discount, but the provisions of S. 57 would be contravened if such debentures carried the right to convert them into shares of equal nominal value (*Mosely v. Koffyfontein Mines* (1904)).

Issue of Shares at a Premium

Shares may be issued at a price above their nominal value and the aggregate of such premiums must be transferred to a **share premium account**. The rules relating to reduction of capital apply also to this account, but the account may be applied:

(*a*) In paying up unissued shares to be issued to members as fully paid shares in the form of a scrip issue;

(*b*) In writing off the preliminary expenses of the company or the expenses of commissions paid or discounts allowed on any issue of shares or debentures;

(*c*) In providing for a premium payable on the redemption of redeemable preference shares (S. 56).

The amount of any premium must be included in the return of allotments (S. 52 as amended) and in any prospectus issued (S. 33 (1976)).

Underwriting

The possibility of not all the shares or debentures offered in a public issue being taken up may be remote, but it does exist. The 'flop' may be due to a miscalculation of market reaction where, for example, the issue price is too high. A more likely reason would be the occurrence of some unexpected event external to the company, such as a sudden political or economic crisis. Whatever the reason, the failure of a company to receive all the money anticipated could be critical, particularly because it would have made plans (or even entered into commitments) on the assumption that the funds would be forthcoming.

This risk is covered by a form of insurance known as an **underwriting agreement**. Financial interests, known as 'underwriters' when carrying out this function, agree that in the event of the issue not being fully subscribed they will purchase the deficiency. By this method, the company can be assured that the full amount will be received.

Like all insurance, it has to be paid for in the form of a premium, known in this case as underwriting commission. In the event of the underwriters having to take up part of the issue, the effective price to them of the shares or debentures will be the issue price less the commission on the total underwritten. If the shares were issued at par (i.e. with no premium), the net cost to the underwriters would therefore be less than the par value, but this is not regarded in law as an illegal issue at a discount.

Because of their possible liability, the underwriters will require to approve the prospectus. They would also wish to be assured that the contents of the prospectus would be likely to result in a successful issue. It is normal practice to include in the underwriting agreement a condition that if an alteration is made to the draft prospectus as agreed with the underwriters, the underwriters would continue to be bound. If, however, the alteration *materially* altered its terms, the underwriters would be released (*Warner International and Overseas Engineering Co. Ltd v. Kilburn Brown & Co.* (1914)).

A **firm underwriting** means an agreement by an underwriter to take up a specified number of shares irrespective of the success or failure of the issue. Although he would not be 'on risk' to the extent of such shares, his commission would include that for those to be taken firm.

Subject to the terms of the agreement, the main underwriters may be relieved from part of their potential liability by entering into sub-underwriting agreements with other parties. The requirement of paragraph 11 of the Fourth Schedule relevant to the payment of commission (see below) does not include commission payable to sub-underwriters.

Payment of Commission

On an issue of *shares*, commission is sometimes paid to persons who introduce capital into a company (e.g. a broker procuring subscriptions from his clients). S. 53, however, provides that shares or capital money may not be applied, directly or indirectly, in payment of commission, discount or allowance, to any person in consideration of his subscribing for shares in the company or for procuring subscription for shares, unless certain conditions are met. These are as follows:

(*a*) Payment of commission must be authorised by the Articles.

(*b*) The rate must not exceed 10 per cent of the issue price of the shares or the rate authorised in the Articles, whichever is the less.

(*c*) The rate or amount must be disclosed in

(*i*) the prospectus, if the shares are offered to the public; or

(*ii*) the statement in lieu of prospectus if the shares are not offered to the public; or

(*iii*) a statement in the prescribed form in the case of a private company. (This is unlikely to obtain because, of course, a private company may not invite the public to subscribe.)

(*d*) The number of shares persons have agreed, for a commission, to subscribe *absolutely* must be disclosed in the above-mentioned manner.

Commission may be paid in respect of an issue of *debentures*, unless forbidden by the Memorandum or the Articles. Particulars of any commission paid must be registered with the Registrar within twenty-one days of the issue (S.95(9)). Disclosure must be made in the prospectus or statement in lieu as for shares.

Generally

The total amount of commission paid must be stated in the Annual Return (S.124) and, to the extent it has not been written off, in the balance sheet (S.149 and Second Schedule, para 3 (1967)). Disclosure must be made in the prospectus or statement in lieu of amounts or rates of commission paid in the two years preceding issue of the prospectus.

The provisions of S.53 apparently do not apply to the payment of commission out of *profits*, as the restrictions of that section are applicable if payment of commission is at the expense of the company's capital. S.53 also does not apply in respect of *brokerage* paid to brokers or an issuing house which places the company's shares or debentures with their clients. The amount must, however, be disclosed in any prospectus or statement in lieu issued within two years.

The share premium account may be used to write off commission (S.56(2)).

Financial Assistance for the Purchase of Shares

S.54 makes it unlawful for a company to give any financial assistance towards the purchase of shares in the company or its subsidiary company. 'Financial assistance' includes the lending of money to the purchaser and the giving of a guarantee or security to a third party who, as a consequence, lends money to the purchaser. Exceptions are:

(*a*) Where the lending of money is part of the company's ordinary business (e.g. a bank);

(*b*) Where, as part of a scheme in force, the company provides money to trustees for shares to be held for benefit of the company's employees, including a director in a salaried office (e.g. a staff pension scheme);

(*c*) The making of loans to bona fide employees (but *not* directors) to enable those persons to purchase fully-paid shares to be held by them as beneficial owners (i.e. not as part of a trust).

The aggregate of (*a*) and (*b*) above, to the extent the loans are outstanding, must be shown in the balance sheet (Second Schedule 1967 Act, para 8(*c*)).

The company and any officer in contravention of S.54 is liable to a fine not exceeding £100. Any contract in contravention of the Section *is unenforceable* (*South Western Mineral Waters Ltd v. Ashmore* (1967)).

It has been held that where a vendor of shares agrees to lend the purchaser part of the purchase money provided that the company issues to him a debenture secured by a floating charge over its assets, the debenture is illegal, whether it is *ultra vires* of the company to issue it or not. If the purchaser guarantees that the company will repay the sum secured, the guarantee is also void and unenforceable (*Heald v. O'Connor* (1971)).

7

MEMBERSHIP

The Status of Membership

Membership of a company must be the result of a *voluntary action* whereby a person is assumed to be aware of the conditions to which he subscribes upon becoming a member. No matter what the circumstances in which a person becomes a member, there must be evidence of his willingness to do so, and, as shown later, a person can claim not to be a member if that evidence is not forthcoming.

The rights of members *generally* which are specific to a company are laid down in the Articles of that company. Those rights which are specific to a *class* of member may be prescribed in the Articles or the terms of issue. The law relevant to any variation of class rights is set out on page 172.

In general, the liability of a member is limited to any amount unpaid on his shares. This subject is dealt with on page 191.

Date of Commencement of Membership

The principle for determining when membership commences for the *subscribers* and the *first directors* is different from that applicable to other members.

Commencement of Membership before Registration as a Member

In respect of subscribers and the first directors, membership may commence before entry in the Register of Members.

(*a*) *As subscribers*. Subscribers to the Memorandum are deemed to have agreed to become members of the company and must be entered in the Register of Members upon registration of the company (S.26(1)), but, irrespective of the date of entry, membership will be deemed to commence *on the date of the company's incorporation* (*Re Tyddyn Sheffrey Slate Quarries Co.* (1868)). Also, membership does not have to await allotment of shares subscribed by signatories, because a signatory binds himself to take and pay for that number of shares. The only exception would be if it was impossible to allot him shares because the shares had been allotted to other persons (*Tuffnell's Case* (1885)).

(*b*) *As directors*. A person who has delivered to the Registrar a signed undertaking to take and pay for qualification shares (see page 81), is in the same position as if he had subscribed to the Memorandum for that number of shares (S. 181 (2)). Persons who are named as directors in the statement to be delivered with the Memorandum upon registration of a company are deemed to have been appointed as the first directors *upon the incorporation of the company* (S. 21 (5) (1976)).

Commencement of Membership upon Registration as a Member

'*Every other person* who agrees to become a member and whose name *is entered in the Register of Members* shall be a member of the company' (S. 26 (2)). Thus, except in the case of the subscribers and the first directors, a person may not be regarded as being a member until he is registered as such, and until that time he acquires no rights or liabilities of a member. Even if a person has contracted to take shares, the agreement may be rescinded by the *mutual* consent of the company and the allottee, provided it is done before an entry is made in the Register (*Nicol's Case* (1885)).

A person entitled to be registered as a member may compel the company to register him as such if it has refused to do so (see page 66).

Registration of a person as a member may derive from:

(*i*) Subscribing to the Memorandum.
(*ii*) Undertaking to take and pay for qualification shares.
(*iii*) Being named as one of the first directors and consenting to act.
(*iv*) Allotment of shares following application.
(*v*) Transfer of shares from a present holder.
(*vi*) Transmission, whereby ownership of shares is changed by operation of law.
(*vii*) Estoppel, whereby a person holds himself out to be a member, such as allowing his name to remain on the Register after he has ceased to be the owner of the shares.

Capacity to become a Member

Eligibility for membership may be determined as prescribed by law or by the Articles of the company concerned.

(*a*) A **company** may be a member of another company if so authorised by its Memorandum. It cannot hold its own shares, by purchase or otherwise, as this would constitute an unauthorised reduction of capital (*Trevor v. Whitworth* (1887)).

A **subsidiary company** cannot hold shares in its holding company (S. 27), except where the subsidiary is acting as personal representative or trustee and the holding company has no beneficial interest under the trust.

(*b*) An **infant** may become a member but has the right to repudiate any liability when he attains his majority or within a reasonable time thereafter. Any liability could, of course, apply only in respect of partly-paid shares, and an infant is not liable for calls made on the shares before or after the repudiation. Should he repudiate, he cannot recover any money he has paid for the shares unless they never had any value (*Steinberg v. Scala* (*Leeds*) *Ltd* (1923)). Any proposed repudiation may be difficult to sustain if the infant has benefited as the holder of the shares or exercised any rights as a member (e.g. by accepting dividends or by voting).

(*c*) **A partnership** may not be registered in its firm's name because a partnership is not a legal entity (except in Scotland).

(*d*) **Joint holders** may be registered. The order in which the names are to be registered will be prescribed by the joint holders, who are also entitled to have the total holding split so as to provide more than one sequence of names (*Burns v. Siemens Brothers Dynamo Works Ltd* (1919)). Most Articles provide that notices, dividends, etc., will be sent to the first-named of joint holders (the 'senior holder'). Joint holders are jointly and severally liable for calls, and all joint holders must sign any transfer of shares.

Cessation of Membership

The circumstances under which a person will be deemed to have ceased to be a member upon removal of his name from the Register of Members, may be summarised as follows:

(*i*) Transfer.

(*ii*) Death (although the estate of the deceased member assumes any liabilities on the shares).

(*iii*) Forfeiture of shares or surrender where forfeiture would be justified.

(*iv*) Imposition of the company's lien and power of sale.

(*v*) Redemption of redeemable preference shares.

(*vi*) Disclaimer by the holder's trustee in bankruptcy.

(*vii*) Rescission by an allottee because of misrepresentation.

(*viii*) Dissolution of the company.

(*ix*) Repudiation by a minor.

(*x*) Shares belonging to an oppressed minority ordered by the Court to be purchased under S. 210.

(*xi*) Compulsory purchase of the interests of dissenting members in respect of takeover bids and reconstruction schemes (Ss. 209 and 287).

The Register of Members

Every company must keep a register of its members, which must contain the following information:

(*a*)(*i*) The names and addresses of the members. (*ii*) The number of shares held by each member (giving the distinguishing numbers, if any).

(*iii*) The amount paid or agreed to be considered as paid on the shares of each member.

(*b*) The date on which each name was entered.

(*c*) The date on which each person ceased to be a member.

If the company has converted any if its shares into stock, the Register must show the amount of stock held by each member (S. 110).

Location

It must be kept at the company's registered office unless it is maintained at another office of the company or by some person authorised to undertake the work of making up the Register. It must be within the domicile of the company. A company must notify the Registrar where the Register is kept and of any change in that place within fourteen days (S. 110).

Index

A company having more than fifty members must maintain an index of members, unless the Register is in the form of an index. The index must be altered within fourteen days of any alteration to the Register (S. 111).

Right to Inspect and Obtain Copies

The Register and the index must be open during business hours (at least two hours a day) for *inspection* by (*a*) any member, without charge, and (*b*) any other person, on payment of a fee not exceeding 5p.

Any person may demand a *copy* of the Register or any part thereof for a fee not exceeding 10p for every one hundred words or fraction thereof (S. 113(2) as amended by S. 52(2)(1967)). Any copy so required must be provided within ten days commencing the day after the day of the request. If inspection is refused or a copy not provided within the prescribed time, the company and every officer in default is liable to a fine not exceeding £2 and a default fine of £2 a day while the refusal or non-provision continues. The Court may compel inspection or the provision of copies (S. 113).

The right to demand copies does not bestow the right to make copies on inspection (*Re Balaghat Gold, etc., Co.* (1901)). Suspicion as to the motive for inspection does not give the right to refuse inspection (*Davies v. Gas Light & Coke Co.* (1909)). The right of inspection is not available when a company is in liquidation (*Re Kent Coalfield Syndicate* (1898)).

A company may give notice by advertisement of the closing of the Register for any times not exceeding in total thirty days in each year, and no right of inspection or to copies is available during those times (S. 115).

Rectification

The Register is *prima facie* evidence of any matter directed or authorised to be entered therein (S.118), but application may be made to the Court for rectification of the Register if (*a*) the name of any person is *entered in* or *omitted from* the Register without sufficient cause, or (*b*) there is default or unnecessary delay in entering the fact that a person has *ceased* to be a member.

Such application may be made by the aggrieved person, by any member or by the company. If the Court orders rectification, it may require the company to pay damages to the party aggrieved. At the same time, it may decide any question concerning title to the shares. The Court order will direct notice of the rectification to be given to the Registrar (S.116).

Rectification can be made if the company is in liquidation, and the Court may even antedate the alteration (*Re Sussex Brick Co.* (1904)).

Notice of Trust

Shares are frequently entered in the names of persons who are acting on behalf of the beneficial owners. S.117 prescribes that no notice of a trust—expressed, implied or constructive—may be entered in the Register of Members. Even though the company may be aware that a trust exists it must not recognise it in any way, and it must deal with the registered holders only as though they were the beneficial owners. The company is not put upon enquiry as to whether the trustees are acting within their authority in any action they take concerning the shares, unless it is fixed with official notice (*Simpson v. Molson's Bank* (1895)).

There *are* certain circumstances where the law requires notification to be made of an 'interest' in shares but the particulars are to be shown, not in the Register of Members, but in the Register of Interests in Voting Shares (see page 160) and the Register of Directors' Interests (see page 90).

Dominion Register

A company may keep a branch register of members in any part of the Dominions in which the company is permitted by its objects to transact business (S.119). Notice must be given to the Registrar of the situation of a Dominion Register, any change in its situation and any discontinuation of such a register.

A Dominion Register is deemed to be part of the company's Register (referred to as 'the principal register') and must be kept in the same manner. A copy of every entry in the Dominion Register must be transmitted to the registered office after entry and a duplicate of the Dominion Register must be kept with the principal register.

Share Certificates

A share has been defined as 'the interest of a shareholder in the company, measured by a sum of money for the purpose of liability in the first place and of interest in the second, but also consisting of a series of mutual covenants entered into by all the shareholders *inter se*' (*Borland's Trustees v. Steel Brothers* (1901)). A share is *personal* property, transferable in the manner prescribed in the Articles (S.73). Each share in a company with a share capital should have a distinguishing number, although this need not apply if all the shares or all the shares of a class are fully paid up and rank *pari passu* for all purposes (S.74).

A share certificate issued under the common seal of the company, specifying the shares held by a member, is *prima facie* evidence of title to the shares (S.81). It is not conclusive evidence, but by the issuing of a share certificate under the above conditions a company may be *estopped* from denying the authenticity of the particulars specified in the certificate. The following are some illustrations of the effect of this principle:

(*a*) If the certificate states that the shares are fully paid, the company may not deny they are fully paid against a person who has *bona fide* relied on the truth of the statement (*Bloomenthal v. Ford* (1897)).

(*b*) In *Dixon v. Kennaway & Co.* (1900), the plaintiff instructed Liddell, a broker and secretary of the defendant company, to purchase shares in the company. Liddell's clerk (who owned no shares) executed what purported to be a transfer of shares to the plaintiff. The company registered the transfer without requiring production of a share certificate from the clerk and issued a share certificate to the 'transferee'. It was held that the company was estopped from denying the validity of the certificate and was liable for damages.

(*c*) Where a certificate was not issued *by the company* or by someone authorised by the company, the company was *not* estopped from denying the holder's right to be regarded as a member. In *Ruben v. Great Fingall Consolidated Co.* (1906) the secretary forged the directors' signatures and fraudulently affixed the company's seal to the certificate.

(*d*) No estoppel can be applied against a company if the claimant is aware of the true position. Thus, an allottee could not rely on a certificate stating shares were fully paid when he, as the allottee, knew he had not paid the full amount (*Crickmer's Case* (1875)).

(*e*) No title can be acquired by a person who has submitted a forged transfer. In that event, the company must restore the name of the true owner to the Register and may seek indemnity against the person lodging the transfer for any loss sustained (*Sheffield Corporation v. Barclay* (1905)). If, however, before the forgery is discovered, the holder of the certificate transfers it to an innocent party, the doctrine of estoppel will operate against the company. It cannot deny the authenticity of the certificate to an innocent party and the company would have to acquire shares for that party or, where that is not possible, pay him compensation. This is because, of course, the true owner of the shares must be restored to the Register (see also page 70).

Issue of Certificates

S. 80 requires that share or debenture certificates must be complete and ready for delivery within two months after allotment or lodgment of a transfer, under penalty of a daily fine not exceeding £5. In the event of default by a company, the aggrieved party may serve a notice on the company requiring compliance. If the default continues for a further ten days, the Court may make an order directing the company and every officer in default to rectify the omission within a specified time.

The Stock Exchange requires more prompt issue of certificates, the maximum periods being (*i*) within one month of expiration of any right to renounce; (*ii*) within fourteen days of lodgment of a transfer.

Share Transfers

The Right to Transfer Shares

The principles governing a member's right to transfer shares may be summarised as follows:

(*a*) Every shareholder has a right to transfer his shares in the manner prescribed by the company's Articles (S. 73).

(*b*) A shareholder may transfer his shares to whomsoever he pleases (*Lindlar's Case* (1910)). (This would be subject to any restrictive provisions in the Articles. For example, Table A gives the directors power to decline to register the transfer of a partly-paid share to a person of whom they disapprove and also the transfer of a share on which the company has a lien.)

(*c*) A private company must restrict the right of its members to transfer shares (S. 28).

(*d*) A private company may include a *pre-emption clause* in its Articles, under which a member wishing to transfer his shares must first offer them to the other members.

(*e*) The Articles of a private company may give the right of *expropriation* of shares. Thus, it may provide for acquisition by the other shareholders of the shares of a member deceased or bankrupt at a price determined by a method given in the Articles. Such an expropriation must be in good faith and shown to be for the benefit of the company.

(The purpose of clauses such as (*d*) and (*e*) above is to prevent shares being transferred in such a way as to bring in a new shareholder without the agreement of the others and thereby perhaps destroy the 'family' relationship of the members.)

(*f*) The form for transferring fully-paid shares is prescribed in the *Stock Transfer Act, 1963* (see below).

(*g*) The transfer of shares to a person resident outside the Scheduled Territories without the consent of the Treasury is forbidden under the *Exchange Control Act, 1947*.

(*h*) In respect of fully-paid shares admitted to listing on the Stock Exchange, an absolute power to refuse transfer is forbidden.

(*i*) Directors with the right to refuse transfers may do so without giving any reason for their refusal (*Re Smith and Fawcett Ltd* (1942)). The Court would not interfere with this right unless it could be shown that the power had been used corruptly, fraudulently or with malice (*Re Penny* (1872)).

(*j*) The right exists in law to refuse transfer of partly-paid shares to an infant (*Castello's Case* (1869)).

(*k*) A company must abide by an order of the Court restricting a member's right to transfer his shares (see page 72).

The Instrument of Transfer

A transfer of shares or debentures may not be registered unless a 'proper instrument of transfer' has been delivered to the company (S. 75).

The Stock Transfer Act, 1963, states that:

(*a*) A transfer of fully-paid shares is required to be signed by the transferor only;

(*b*) There is no requirement for witnessing of the transferor's signature;

(*c*) A transfer need not be in the form of a deed (except in the case of a corporate body having a common seal).

The Act over-rides any conflicting clause in the Articles governing the form of transfer of securities to which it applies. Articles drafted before the Act usually prescribe the 'common form of transfer' but such a requirement cannot be imposed. Any rights a company may have to refuse transfers are not abrogated by the *Stock Transfer Act*, except the right to refuse a transfer not in the form demanded in the Articles.

The Act relates, *inter alia*, to securities issued by companies within the meaning of the *Companies Act, 1948*, with the exception of unlimited and guarantee companies.

Blank Transfers

A lender may retain the borrower's share certificate as security for a loan, together with a transfer form 'in blank', i.e. signed by the borrower but otherwise incomplete. In the event of the lender having to realise on his security, he could enter his name or that of some other person on the transfer as the transferee. This would be in accordance with an agreement between the lender and the borrower, such agreement being preferably in writing, although it may be oral or implied.

Effective Transfer

A person is not deemed to be a member until his name is entered in the Register of Members and consequently he does not become the owner of the shares until that date, although the agreement to purchase the shares (and, possibly, payment for them) would have been made prior to the date of entry. Between those two dates, the transferee would have an equitable interest in the shares and the transferor would be regarded as holding them in trust for the transferee. This has given rise to the following decisions:

(*a*) So far as the company is concerned, any dividends declared and payable before registration of the transfer are the property of the transferor and can be remitted only to him or on his instructions. As regards the buyer and the seller, however, the buyer is *prima facie* entitled to all dividends declared after the date of the transfer form (*Black v. Homersham* (1878)). This would be subject to any contrary agreement, i.e. the shares could be bought 'ex dividend' (without the right to dividends declared).

(*b*) In *Musselwhite v. C. H. Musselwhite & Son Ltd* (1962) it was decided that the voting rights attached to shares passed with the transfer agreement and that, accordingly, the transferor must vote at the direction of the transferee. This would not apply, however, if the transferor had not been paid.

(*c*) Any calls made in the interim period must be paid by the transferor. The amount may be recovered from the transferee, however, because it can be implied that the transferee would indemnify the transferor in respect of any liability arising after the transfer agreement (*Hardoon v. Belilios* (1901)).

The position of the company is clear: it may recognise and deal only with the person registered as the owner of the shares, even if it is aware that a transfer has been agreed.

Forged Transfers

No rights can pass to a person named as the transferee on a transfer instrument which is forged. This applies even if the transferee acted in good faith and had received a share certificate from the company in his name. Upon discovery of the forgery, the true owner's name must be restored to the Register and any dividends not received by him during the period when his name was absent must be paid to him (*Barton v.*

North Staffordshire Railway Co. (1888)). He must also receive any rights of which he had been defrauded.

The company would have a right of action against the person lodging the transfer because in so doing he implies that the transfer is genuine. A bank lodging a forged transfer has been held to be so liable (*Sheffield Corporation v. Barclay* (1905)).

Under the *Forged Transfers Acts, 1891–92*, a company is permitted to establish a fund to provide compensation for anyone suffering as a result of a forged transfer. If a company does make compensation, it is subrogated to the rights of the person compensated. The Act allows the company to charge a sum not exceeding 5 per cent on amounts transferred for the purpose of the fund. Few companies have adopted these measures, the usual practice being to take out insurance against the risk of liability for compensation.

The position is different if a person has acquired a share certificate as the result of a forged transfer and then transfers his holding to a third party acting in good faith. The question is then concerned with the validity of the *share certificate*. This is discussed on page 67.

Stamp Duty on Transfers

If any person whose office it is to enrol, register, or enter in or upon any rolls, books or records any instrument chargeable with duty, enrols, registers or enters any such instrument not being duly stamped, he shall be liable to a fine of £10 (*Stamp Act, 1891*).

Duty is assessed on the value of the consideration passing from the transferee to the transferor or, in the case of voluntary disposition, on the value of the property. The instrument must be stamped within thirty days after execution. Where the consideration is a nominal sum and recognised under the Act as being a 'transfer for a nominal consideration', the duty is a fixed amount of 50p.

Certification of Transfers

A seller of shares would ordinarily produce his share certificate as evidence to the transferee that he is the owner of the shares and to enable the buyer to send the document of title to the company for registration of the transfer. This would not be possible, however, in the following circumstances:

(*a*) If the seller was disposing of only part of the holding on a certificate he would not wish to surrender a document which would include those shares he was retaining.

(*b*) If there were more than one buyer of the shares represented by one certificate he obviously could not provide each buyer with a certificate.

(*c*) He may not yet have received a share certificate and holds only a temporary document of title, e.g. an allotment letter.

(*d*) If he is acting in a representative capacity (e.g. executor) the transferee will need to be satisfied that the personal representative has authority to transfer.

In such cases, the procedure would be for the share certificate and the transfer to be sent to the company by the transferor. The secretary would endorse and sign the transfer with the words 'Certificate lodged' and return it to the person who lodged it. The transfer could then be handed to the transferee or his broker as evidence that a certificate for the shares mentioned on the transfer was held by the company. When the transferee submits the certified transfer to the company it would be 'married' to the share certificate held by the company and the transfer effected in the company's books.

The *effect* of certification is to represent to any person acting with reliance on it that there has been produced to and is held by the company a document which, *prima facie*, shows that the person named has title to the shares. It does not warrant the person named as *having* title (S. 79(1)) and the company is not estopped from subsequently denying that the person has a right to transfer. Certification merely confirms that the document of title appears to be in order and agrees with the related transfer form.

If certification is effected by an *authorised* person (e.g. the secretary), the company will be liable for damages to a person acting on the faith of any certification which is made *fraudulently or negligently* (S. 79(2)). Certification is deemed to be made by the company if (*a*) the person issuing the instrument of transfer is authorised to issue certified transfers on behalf of the company, and (*b*) the certification is signed by the person so authorised (S. 79(3)).

Restrictions on Members' Rights to Transfer

A person who has an equitable interest in shares registered in the name of another person may protect that interest by serving on the company a **stop notice** (previously known as a 'notice in lieu of distringas'). Such a notice is obtained from the Court by filing an affidavit reciting the nature of the applicant's interest and the threat to it. Serving a stop notice has the effect of preventing the company from acting on a transfer of the shares or paying a dividend on them without first notifying the applicant. Within eight days of that notification, the applicant may apply for an injunction restraining the transfer or payment of the dividend. Failing any action by the applicant within that period, the company is released from the restraint of the order.

A **charging order** can be obtained from the Court by a judgment creditor of a person registered as the owner of the shares. Such an order has the effect of prohibiting transfer of the shares.

A **garnishee order** restrains the payment of a dividend or interest or any other sum payable by the company to the registered owner.

An **injunction** or **restraining order** may be made by the Court forbidding the transfer of shares pending a decision in a legal action to decide the beneficial ownership of the shares.

Where the Department of Trade is conducting an investigation under S.172 or S.173 (see page 162) and difficulty is encountered in establishing certain facts about securities, the Department may make an order prohibiting all rights of transfer, renunciation, voting, dividends and return of capital, and the company may not make any scrip or rights issues of shares (S.174).

Forfeiture of Shares

A company may have authority in its Articles to forfeit the shares of a member for non-payment of calls or instalments on his shares. Forfeiture may not be resorted to unless the Articles so prescribe, and the conditions and procedure laid down in the Articles must be strictly complied with (*Johnson v. Lyttle's Iron Agency* (1877)). Forfeiture *for any other reason* would constitute an illegal reduction of capital (*Hopkinson v. Mortimer Harley & Co.* (1917)).

A former holder of forfeited shares ceases to be a member from the date of forfeiture and is relieved of liability for past calls (*Stocken's Case* (1868)). Articles may, however, provide that the ex-holder will continue to be liable for monies due by him to the company at the time of forfeiture (as in Table A). In such a case, he may be sued as a *debtor* but not as a *contributory* (*Ladies' Dress Association v. Pulbrook* (1900)). Any liability would be limited to the difference between the amount due to the company and the amount received by it upon reissue of the shares (*Re Bolton* (1930)). Thus, the company may credit the purchaser of forfeited shares with the amount already paid but must, in total, receive an amount not less than the nominal value of the shares. To do otherwise would effectively mean issuing shares at a discount.

Surrender of Shares

There is no provision in law for the surrender of shares because, without permission of the Court, it would constitute an illegal reduction of capital. It would be permitted, however, where the circumstances were such as would justify forfeiture (*Bellerby v. Rowland & Marwood Steamship Co.* (1902)).

A surrender of shares in exchange for other shares of an equal nominal value, as part of a scheme, would not be unlawful as it would not constitute a reduction of capital (*Rowell v. John Rowell & Son* (1912)).

Lien on Shares

A company may take power in its Articles to exercise a lien on its shares in respect of amounts due on the shares or on any other amounts due to the company from members (Table A gives this right). Stock Exchange regulations do not allow a lien on *fully-paid* shares.

The right of lien is a right to *retain*, but it is in doubt as to whether such a right implies a *power of sale*. Articles including the right of lien therefore usually give the power of sale also. Such Articles must also give the directors power to authorise someone to execute the transfer, because S. 75 requires a written instrument to effect any transfer.

If a member's debt, threatened by lien by the company, is discharged by a third party, the company's lien must be transferred to that party (*Everitt v. Automatic Weighing Machine Co.* (1892)).

Table A gives a company a 'first and paramount' lien on its shares and on dividends payable, although in the case of joint holders the lien extends only to amounts owing on the shares. The provision of S. 117 that no notice of trust may be entered in the Register of Members is reinforced in Table A, which states that the company is not bound to recognise, even after notice thereof, any interest in any share or any right except as absolute rights of the registered holder. There is some doubt as to the extent to which the Court would recognise such priority of lien, however. It is possible that the priority could be relied upon only in respect of amounts due on the shares.

Transmission

Whereas transfer of shares is a voluntary action, transmission relates to a change of ownership by operation of law whereby a company can deal with a person acting in a representative capacity for the registered holder.

Concerning the Death of a Member

(*a*) A transfer of shares of a deceased member by the personal representative (the executor or administrator) shall be as valid as if he were the registered holder (S. 76).

(*b*) A company may accept as sufficient evidence any document which by law is sufficient evidence of probate or letters of administration (S. 82).

Upon the death of a joint holder, the shares vest in the survivor(s). The company *may not* recognise a personal representative of a deceased joint holder.

If the personal representative of a deceased member requires the shares to be registered *in his own name*, a company may not refuse to do so unless its Articles give that power.

Other personal representatives may be brought into existence as follows:

(a) A trustee or receiver in the case of bankruptcy.
(b) A liquidator upon winding up of a company which is a member.
(c) A receiver upon a shareholder becoming of unsound mind.

In general, personal representatives acquire the same rights and obligations as of any member except that they apply only *on behalf* of the registered holder. Thus, any dividends paid to a personal representative of a deceased member must be applied for the benefit of the estate of the member and any calls would be a liability of the estate. The Articles may stipulate conditions as to the right to receive notice of meetings, to vote, etc.

Any note in the Register of Members that a personal representative was acting as *trustee* would contravene S. 117 concerning notice of trust.

8

DIRECTORS AND SECRETARIES

The Fiduciary Relationship

Directors have delegated to them, by the shareholders, wide powers for managing the affairs of the company, including the making of major policy decisions. This act of faith on the part of investors is evidenced by their action in entrusting money to the company in the expectation that the directors will put it to profitable use and with the exercise of circumspection. The extent of such trust may be more fully recognised when the following facts are taken into consideration:

(a) Any action by the directors within their authority, no matter how unwise such action may be, *is binding upon the company*. Any consequent financial loss to the shareholders can give rise to no more than a protest from them.

(b) Shareholders have very little direct influence on policy-making. In general, *their only power to control the direction of the company is that of appointing and removing directors*. To do either requires the agreement of holders of more than fifty per cent of the shares with voting rights, but not all shares necessarily carry votes and the directors and their supporters may hold the majority of voting shares.

(c) By reason of their duties, *directors must be in possession of information concerning the company which is not available to the other shareholders*.

Bearing these facts in mind, the necessity for a high degree of accountability and responsibility on the part of the directors, no matter how honest and diligent they may be, is obvious. Control of directors to that end is exercised by measures such as the following:

(a) The personal information about directors which has to be placed on public record in the form of returns to the Registrar.

(b) The information about the directors and their interests which has to be disclosed in sundry registers kept by the company, in the annual accounts, in the directors' report and in any prospectus which is issued.

(c) Relevant regulations contained in the Articles of Association of the company.

(d) The reporting by the auditors of any matters which they consider should be known by the investors.

(*e*) The additional requirements imposed by the Stock Exchange if the company's shares have been admitted to listing.

(*f*) Sundry measures prescribed by law for protecting minority interests and for the detection of fraud.

There is an understanding, apart from the specific requirements mentioned above, that directors will act in good faith in the discharge of their duties. They may therefore be regarded as being in a fiduciary relationship with the members. It was established in *Percival v. Wright* (1902) that directors are not trustees for individual shareholders, nor are they trustees for third parties who contract with the company (*Bath v. Standard Land Co. Ltd* (1911)). Nevertheless, directors may be regarded as *trustees of the company's assets*, since they are required to administer such assets in the interests of the company and may incur liability for breach of trust if they misapply the assets.

A director must not profit by reason of his position without disclosure being made to the company and he must always act in the best interests of the company. In common law, he is not, however, required to exercise any greater skill than may reasonably be expected of a person of his knowledge and experience. (Further consideration of the fiduciary position of directors in relation to the *exercise* of their powers is given on page 85.)

Definition of 'Director'

In specifying those provisions which are relevant to directors, the Acts refer to 'directors' in the appropriate sections. However, a person who is a director in *fact* may not escape the strictures of those sections by being referred to by some other title than that of 'director'—such as 'governor' or 'manager'. S.455(1) defines a director as 'including any person occupying the position of director *by whatever name called*'.

This definition is widened in Ss.200 and 201 and S.27(1967) to include any person *in accordance with whose directions or instructions the directors are accustomed to act*. Thus, a person not referred to as a director and not generally regarded as being a director, may be considered in law to be subject to the liabilities of a director if his actions come within the above definition. An official adviser to the board or a major shareholder who joins in discussions with the directors (even in board meetings) would not be regarded as being a director, *provided*, even after taking account of his observations, the directors made their own decisions. It would be a question of degree, however, because if that person's influence was so strong as to determine the decision of the board he may possibly be regarded as being a director as recognised by law.

A director is an 'officer' of the company (S.455(1)) and liable as such where the Acts prescribe penalties and responsibilities in respect of officers. The general provisions of Ss.205 and 448 therefore apply (see page 85).

Appointment of Directors

In general, the method of appointing directors is laid down in the Articles. The almost invariable rule is for directors (other than the first directors) to be appointed by members in general meeting and for casual vacancies to be filled by the directors, but there is no legal prohibition on a company having 'life directors' or a managing director not subject to retirement by rotation.

The secretary cannot also be a sole director (S.177) nor can a corporation be a sole director if the corporation has only one director and he is secretary of the company (S.178). Other prohibitions are those relevant to disqualification of directors (see page 82).

Consent to Act

S.181 (as amended) requires that in the case of a person being named as a director or proposed director in a prospectus or statement in lieu of prospectus, a consent to act must have been signed and delivered to the Registrar. This does not apply to a private company or to a public company where the prospectus was issued more than a year from the date of entitlement to commence business or to a company which was a private company before becoming a public company.

The provisions relevant to the first directors and to subsequent directors are given below.

Appointment of the First Directors

The first directors are those named in the statement required under S.21(1976) to be delivered with the Memorandum upon the registration of the company (see page 16). Each person named therein must submit a consent to act. The section also provides that a person so named is deemed to be appointed as a first director *upon the incorporation of the company*. Thus, the responsibilities and legal obligations of a director commence from that time, without the necessity for any resolution. If the Articles should name the first directors, such 'appointments' are void unless the above statement is made.

Appointment of Subsequent Directors

These may be made under the following circumstances:

(*a*) *By the company in general meeting* if directors are subject to *retirement by rotation*. Articles usually provide that a proportion of the directors retires each year. Table A requires the retirement of one third of the directors at each annual general meeting after the first annual general meeting (when all retire), and states that retiring directors are eligible for re-election. Any nominee other than a retiring director must be one recommended by the board of directors or one proposed to the board in writing by a member entitled to vote at that meeting. Thus, Table A makes provision to avoid the automatic reappointment of directors by the board. (Under Table A, a managing director is not required to retire by rotation.)

(b) *By the company in general meeting to replace a director removed at that meeting* (see page 83).

(c) *By the directors* to fill a *casual vacancy.* These are board vacancies arising from causes other than retirement by rotation or removal in general meeting. They thus relate to circumstances occurring between annual meetings and will include the death, resignation and disqualification of directors. The power to appoint is invariably vested in the directors, but it is usually prescribed that the person appointed shall retire at the next annual general meeting but may offer himself for reappointment. Thus, an appointment made in an emergency must, in effect, be confirmed by the members at the earliest possible time, thereby reducing the possibility of abuse of their powers by the directors in making unwelcome appointments.

(d) *By the directors* appointing an *additional* director. Powers similar to those relevant to casual vacancies are usually given to the directors to appoint additional directors up to the maximum permitted by the Articles.

Any change in the board notified to the Registrar must be accompanied by a consent to act signed by the director (S. 22 (1976))—see page 97.

Appointment of Alternate Directors

There may be circumstances where a director expects to be unable to attend board meetings for some time and therefore wishes another person to act in his place during his absence. There is no provision under the Act for this to be done and an alternate director can be appointed only if the Articles permit. An alternate director acquires all the responsibilities of a director as prescribed by law and his appointment is subject to all the procedures required under the Acts.

Appointment Resolutions

If more than one director is to be appointed at a general meeting of a company other than a private company, there must be a separate resolution for the appointment of each director (S. 183). An exception is allowed in the event of the meeting having first resolved otherwise, with no one voting against. To put a resolution containing the names of more than one nominee would obviously place in an unfair position any member who favoured one or more but not all the nominees.

Defective Appointments

S. 180 provides that the acts of a director shall be valid notwithstanding any defect in his appointment or qualification which may afterwards be discovered. This does not apply where no true appointment had been made, but only where the board or the director acted in good faith and the defect is one which can be rectified when discovered (*Morris v. Kanssen* (1946)).

Service Contracts

Under S. 26(1967) every company is required to keep a copy of every director's service contract and variations thereof or a memorandum of such a contract if it is not in writing. The Registrar must be notified as to where the contracts are kept, which may be at the registered office; where the Register of Members is kept, if different; or at the principal place of business within the domicile of the company. Any member may inspect the contracts without charge.

This section does not apply to contracts requiring a director to work wholly or mainly outside the United Kingdom, or contracts which are capable of being terminated by the company within the next twelve months without payment of compensation.

Assignment of Office

This differs from the appointment of an alternate director (see page 79) in that a director assigning his office ceases to be a director, whereas the appointing director of an alternate director remains a director and merely authorises his alternate to act in his absence. Assignment may not take place unless there is power to do so in the Articles or it derives from an agreement between a person and the company, and must be sanctioned by a special resolution in general meeting (S. 204). Assignment of office is rare.

The Number of Directors

A public company must have at least two directors (S. 176). A private company must have at least one director, but a sole director may not also be the secretary (S. 177).

Most Articles prescribe the minimum and maximum number of directors, but usually with the proviso that any other numbers may be decided upon by the company in general meeting. Thus, any change in the numbers would not require alteration of the Articles; an ordinary resolution to fix the numbers would be required and not a special resolution to change the Articles.

Problems may ensue if the number of directors falls below the minimum, because this could mean the board would be unable to act (*Re Alma Spinning Co.* (1880)), but Articles usually provide for this. Table

A states that if the number falls below the set minimum, the remaining directors can act but *only* to appoint additional directors or to call a general meeting of the members to resolve the difficulty.

Share Qualification

There is no legal requirement for a director to hold shares. Table A does not stipulate that directors must hold shares nor does the Stock Exchange require Articles so to provide. If a director is required to hold shares as a qualification, it will be so stated in the Articles.

The principle of demanding a qualification in the form of shares was that a person with the responsibilities of a director should have a 'stake' in the company and so be at risk in the same way as any other member, but the effectiveness of such a requirement became lessened with the practice of fixing merely a nominal amount as the qualification.

Where a share qualification is stipulated, the provisions of S.181 concerning a person named as a director in a prospectus or statement in lieu of prospectus will apply (see page 17). S.182 states that if a person does not obtain his qualification shares within two months of appointment (or such shorter period as the Articles may fix), he must vacate office and cannot be reappointed until he has obtained his qualification. Furthermore, such a person is liable to a fine of £5 for every day he illegally acts as a director.

The section also states that the holding of a share warrant does not count as a share qualification.

The Test as to whether a person holds such shares is that they are registered in his name. This would apply even if the director was not the beneficial owner of the shares but, for example, held them as a trustee (*Pulbrook v. Richmond Consolidated Mining Co.* (1878)). The shares must be held in such a manner as to allow the company to deal with the director as the owner of the shares (*Sutton v. English and Colonial Produce Co.* (1902)).

Shares held jointly are a sufficient qualification unless the Articles state otherwise (*Grundy v. Briggs* (1910)).

The shares must have been paid for and not acquired by way of gift from the promoter or any person having contracts with the company unless this is approved by the company (*Carling's Case* (1876)).

Any prospectus issued within two years of a company being entitled to commence business must disclose the share qualification (if any) of each director (Fourth Schedule, para 2).

'Over-age' Directors

The 1948 Act introduced the suggestion that it may not be beneficial for a *public* company to have elderly directors. S. 185 therefore prescribes that a person who had attained the age of 70 could not be appointed a director of a public company, and that a serving director must resign at the conclusion of the next annual general meeting after he had attained that age. An exception allows an 'over-age' director to be appointed or to continue in office provided it is approved in general meeting by a resolution of which Special Notice, stating his age, has been given.

A person over the age of 70 who is appointed or proposed to be appointed as a director of a company which is subject to S. 185, must give notice of his age to the company. Should he fail to do so and acts as a director without authority, he is liable to a fine of £5 a day while the failure to disclose continues or while he continues to act as a director (S. 186).

The principle was acknowledged to be one about which there could be no unanimity of opinion and, accordingly, the Act allows a company to provide in its Articles that the section would not apply. As an alternative to 'contracting out' of S. 185, a company may prescribe a retirement age other than that of 70.

Disqualification of Directors

The circumstances listed **by statute** under which a person may be disqualified from holding office as director are as follows:

(*a*) Failure to obtain a share qualification within the prescribed period or, having a qualification, upon subsequently disposing of it (S. 182).

(*b*) A director of a company which is subject to S. 185 reaching the age of 70, the disqualification being operative after the next following annual general meeting, unless Special Notice of the reappointment had been given.

(*c*) A director being an undischarged bankrupt, unless he is permitted by the Court to remain in office (S. 187).

(*d*) A director having a Court Order made against him under S. 188. This relates to a disqualification (for a period of up to five years) from acting as a director, of a person

(*i*) convicted of an offence in connection with the promotion, formation or management of a company; or

(*ii*) who appears, in the course of a winding up, to have been guilty of fraudulent trading, as set out in S. 332 (see page 195); or

(*iii*) who has otherwise been guilty of fraud or breach of duty in relation to the company.

(*e*) A director being made subject to a Court Order under S. 28 (1976) for being persistently in default in the making of returns, etc., to the Registrar (see page 177).

Concerning (*d*) and (*e*) above, the Secretary of State is required to maintain a Register of Disqualification Orders (see page 178).

Most **Articles** follow Table A, where the grounds for disqualification of a director are those set out above, with, in addition, where he:

(*a*) Becomes of unsound mind.

(*b*) Resigns by notice in writing. The resignation is effective from the date the letter is received or any date quoted in the letter. A verbal resignation is sufficient, whether or not the Articles contain a clause as above (*Latchford Premier Cinema v. Ennion* (1931)). Any resignation is irrevocable without the consent of the company (*Glossop v. Glossop* (1907)).

(*c*) Is absent from meetings of the board for more than six months without permission. The vacation of office is effective from the date of the board resolution.

Removal from Office

The Statutory Provisions

The powers stated above by which a person may not continue in office as a director operate as a consequence of statutes imposed on a company or as a result of action by the directors pursuant to the Articles. A basic right contained in the Act gives the power of **dismissal** to those shareholders with voting rights. No clause in the Articles or any agreement between a director and the company can deprive those members of that right.

S. 184 states that a director may be removed from office by the passing of an ordinary resolution—that is, by a simple majority. Because of the power of the directors to manage the affairs of the company, it may be said that effective control of a company is in the hands of those entitled to appoint and remove directors. The object of S. 184 is to place that power with those bearing the greatest risk. These are ordinary shareholders, who usually, although not always, have voting rights exclusively. In practice, the power rests with the holders of the majority of voting shares who can act in concert. Thus, the power depends upon the number of voting shares and not the number of holders; and it requires coordination between the majority-holders.

The section provides safeguards to prevent what may be termed a 'coup'. These are as follows:

Advance notice of the intention to put the motion must be given to the directors in the form of a Special Notice. A copy of that Notice must be sent to the director concerned and of any proposal to appoint someone in his stead. The threatened director thus has the opportunity of 'preparing his defence'. He is permitted to submit representations in writing (of a reasonable length) to the company, which must then:

(*a*) state, in any notice of the resolution sent to the members, that representations have been made; and (*b*) send a copy of the representations to every member to whom notice of the meeting is sent.

In the event of the representations being received too late to send to the members or because of default by the company, the director may demand that the representations be read at the meeting. This is additional to the right the director has under S. 184 to be heard at the meeting on the resolution for his removal.

To prevent a director abusing his rights to make representations, the Court may, on application by the company or any person claiming to be aggrieved, deprive the director of those rights if it is satisfied that the director is aiming to obtain needless publicity for defamatory matter.

Powers in the Articles

The Articles may contain the power to remove directors. This would be additional to the powers given in the Act. If the removal was based on a ground contained in the Articles, the director would not be entitled to the facilities available under S. 184. If the Articles state that a director may be removed 'for reasonable cause', the Court will not normally question the interpretation of the phrase by the company in general meeting (*Osgood v. Nelson* (1872)).

The Directors as Agents

The board of directors is a committee with delegated powers to conduct the affairs of the company. Although a company is a legal entity, it obviously cannot act personally. Its relationship with the directors in that respect was underlined over a century ago: 'The company cannot act in its own person . . . it can only act through directors' (*Ferguson v. Wilson* (1866)).

A director is therefore an agent of the company. He is not, however, an agent of the *shareholders*, unless he was appointed to act for them in a specific instance, such as negotiating the sale of shares (*Briess v. Woolley* (1954)).

The ordinary rules of agency apply in that when directors are acting on behalf of the company within their authority the company is thereby bound. In such circumstances, no personal liability to the other party is attached to the directors. The position obtaining when directors act on behalf of the company and the other party assumes such action does not conflict with the internal regulations of the company or that the director has the necessary authority, is relevant to *Royal British Bank v. Turquand* (1856) and Section 9 of the *European Communities Act, 1972*. (This is discussed on page 33.)

If directors act beyond their powers but the action is within the powers of the company, such action will become binding upon the company if it is ratified or approved by the company in general meeting (*Bamford v. Bamford* (1969)).

Delegation of some of its functions by the board to committees or individuals is usually permitted by the Articles. Under the rules of agency, any action within delegated authority becomes the collective responsibility of the board and, in turn, the company.

Because actions by directors derive from the decisions made by them as a body, the rules relevant to board meetings are of importance (see page 86).

Liability of Directors

Abuses in the exercise of their authority by directors or their negligence, result in liabilities and penalties, and no provision in the Articles can protect directors in respect of such failings. Thus, S.205 provides that 'any provision in the Articles or in any contract with a company or otherwise for exempting any officer of the company, or indemnifying him against any liability which by virtue of any rule of law would otherwise attach to him in respect of any negligence, default, breach of duty or breach of trust of which he may be guilty in relation to the company, is void.'

S.448, however, permits the Court to grant relief to an officer, on such terms as it thinks fit, in proceedings for negligence, default, breach of duty or of trust, if it appears that he acted honestly and reasonably, and that in view of the circumstances he ought fairly to be excused. It has been held that a director may be granted relief if his breach was due to his reliance upon advice of counsel which proved to be incorrect (*Re Claridge's Patent Asphalte Co.* (1921)).

With regard to breach of duty or of trust or negligence, the following decisions have been made:

(*a*) In addition to being liable if he is directly implicated, a director may be liable even if he had had only *notice* of the breach. If a director had been put on enquiry and neglected to take action to discover the facts for himself, he may be regarded as having had notice of a breach of trust (*Land Credit Co. v. Lord Fermoy* (1870)).

(*b*) The general rule is that directors jointly implicated in a breach of trust are jointly and severally liable, but a director is not liable for more than the consequences of his own acts or defaults when the breach by him is separable from breaches committed by his fellow directors (*Madrid Bank v. Pelly* (1869)).

(*c*) A director is not liable for any breach of trust that occurred before he became a director (*Re Forest of Dean Coal Co.* (1878)).

(*d*) A director is required to exercise the same degree of prudence which he would apply on his own behalf (*Re Liverpool Household Stores* (1890)).

(*e*) A director is not liable for errors of judgment, provided he acts honestly for the benefit of the company (*Lagunas Nitrate Co. v. Lagunas Syndicate* (1899)).

Sundry offences may be identified in the course of a winding up. These are itemised under *Offences by Officers of Companies in Liquidation* on page 194.

Meetings of Directors

Directors usually act by resolutions in board meetings, but it is frequently permitted in Articles for a decision to be made and recorded by all the directors signing a document containing the resolution. The rules relevant to board meetings cover the following.

Notice

The length and form of notice may be prescribed in the Articles; or board meetings may be held at regular intervals and require no notice; or both methods may be used. A director is entitled to have reasonable notice of meetings.

Unless stipulated otherwise, the nature of the business need not be specified (*La Compagnie de Mayville v. Whitley* (1896)). (In this respect it differs from the rule concerning notice of *general* meetings.)

It is common (as in Table A) to make unnecessary the serving of notice on directors who are abroad.

Quorum

If the Articles allow, the quorum may be one (*Re Fireproof Doors Ltd* (1916)). Table A permits the directors to fix the quorum, failing which the quorum would be two. The quorum must consist of 'disinterested directors' unless Articles permit 'interested directors' to vote (see *Disclosure of Interests in Contracts*, below).

Ratification

Any action taken at a board meeting which contained irregularities may be ratified by a subsequent valid meeting.

Voting

Voting is by a simple majority of votes cast unless the Articles provide otherwise. Table A gives the chairman a casting vote in the event of equality of voting.

Minutes

These must be kept. If signed by the chairman of that or the next succeeding meeting, they are evidence of the proceedings and may be produced in Court as such. Minutes are *prima facie* evidence that a meeting has been duly convened and held, all proceedings thereat duly taken place and that any appointments of directors, managers or liquidators are valid (S. 145).

Disclosure of Interests in Contracts

In dealing with the company's business in board meetings, directors must not place themselves in a position where conflict exists between the interests of the company and their personal interests (*Parker v. McKenna* (1874)). Thus, if a director has a personal interest in a transaction with the company he would be biased in any voting on that contract.

S. 199 states that a director may be interested in or be a party to a contract with the company and may retain any profit therefrom, *provided he declares that interest at a board meeting*. In the case of a *proposed* contract, such a declaration must be made at the meeting at which the contract is first discussed. If the director was not interested at the time of that meeting, he must declare his interest at the first board meeting after he becomes interested. In the event of a director becoming interested after the contract has been *made*, he must make his declaration at the first board meeting following acquisition of the interest.

Provision is made under the section for a director to give a 'general notice' that he is a member of specified firms and is to be considered as being interested in any contract made with those firms. The usual procedure is to require a director to make a written declaration of this sort at the first board meeting he attends. Any interests acquired subsequently must, of course, also be declared.

It is common for Articles, as in Table A, not to allow an 'interested' director to vote on a contract, although he may join in the discussion. This does not affect a director's right to vote in general meetings on matters in which he is interested, because, of course, he then has the same rights as has any other member.

Disclosure of Directors' Interests in the Company's Securities

It may be important to know the extent of a director's financial interests in his company. Because a director may, for example, have knowledge of an event which will cause the price of the securities to move, he could gain an advantage by buying or selling securities before the information became generally available. There are other obvious reasons why a director's financial involvement should be disclosed.

The law requires that a director must notify the company of all acquisitions and disposals of his interests and, further, that such movements be recorded in a register which is available for inspection.

Information to be Disclosed

S. 27(1967) as amended by S. 24(1976) requires that a director, *when appointed*, gives written notice to the company of his interests in the shares or debentures of the company, its subsidiary, its holding company or fellow subsidiary (but not of a wholly-owned subsidiary). This notice must be given within five days of his appointment. *Thereafter*, he must give written notification, within five days after the date of the event, of the occurrence of the following events. The number or amount, and class, of shares or debentures must be specified, as it must be in the notice given on appointment mentioned above:

(*a*) Any event as a consequence of which he becomes interested or ceases to be interested in the shares or debentures of a company as specified above. In the case of a purchase, the price to be paid must be stated.

(*b*) Entry into a contract to sell any such shares or debentures, and the price to be received.

(*c*) The assigning of a right granted to him by the company to subscribe for shares or debentures of the company, and the consideration therefor.

(*d*) The grant to him by the company's subsidiary, holding company or fellow subsidiary of a right to subscribe for shares or debentures in that company, the date and currency of the grant, the consideration therefor and the price to be paid for the securities. If he exercises the right, the amount or number of the securities must be stated. If he assigns the right, the consideration must be stated.

If a director is not immediately aware of any of the above events or of his liability to notify it, he must give the notice within five days of his becoming so aware.

A person in accordance with whose directions or instructions the directors are accustomed to act is deemed to be a director for the purpose of the above provisions.

Defining 'Directors' Interests'

The above provisions could be avoided to some extent if a director declared only those interests which were registered in his own name. There are obvious possibilities of securities being effectively owned by a director but registered in other names. To guard against such deception, S.28(1967) states that a person is deemed to have an interest in shares or debentures where:

(*a*) He has an interest under a trust deed whereof the property consists of shares or debentures (other than a discretionary interest).

(*b*) A body corporate has an interest and that body or its directors are accustomed to act in accordance with his instructions or directions, or he is entitled to exercise one third or more of the voting power in general meeting of that body.

(*c*) He enters into a contract for the purchase of securities; or has a right (other than through an interest under a trust) to call for their delivery to himself or his order, presently or in the future; or is entitled to exercise or control the exercise of any right conferred by the holding (other than as a proxy or representative of a corporation).

Persons with a joint interest are deemed to each have that interest.

The section further states that references to a person being interested shall be construed 'so as not to exclude an interest on the ground of its remoteness or the manner in which it arises or by reason of the fact that the exercise of a right conferred by ownership thereof is, or is capable of being, in any way subject to restraint or restriction'.

The following 'interests' are to be disregarded:

(*a*) An interest in reversion or remainder or in fee, so long as the person is entitled to receive during his or another's lifetime income from trust property comprising shares or debentures.

(*b*) Securities held under the law of England and Wales as a bare trustee or custodian trustee, or under the law of Scotland as a simple trust.

(*c*) Those subsisting by virtue of an authorised unit trust scheme; schemes under S.22 of the *Charities Act, 1960*; S.11 of the *Trustee Investments Act, 1961*, or S.1 of the *Administration of Justice Act, 1965*, or as set out in the *Church Funds Investment Measure, 1958*; interests of the Church of Scotland Trustees or of the Church of Scotland Trust.

An interest is deemed to cease upon delivery to a person's order of shares or debentures in fulfilment of a contract for their purchase or in satisfaction of his right to call for their delivery, or upon failure to deliver shares or debentures in accordance with such a contract or on which such a right fails to be satisfied, as does the lapse of a right to call for delivery.

Interests of Spouses and Children

S.31(1967) as amended by S.24(1976) extends the requirements of S.27(1967) regarding disclosure of interests. It states that the interests of the wife or husband of a director (not being herself or himself a director) and the interests of any infant son or daughter of a director (including stepchildren and adopted children) are treated as being the *director's* interests. Any contract, assignment or right of subscription entered into, exercised or made by or grant made to any such person shall be regarded as being performed by or to the director.

The section also requires a director to notify the company, within five days of his becoming aware of the event, (*a*) of the grant to the spouse or infant child of a right to subscribe for shares or debentures of the company, and (*b*) of the exercise of such right. The notice must give, in the case of a *grant* of a right, the information required by S.27(1967) concerning a grant to a director by another body corporate to subscribe for securities in that body; and in the case of *exercise* of a right, the information required by that section in respect of the exercise of such rights by a director.

The Register of Directors' Interests in Company Securities

S.29(1967) requires every company to keep a register and to enter therein the information provided by directors under S.27(1967). The date of entry must be recorded. An index must be provided unless the register is in a form of self-indexing. The entries against each name must appear in chronological order.

Although it is the company's responsibility to enter up the register, the responsibility for *making the declarations* is that of the director. The company is also required to enter in the register against each director's name:

(*a*) The date it *grants* the director a right to subscribe for shares or debentures of the company; the currency of the grant; the consideration for it (if any); the number or amount and description of the securities; and the price to be paid.

(*b*) The date of the director *exercising* such a right; the number or amount of the shares or debentures concerned; whether registered in his name or in the name or names of specified persons, with the number or amount registered in each name.

Any entry in the register must be made within three days of the obligation to do so arising.

A director has the right to require that the nature and extent of his interest is noted in the register.

Entry in the register does not effect the company with notice of the rights of any person in relation to the shares or debentures.

The register must be kept at the registered office of the company or where the register of members is kept. Notice of the location of the register and any change must be given to the Registrar unless it is kept at the registered office at all times. It must be open to inspection during business hours to any member without charge and to any other person on payment of a fee. Any person may require a copy of the register or any part of it on payment of a fee. A copy must be provided by the company within ten days of the requirement.

The register must remain open throughout the annual general meeting and be accessible to any person attending the meeting.

Notification to the Stock Exchange

The 1976 Act introduced a measure to ensure that, in certain circumstances, there is an element of publicity when an entry is made.

S.25(1976) refers to shares and debentures which are listed on the Stock Exchange. It states that when a notification is made by a director under S.27(1967) or S.31(1967) and it refers to listed securities, the company must notify the Stock Exchange accordingly. This must be done before the end of the day next following the day of notification.

The Stock Exchange may then publish 'in such manner as it may determine' any information received thereby.

Penalties

A person who fails to fulfil the obligation imposed by sections 27 and 31 of the 1967 Act as amended by the 1976 Act or who knowingly makes a statement falsely or recklessly is liable to a fine or imprisonment or both.

If the Department of Trade considers there are circumstances suggesting contravention of the above sections, it may appoint inspectors to investigate whether contraventions have in fact occurred (S. 32(1967)) —see page 168.

Disclosure of Interests in Voting Shares

The provisions of S. 33(1967) as amended by S. 26(1976) relevant to the disclosures to be made concerning interests in voting shares by *any* person (see page 158), also apply to any director who may come within the scope of those sections. An interest in shares held by a director may therefore require him to make two declarations.

Remuneration of Directors

Directors have no automatic right to remuneration. It is usual for the Articles to provide that remuneration of directors be fixed from time to time in general meetings, or it may be fixed by service agreements. Once agreed, the debt becomes a liability of the company, irrespective of whether or not profits have been made (*Re Lundy Granite Co.* (1872)). In a winding up, however, directors may prove for due fees but only as unsecured creditors; they may not, as directors, claim preference under S. 319 as 'clerks or servants' of the company (*Ex parte Beckwith* (1898)).

The directors may not vote themselves remuneration or appoint one of their number to a paid position in the company unless authorised by the Articles or agreed in general meeting. Any such appointment is void and any sums paid must be refunded (*Kerr v. Marine Products Ltd* (1928)).

Apportionment of Remuneration

If the agreement is 'to be deemed to accrue from day to day' (as in Table A) or is 'at the rate of £x a year', a director who acts for part of a year is entitled to payment for that period. If, however, the remuneration is expressed as being '£x per annum', a director is not entitled to remuneration in respect of any period less than a full year (*Inman v. Ackroyd & Best Ltd* (1901)). (The latter legal ruling is, however, in some doubt as it may conflict with the *Apportionment Act, 1870.*)

Payment of Expenses

A director may not claim for expenses incidental to his duties unless expressly provided for in the Articles or by agreement (*Young v. Naval, Military and Civil Service Co-operative Society of South Africa* (1905)).

Tax-free Payments

It is unlawful to pay a director (as a director or otherwise) remuneration free of income tax (S. 189).

Disclosure of Directors' Emoluments and Pensions

Disclosure must be made in the accounts of the aggregate of directors' emoluments, distinguished as between amounts received *as directors* and other emoluments (such as salaries). Disclosure must also be made of the aggregate of pensions. Particulars of any waiver of future fees by any director must also be disclosed in the accounts (see page 130).

Compensation for Loss of Office

A practice which has sometimes been abused is that of paying compensation to directors for loss of office or upon retirement (irreverently known as 'golden handshakes'). Specific provisions against suspect arrangements are afforded by law as follows:

(*a*) No payment may be made to a director as compensation for loss of office or in connection with his retirement unless the amount is disclosed to members and approved by the company (S. 191).

(*b*) Ss. 192 to 194 contain provisions relevant to payment of compensation to a director who resigns his office as part of an agreement to transfer the undertaking of the company. These are detailed on page 188.

(*c*) Any payments made to directors under Ss. 191–193 as *bona fide* payments of damages for breach of contract or by way of pension for past services, are not included in the payments envisaged in those sections. The expression 'pension' includes any superannuation allowance, superannuation gratuity or similar payment (S. 194).

Loans to Directors

Because directors have control of the management of the company, there could be opportunity for malpractice in the use of company funds to make loans to themselves. Under S. 190, however, it is unlawful for a company to make a loan to any of its directors or to a director of its holding company, or to enter into a guarantee or provide security in connection with a loan by any other person. The prohibition is subject to the following exceptions:

(*a*) Where the company is a subsidiary and the director is its holding company.

(*b*) Where the loan is made in the ordinary course of the business of the company (such as a bank or finance house lending to one of its directors *as a customer*).

(*c*) Where the loan is made to enable the director to perform his duties or to meet expenditure for company business. In this instance, the loan must first be approved by the company in general meeting or so approved at or before the next annual general meeting, failing which the loan must be repaid within six months of that meeting.

The section allows a holding company to make loans or give guarantees or security for loans to a director of a subsidiary company, provided he is not also a director of the holding company. Also, a subsidiary company may do the same for a director of a co-subsidiary, provided the director is not a director of the lending company or the holding company.

There is a general requirement for directors to disclose to the company any loans so made (S. 198) and for details to be shown in the published accounts (S. 197) (see page 131).

Managing Directors

Directors have no power to appoint one of their number as managing director unless the Articles so prescribe (as in Table A), but the *company* may always appoint one by resolution. In his capacity as *manager*, a managing director is an employee of the company. In a winding up he may prove for any remuneration owing to him in that capacity but he would not be classed as a preferential creditor as a 'clerk or servant' (*Re Newspaper Proprietary Syndicate* (1900)).

Directors Dealing in Options

An option is a form of speculation whereby a person may purchase the option of buying or selling securities within a specified period at a price fixed when the option is purchased. Because it is an *option*, the speculator need not buy or sell (as may be) if the price is then unfavourable to him; if he abstains he would merely lose what he had paid for the option. If he does opt, however, the other party is bound by the terms of the agreement and must sell or buy as the case may be.

Because of their privileged position concerning information about the securities of their company, directors could enter option agreements with more certainty of profit than could others not privy to such information. S. 25 (1967) makes it an offence for a director to deal in options in respect of listed shares or debentures of the company or associated companies. This prohibition extends to the director's spouse and infant children (S. 30 (1967)).

The ruling does not preclude a director from buying a *right to subscribe* for shares or from buying debentures carrying the *right to convert into shares* or buying debentures with an *option to subscribe*. In such cases, the director's 'inside information' would not place him in a privileged position.

Suspected contravention of S.25(1967) may lead to the appointment of inspectors to investigate the circumstances (S.32(1967))—see page 168.

Unlimited Liability of Directors

Directors, managers or a managing director may have their liability made unlimited by providing therefor in the Memorandum (S.202) or, if the Articles permit, by passing a special resolution altering the Memorandum to include such a provision (S.203). Any person proposed as a director with unlimited liability must be notified in writing of that fact before he accepts office. This liability is, of course, in respect of company debts and is contrary to the general principles concerning shareholders' limited liability. Instances of unlimited liability are very rare.

Published Information Concerning Directors

Recognising the advantageous position of directors as compared with that of other shareholders and the creditors, the Acts require specific information about directors to be available. These requirements may be summarised as follows:

The Register of Directors and Secretaries (S.200) (see page 96). (Note that S.21(1976) requires this information to be filed *before* the Register is opened in the case of the first directors.)

The Register of Directors' Interests in Company Securities (Ss.27, 28, 29 and 31(1967) and Ss.24 and 25(1976) (see page 90).

Particulars in the accounts of directors' emoluments (S.196) and of *loans to directors* (S.197) (see pages 130 and 131).

Particulars of directors in the Annual Return (S.124) (see page 180).

Particulars of directors in a prospectus (S.38) (see page 39).

Particulars of interests and any special rights of directors in the Directors' Report (S.16(1967)) (see page 133).

Copies of service contracts (S.26(1967)) (see page 80).

The Register of Interests in Voting Shares (so far as it relates to directors) (Ss.33 and 34(1967) Ss.26 and 27(1976)) (see page 160).

Publication of Directors' Names

S.201 requires that on all documents which are circulated generally in the course of business (such as letter heads, etc.) and which contain the company's name, there must be shown the names and any former names of the directors. By the *Companies* (*Disclosure of Directors' Nationality*) (*Exemption*) *Order, 1974*, the nationality of a director need not be disclosed if he is a national of a member state of the European Economic

Community. There is provision for the Department of Trade to grant exemption from the requirements of the Section.

The Secretary

The Status of the Secretary

The change in recognition of the status of the company secretary is shown when remarks made in two cases are compared. In 1887 in the case of *Barnett Hoares & Co. v. The South London Tramways Co.*, Lord Esher described the secretary as follows:

> 'A secretary is a mere servant. His position is that he is to do what he is told, and no person can assume that he has any authority to represent anything at all; nor can anyone assume that statements made by him are necessarily to be accepted as trustworthy without further enquiry.'

In 1971, however, it was considered that the secretary is the chief executive officer of a company with extensive duties and responsibilities including ostensible authority to sign administrative contracts on behalf of the company (*Panorama Developments (Guildford) Ltd v. Fidelis Furnishing Fabrics* (1971)).

In a winding up, a secretary is considered to be a preferential creditor as a 'clerk or servant' in respect of unpaid salary, but this does not apply to a part-time secretary (*Cairney v. Back* (1906)).

A secretary is an 'officer of the company' (S. 455) within the meaning in the Act and may be liable to such penalties as the Act prescribes in respect of officers. The general provisions concerning liabilities of officers contained in Ss. 205 and 448 are therefore applicable (see page 85).

Appointment

A person may not be appointed as secretary unless he has filed a consent to act as such. This must be done in the case of the first secretary when his personal details are registered before incorporation of the company (see page 16). These personal details must be entered in the Register of Directors and Secretaries as prescribed by S. 200, and in the event of any change of secretary the Registrar must be notified and a consent to act filed by the new secretary (S. 22(1976)) (see page 97).

Termination of Appointment

A compulsory winding-up order by the Court operates as a dismissal of the secretary (*Chapman's Case* (1866)), as does the appointment of a receiver and manager in a debenture-holders' action (*Reid v. Explosives Co. Ltd* (1887)). A voluntary winding up because of the company's insolvency terminates the employment of all officers and servants (*Fowler v. Commercial Timber Co.* (1930)).

Other Statutory References

Every company must have a secretary but a sole director may not also be the secretary (S. 177). A corporate body may be the secretary, but not if the sole director of the body is also the secretary. Similarly, a corporation the sole director of which is the sole director of the company may not be the company's secretary (S. 178).

In the event of there being no secretary or no secretary capable of acting, his functions and duties may be assumed by an assistant or deputy or by any officer authorised generally or specifically by the directors (S. 177).

Where something is required to be done by or to a director *and* the secretary (for example, affixing the seal), it cannot be done by one person acting in *both* capacities where that person holds both offices (S. 179).

The Register of Directors and Secretaries

S. 200 requires every company to maintain a register of its directors and secretaries at its registered office. It must contain the following information concerning **directors**:

(*a*) In the case of an individual,

(*i*) His present and any former Christian names and surname. (Former names are not required where a change was due to marriage or acquisition of a title; where the change occurred before the person was 18 years of age; or where the change was effected more than twenty years previously.)

(*ii*) His residential address.

(*iii*) His nationality, unless he is a national of a member state of the EEC.

(*iv*) His business occupation.

(*v*) Any other directorships held by him but excluding those of the company's wholly-owned subsidiaries or its fellow subsidiaries; or a holding company of which the company is a wholly-owned subsidiary.

(*vi*) His age, unless the company is not subject to S. 185 (see page 81).

(*b*) In the case of a corporation, its corporate name and registered or principal office.

The following information must be entered concerning a **secretary**:

(*a*) In the case of an individual, his present and former Christian names and surname, and his residential address. (If all the partners in a firm are joint secretaries, the firm's name and principal office may be given.)

(*b*) In the case of a corporation or a Scottish firm, its corporate or firm name and its registered or principal office.

The register must be open to inspection by any member without charge and by any other person for a fee.

A statement of the above particulars concerning the *first* directors and secretaries must be delivered on application for registration of a company, as required by S. 21 (1976) (see page 16).

Changes in the Register

Any change of directors or secretaries or any change in the particulars in the register must be notified in the prescribed form to the Registrar within fourteen days of the change. Where the change is of a person becoming a director or secretary, the notification must contain a consent to act signed by that person (S. 22 (1976)).

The date on which a notification of a change of directors becomes effective, as against any person who cannot be shown to have knowledge of the change, is the fifteenth day after publication by the Registrar in the *Gazette* (*European Communities Act, 1972*).

9

SHARE CAPITAL

Forms of Share Capital

Nominal or Authorised capital relates to that amount of capital which is stated in the Memorandum and is there shown in its division into shares of fixed amounts. As such, it represents the maximum amount the company may issue and which can be increased only as prescribed by law. (The amount of share capital of an *unlimited* company is stated in the *Articles* (S. 7).)

Issued capital is the nominal amount of the shares allotted, irrespective of the amount deemed to have been paid up on the shares.

Paid-up capital represents the amount received, in cash or for other consideration, on shares issued.

Reserve capital is part of the *uncalled* capital which can be called up only on a winding up. The creation of such capital must be by special resolution (S. 60). Reserve capital cannot be charged as security for borrowing. Reserve capital is also referred to as 'reserve liability'.

Types of Shares

Shares may be divided broadly into two groups: **preference shares**, which pay a dividend at a fixed rate in priority to those in the other group, and **ordinary shares**, which carry a dividend payable from the balance of profits, the rate being largely dependent upon the amount of that balance. There is also another category of shares, known as **founders'** or **deferred shares** (now rarely in issue), the special features of which are stated on page 44.

Preference Shares

The precise conditions of an issue of preference shares are as specified in the terms of issue and in the Memorandum and Articles. The common factors of all preference shares are their priority as regards payment of a dividend and the fixed dividend rate. Variations between different terms of issue may be summarised as follows.

Arrears of Dividends

Unless the shares are declared to be 'non-cumulative', they are assumed to be cumulative (*Webb v. Earle* (1875)). This means that if the agreed rate of dividend was not paid in any year, such arrears must be paid before a dividend can be paid on lower-ranking classes of share. It has been held that if the terms prescribe payment of a dividend 'out of the profits of each year', the shares are non-cumulative (*Staples v. Eastman Photographic Materials Co.* (1896)). The amount of any arrears must be disclosed in the accounts.

In general, a dividend is not payable unless it has been declared. In the event of winding up, therefore, there would be no right to arrears unless the dividend had been declared before winding up (*Re Roberts & Cooper Ltd* (1929)). If, however, as in *Re E.W. Savory Ltd* (1951), the Articles prescribe that shares 'shall rank both as regards dividend and capital in priority to all other shares, both present and future', it must refer to rights in winding up. The preference shareholders were, therefore, entitled to the arrears even though no dividend had been declared.

Any arrears which are payable may be paid from the surplus assets in winding up; they do not have to come from available profits (*Re Wharfdale Brewery Ltd* (1952)).

Return of Capital

Unless there is provision for the preference shareholders to rank in priority to other shareholders for the return of capital, they will rank *pari passu* with them (*Birch v. Cropper* (1889)). Where priority does exist, the *whole* of the preference capital must be repaid before other share capital.

Share in Surplus Assets

After all creditors have been paid, the expenses of the winding up discharged and share capital refunded, any surplus from the realisation is distributed to the shareholders. The general rule is that, subject to any contrary terms, preference shareholders have no right to share in the distribution of surplus assets (*Scottish Insurance Corporation Ltd v. Wilsons and Clyde Coal Co.* (1949)). Accordingly, in such instances the repayment of the preference share capital exhausts the rights of the holders and all the surplus accrues to the ordinary shareholders.

Redeemable Preference Shares

Share capital generally may not be returned to the shareholders except under conditions as provided by law. The exception is capital in the form of redeemable preference shares, which are issued on terms whereby they are redeemable on a specified date or within specified dates. A company issuing such shares is subject to the following rules as laid down in S. 58:

(*a*) The issue must be authorised by the Articles.
(*b*) Redemption must be made out of

(*i*) profits which are otherwise available for dividend; or

(*ii*) the proceeds of an issue of shares made for the purpose of the redemption.

(*c*) The shares must be fully paid before being redeemed.

(*d*) Any premium payable on redemption must be provided out of

(*i*) profits; or

(*ii*) the share premium account (see page 58).

(*e*) In the case of redemption being made from profits, an amount equal to the nominal value of the shares redeemed must be transferred out of profits otherwise available for dividends to a 'capital redemption reserve fund'. This fund may only be used to pay up unissued shares to be issued as fully paid shares to the members (a scrip issue). Otherwise, the fund may be reduced only in the same manner as the Act prescribes for reducing capital.

Calls and Instalments

Most public company shares are payable in full upon application, but provision may exist for any balance of the issue price after payment of application and allotment monies to be paid by (*a*) **calls**, whereby the directors demand payment when they so decide, or (*b*) **instalments**, whereby the balance becomes payable on dates specified in the terms of issue. A call is in the nature of a specialty debt (S.20(2)).

S.59 provides that a company, if permitted by its Articles, may:

(*a*) Make arrangements which differentiate between members as to the amounts and due dates of calls. This is interpreted so as not to permit differentiation between members holding the *same class* of share, however (*Galloway v. Hallé Concerts Society* (1915)).

(*b*) Accept calls in advance of the due date. Interest can be paid on such payments (subject to the Articles) even if there are no available profits (*Lock v. Queensland Investment Co.* (1896)). Calls paid in advance cannot be repaid while the company is a going concern (*London and Northern Steamship Co. v. Farmer* (1914)), but in a winding up they can be repaid after the creditors and winding-up costs have been paid and before any capital is returned to any member (*Re Wakefield Rolling Stock Co.* (1892)).

The right may exist to forfeit shares for non-payment of calls or instalments (see page 73).

Alteration of Capital

A company limited by shares or a guarantee company with a share capital may, if authorised by its Articles, alter its share capital. The capital clause in the Memorandum can be altered only in the mode and to the extent provided for in the Act (S.4).

S.61 provides that a company may:

(*a*) **Increase** its share capital by issuing such number of new shares as it considers expedient.

(*b*) **Consolidate and divide** all or any of its share capital into shares of larger amounts.

(*c*) **Convert** all or any of its paid up shares into stock, and **re-convert** that stock into paid up shares.

(*d*) **Subdivide** any of its shares into smaller amounts.

(*e*) **Cancel** shares not taken or agreed to be taken.

The decision to alter the capital can be taken only in a general meeting of the company. Unless the Articles prescribe otherwise, an ordinary resolution will suffice.

With the exception of an increase in capital (see below), notice and details of any of the above alterations must be given to the Registrar within one month (S. 62). Every copy of the Memorandum subsequently issued must include the alteration (S. 25).

(A **reduction** of capital is not an alteration as permitted under S. 61—see page 101.)

Increase of Capital

This is, of course, an increase in the *Authorised* capital as set out in the Memorandum.

Within fifteen days of passing the resolution, notice of the increase must be given to the Registrar, with such particulars as may be prescribed concerning the shares affected and the conditions subject to which the shares have been or are to be issued. It must be accompanied by a printed copy of the resolution (S. 63).

Subject to any contrary conditions in the Memorandum, the increased capital may consist of a new class of shares (*Andrews v. Gas Meter Co.* (1897)).

Consolidation and Division

Consolidation entails the merging of shares into larger units. This is rarely done in isolation, the modern tendency being for shares to be in smaller units. Consolidation is usually resorted to when it is combined with division of shares following a reduction of capital. A reduction of capital may have reduced the nominal value of the shares to an odd amount, says 55p. Ten of the reduced shares could be consolidated into one share of 550p and then divided into eleven shares of 50p each.

Conversion and Re-conversion

Stock may not be issued initially; it can derive only from a conversion of shares. In the past, the existence of stock reduced the work of a transfer department because there was no legal requirement for distinguishing numbers on stock. As, however, the 1948 Act removed the necessity for distinguishing numbers for fully paid shares (see page 67), the advantage no longer exists.

Upon conversion, the register of members must show the amount of stock in the name of each member (S. 110). The Annual Return must give similar information (S. 124).

Stock may be re-converted into paid-up shares. The new shares may be of a different nominal value from the original shares. They may even be of a different class although, of course, the prescribed procedure would be necessary if this involved a variation of rights.

Subdivision

This results in an increase in the number of shares with a corresponding reduction in the nominal value of each share. Where the market value of a share is exceptionally high, reduction of the nominal value will reduce the market price to a more manageable figure.

If the shares are partly-paid, the proportion paid must remain the same after the reduction.

Cancellation

Creditors look to the *issued* share capital as the company's funds available for satisfaction of company debts if necessary. Accordingly, cancellation so as to *prohibit issue* of certain shares is not a reduction of share capital. The reason for cancellation could be to prevent the issue of shares which would carry burdensome rights.

Reduction of Capital

Creditors are entitled to regard the issued share capital as a fund available to them in the event of the liquidation of the company. Consequently, there are specific and stringent legal provisions applicable. The basic requirements are that:

(*a*) The decision to reduce the capital must be taken by the passing of a special resolution in general meeting.

(*b*) The Court must be petitioned for its approval.

(*c*) The Court's decision may take account of objections by the company's creditors.

S. 66 states that the share capital may be reduced *in any way*. It then goes on to specify three particular methods (which, in practice, encompass those usually adopted). They are:

(*a*) To extinguish or reduce liability on any shares not fully paid up.

(*b*) To cancel paid-up share capital which is lost or unrepresented by available assets, with or without extinguishing or reducing liability on any shares.

(*c*) To pay off any paid-up capital in excess of the wants of the company, with or without extinguishing or reducing liability on any shares.

It may, if and so far as is necessary, alter its Memorandum by reducing the share capital accordingly.

The resolution (referred to in the Act as 'a resolution for reducing share capital') must be a *special* resolution and can be passed only if reduction of capital is authorised by the Articles. If the required authority is not available, then the Articles must be altered to give that power *before* the resolution to reduce is placed before the meeting (*Re Oregon Mortgage Co.* (1910)). A power in the *Memorandum* is insufficient authority (*Re Dexine Patent Packing and Rubber Co.* (1903)).

Petition to the Court

Having passed a resolution to reduce the share capital, a company may ask the Court to confirm the reduction (S. 67(1)).

(1) *If the reduction is likely to prejudice the interests of creditors* (i.e. on a diminution of liability on unpaid share capital; on repayment of any paid-up share capital; or in any other case if the court so directs), the creditors will have the right to object. In such circumstances S. 67(2) prescribes as follows:

(*a*) Every creditor whose debt would have been admissible in proof in a winding up may object.

(*b*) The Court will settle a list of creditors so entitled, with the nature and amount of the claims.

(*c*) The Court may publish notices to fix a time within which creditors not entered on the list may claim entry therein.

(*d*) In the case of a creditor who does not consent to the reduction, the Court may dispense with his consent if the company secures payment of his debt by setting aside the full amount of the claim or, if the amount is disputed or contingent, pays into Court such amount as the Court directs.

(*e*) The Court may, in special circumstances, withhold the right to object.

It is an offence for an officer of the company wilfully to conceal the name of any creditor entitled to object, or to misrepresent the nature or amount of any debt or claim (S. 71).

(2) *If the reduction does not involve creditors*, the Court will take account only of the following, it being a purely domestic matter (*British and American Trustee and Finance Corporation Ltd v. Couper* (1894):

(*a*) To consider the interests of *members of the public* who may be induced to take shares.

(*b*) To consider whether the reduction is fair and equitable *as between different classes of shareholders*. In deciding this, the Court would normally take account of the order of priority in a winding up.

(*i*) If surplus capital is to be repaid, shareholders with priority in a winding up would be paid first (*Prudential Assurance Co. v. Chatterley-Whitfield Collieries* (1949)).

(*ii*) If preferential shareholders have no priority in the repayment of capital, the reduction should be borne in the same proportion as that of the nominal value of the ordinary share capital and the preference share capital (*Bannatyne v. Direct Spanish Telegraph* (1886)).

(*iii*) If the preference shareholders have priority as to repayment of capital, the ordinary shareholders must first bear the loss (*Re London & New York, etc., Corporation* (1895)).

The Court Order

When the Court is satisfied that each creditor entitled to object has given his consent or his debt has been discharged or secured, it may confirm the reduction on such terms and conditions as it thinks fit. It has the right to order (*a*) that the words 'and reduced' be added to the company's name for a specified period, and (*b*) that the company publish reasons for the reduction (S. 68).

The reduction does not become effective until the order has been produced to the Registrar, and a copy of the order and a minute approved by the Court delivered to the Registrar and registered by him. The minute must show, in respect of the share capital as altered: (*i*) the amount of the share capital; (*ii*) the number of shares into which it is divided; and (*iii*) the amount of each share and the amount deemed to be paid up thereon.

A certificate given by the Registrar and authenticated by a seal prepared under S. 424(5) shall be conclusive evidence that the requirements of the Act have been complied with. The minute shall be deemed to be substituted for the corresponding part of the Memorandum (S. 69 as amended) and all copies of the Memorandum issued thereafter must include the alteration (S. 25).

Following the reduction, a shareholder, past or present, cannot be liable for any amount exceeding the difference between the amount of the shares as reduced and the amount paid or the reduced amount deemed to be paid. But if the company is wound up within one year of the reduction, any creditor not entered on the list of creditors because of his ignorance of the reduction may claim against those who were members at the time of the reduction if the company is unable to pay him (S. 70).

10

LOAN CAPITAL

The Power to Borrow

The right to borrow and the extent of borrowing are determined as follows:

(*a*) **Implied powers.** A company engaged in trading has implied power to borrow and to give security (*General Auction Estate & Monetary Co. v. Smith* (1891)). A non-trading company has no such powers unless they are bestowed by the Memorandum, although this does not debar the company from trading on normal credit terms.

(*b*) **Power in the Memorandum.** It is usual expressly to bestow the power of borrowing in the Memorandum even if the company has implied power. The Memorandum may contain a restriction on the amount which may be borrowed.

(*c*) **Power in the Articles.** Any restriction on the amount which may be borrowed is usually contained in the Articles. It is normal to permit the directors to exercise borrowing powers up to a specified or ascertainable amount (such as the amount of the issued share capital) and to require the approval of members in general meeting for any borrowing in excess of that figure. Clause 79 of Table A makes provisions on these lines.

(*d*) **The Act.** A company may not borrow until it is entitled to commence business, but it may receive application moneys for debentures (S. 109).

The Power to Charge Assets

A company with power to borrow has also power to mortgage or charge assets as security for loans (*Re Patent File Co.* (1870)), subject to any restriction in the Memorandum or Articles.

Reserve capital (see page 98) cannot be charged (*Re Mayfair Property Co.* (1898)) and uncalled share capital cannot be charged unless authority to do so is contained in the Articles.

Ultra Vires Borrowing

Any borrowing by a company beyond its powers (or if it has no powers) is null and void, and does not create an actionable debt. Any security given is also void. A lender may, however, have certain rights as detailed below.

(*a*) If the borrowing is *ultra vires* the **Memorandum**, the lender may be able to rely upon the provisions of S. 9 of the *European Communities Act, 1972*. This states that an agreement, decided upon by the directors and affecting dealings with those acting in good faith, may not be set aside as being beyond the objects clause in the Memorandum (see page 34).

(*b*) If the directors exceed their powers as defined in the **Articles**, the same Act relates also to directors so acting. The lender may also be able to rely on the rule in *Royal British Bank v. Turquand* in that he may have reasonably assumed that any necessary internal procedures of the company had been carried out (see page 33). In fact, Clause 79 of Table A states that no lender shall be concerned to see whether any limit of the directors' borrowing powers is observed and no debt or security in excess of any such limit shall be invalid, unless the person concerned had express notice of such excess.

(*c*) If the money, or any assets purchased with it, is identifiable and still in the company's possession, application can be made for an injunction to restrain the company from parting with it, and for a 'tracing order' to trace and recover it.

(*d*) The right of 'subrogation' may exist if the money has been used to pay off creditors, whereby the lender may 'stand in the shoes' of the creditors paid off and sue the company for the amount of the debts (*Sinclair v. Brougham* (1914)). This would not, however, enable the lender to have priority over other creditors which the creditors paid off may have had (*Re Wrexham, Mold & Connah's Quay Railway* (1899)).

(*e*) An action for damages may be taken against the directors for breach of warranty of authority (*Firbank's Executors v. Humphreys* (1886)). Any damages will be limited to such amount as is required to place the creditor in the position he would have occupied if the representation had been true. Thus, any recompense made by the company would be set off against the lender's original loss.

Debentures

Debentures are not precisely defined in the Act, although S. 455 states that the term includes debenture stock, bonds and other securities, whether constituting a charge on the assets or not. It has been described as 'a document which creates or acknowledges a debt' (*Levy v. Abercorris Slate and Slab Co.* (1887)).

A debenture-holder is a *creditor* of the company, and interest on debentures is payable whether or not the company makes profits.

A debenture is a 'chose in action' and accordingly is subject to equities. A transferee takes a debenture subject to any rights the company may have against the transferor, but it is usually provided that repayment will be made to a registered holder *irrespective* of any equities existing between the company and the previous holder.

Types of Debentures

Bearer debentures are rarely issued because they are subject to Exchange Control restrictions, being transferable by delivery.

Registered debentures are registered in the name of each holder. There may be a single lender or a series of debentures may be issued if there is more than one lender. Usually, the provisions concerning transfer are similar to those applicable to shares, except that the name of the new holder is endorsed on the debenture instead of a new document being issued.

Mortgage debentures are debentures secured by a fixed charge on the assets of the company.

Debenture stock relates to a public issue of debentures, supported by a trust deed made between the company and trustees acting for the lenders (see page 112).

Unsecured loan stock is debenture stock issued without a charge. Frequently, such debentures carry the right, exercisable at a holder's option on specified future dates, to convert them into fully paid ordinary shares at prescribed exchange rates.

Debentures are almost invariably due to be redeemed by a fixed date, although S. 89 makes provisions for the issue of **irredeemable debentures**. The term usually means that the debentures can be redeemed only at the company's option and are more properly termed **perpetual debentures**.

Issue of Debentures

Unlike shares, debentures may be issued at a discount. It is not permitted, however, to issue debentures at a discount with the right subsequently to convert them at their par value into fully-paid shares, as this would be tantamount to issuing shares at a discount (*Moseley v. Koffyfontein Mines* (1904)).

A contract to take up and pay for any debentures may be enforced by an order for specific performance (S. 92).

A company may *re-issue* debentures which have been redeemed or it may issue other debentures in place of redeemed debentures, unless (*a*) the Articles or any contract forbids it, or (*b*) the company has manifested its intention to cancel the redeemed debentures (S. 90(1)). The holders of re-issued debentures acquire the same priorities as if the debentures had not been redeemed (i.e. they will rank *pari passu* with the unredeemed debentures in the same issue) and the terms of the original issue remain unaltered. Particulars of any redeemed debentures capable of being re-issued must appear in the balance sheet.

Types of Charges

Security for debentures can take one or both of two forms:

(*a*) **Fixed charge.** This is in the form of a mortgage on specific assets. It may be

(*i*) a legal mortgage, whereby title to the charged property passes to the lender, subject to the right of the company to redeem on payment of the principal and the interest; or

(*ii*) an equitable mortgage, whereby the document of title is lodged with the lender and legal ownership remains with the company.

(*b*) **Floating charge.** This is an equitable charge on the assets, present and future, of the company and is therefore not specific to any asset. The charged assets would constantly change in the ordinary course of business and there would be no restriction on the normal use and disposal of the assets until such time as the debenture-holders took action to enforce their security. A floating charge becomes a fixed charge (or 'crystallizes') when

(*i*) an event specified in the conditions of issue occurs (such as default in payment of interest or in repayment of the principal sum) and the debenture-holders take action to enforce their security;

(*ii*) the company goes into liquidation.

(The circumstances in which a floating charge could be avoided in a winding up are explained on page 194.)

Priorities of Charges

A floating charge is subject to any existing charges on the property.

Unless the conditions prescribe otherwise, a subsequent *floating* charge cannot be made which ranks prior to or *pari passu* with an existing floating charge. However, a *fixed* charge can be subsequently created which will rank prior to a floating charge. It is usual to attempt to prevent a company from doing this by a suitably worded clause in the terms of issue, but such a condition is limited in its effect to the *company and the debenture-holders*. Any subsequent lender who obtains a legal estate or interest without knowledge of the existence of the floating charge or of a restriction on the creating of preferential charges will obtain priority (*English and Scottish Mercantile Investment Co. v. Brunton* (1892)). Registration of the floating charge with the Registrar (see below) does not negate this latter principle because it does not fix the subsequent lender with notice of the restriction concerning future charges (*Re Standard Rotary Machine Co.* (1906)). To do so, it is necessary that the restriction appears on the Form 47 filed with the Registrar.

Registration of Charges

It is obviously necessary that facilities exist whereby persons dealing with a company or contemplating doing so can establish the extent to which the company has charged any of its assets or its undertaking generally. The Act provides for two forms of registration and facilities for inspection. These are the *Registrar's* Register of Charges (see below) and the *company's* Register of Charges (see page 111).

Registration of Charges with the Registrar

S.95(2) states that particulars of the following charges created by a company must be delivered to the Registrar within twenty-one days of their creation, together with the charging instrument, if any. A charge is deemed to be created at the time of execution or at the time of depositing the title deeds (*Esberger & Son v. Capital and Counties Bank* (1913)).

(*a*) A charge for securing any issue of debentures.

(*b*) A charge on uncalled share capital.

(*c*) A charge which if executed by an individual would require registration as a bill of sale.

(*d*) A charge on land or any interest in land, but not a charge for rents or other periodical sums issued out of land.

(*e*) A charge on book debts.

(*f*) A floating charge on the undertaking or property of the company.

(*g*) A charge on calls made but unpaid.

(*h*) A charge on a ship or share in a ship.

(*i*) A charge on goodwill, a patent or licence under a patent, a trademark, copyright or licence.

If a company acquires property which is *already* subject to any of the above charges, it must register particulars of such existing charges (S. 97).

Failure to Register

The responsibility for registering a charge rests with the company and there is a default fine for failing to do so, but *any* interested person may register (S.96). (See also *Rectification of the Register* below.)

In the event of failure to register, the charge is void, but only against the liquidator and any creditor. The obligation on the company to repay remains and, in fact, *the money becomes repayable immediately* (S.95(1)). Upon liquidation of the company, the holder of an unregistered charge becomes an unsecured creditor.

Particulars to be Registered

(*a*) Where a *series* of mortgage debentures has been issued, it is sufficient if the deed containing the charge (or, if there is no such deed, a debenture in the series) is delivered to the Registrar within twenty-one days with the following particulars:

(*i*) The total amount secured by the whole series.

(*ii*) The dates of the resolutions authorising the issue and the date of the covering deed (if any).

(*iii*) A general description of the property charged.

(*iv*) The names of the trustees for the debenture-holders (if any) (S.95 (8)).

(*b*) In the case of *any other* charge, the particulars to be registered are as follows:

(*i*) The date of creation of the charge by the company, or, if a charge already exists on property acquired by the company, the date of the acquisition.

(*ii*) The amount secured.

(*iii*) Short particulars of the property charged.

(*iv*) The persons entitled to the charge (S.95(1)(b)).

Particulars of any discount, allowance or commission paid in consideration of subscribing must also be registered (S.95(9)).

The Registrar's Register of Charges

S.98(1) requires the Registrar to maintain a register of all charges required to be registered, containing the particulars quoted above.

Particulars of the appointment of a receiver or manager under a charge must be notified to the Registrar within seven days and included in the Register, and on the termination of such an appointment (S.102) (see page 113).

Any person may inspect the Register on payment of a fee (S.98(3)).

Certificate of Registration

The Registrar will give a certificate under seal of the registration of any charge, stating the amount secured. Such a certificate is conclusive evidence of registration (S.98(2) as amended). In *Re C.L. Nye Ltd* (1971) the Court of Appeal held that even though the document registered bore the wrong date, the certificate of registration was conclusive evidence that all the requirements of the Act had been complied with.

A copy of every certificate of registration must be endorsed on every debenture or certificate of debenture stock (S.99). (When debenture stock is issued, every lender receives a certificate showing his contribution to the total issue.)

Rectification of the Register

In the event of a charge not being registered within the prescribed period or if there was a misstatement or omission in the registration, the company or any interested party may apply for an extension of the time limit. The Court will grant this concession only if it is satisfied that the default:

(*a*) was 'accidental'; or

(*b*) was 'due to inadvertence or to some other sufficient cause'; or

(*c*) is 'not of a nature to prejudice the position of creditors or stock-holders of the company'; or

(*d*) is such that, on other grounds, 'it is just and equitable to grant relief' (S. 101).

Memorandum of Satisfaction

When the debt is paid, wholly or in part, or part of the property charge is released or ceases to form part of the company's property, the Registrar may enter a Memorandum of Satisfaction on the Register and, if required, will, in respect of satisfaction *in whole*, furnish the company with a copy (S. 100).

The Company's Register of Charges

Every company is required to keep at its registered office a copy of every instrument creating a registrable charge, except that a copy of one debenture in a series of uniform debentures shall be sufficient (S. 103). In addition, S. 104 requires a company to keep a Register of Charges at its registered office (even if no item qualifies for entry) and to enter therein, in respect of *all* specific charges on property of the company and all floating charges, (*a*) a short description of the property charged; (*b*) the amount of the charge; (*c*) the names of the persons entitled thereto.

Thus, there may be charges which have to be registered at the company which are not required under S. 95 to be entered in the Register kept by the Registrar. An example would be the deposit with a bank of share certificates with a memorandum of deposit as security for a loan.

Copies of the charging instruments and of the Register must be available for inspection, without charge, by any creditor or member of the company. Any other person may inspect the Register on payment of a fee (S. 105).

Register of Debenture-Holders

There is no legal requirement to maintain a register of debenture-holders, but S. 86 states that if a register is kept it must be kept at the registered office of the company or at some other place where the work of making it up is done. Notice of that place and of any change must be given to the Registrar, unless the register has always been kept at the registered office. The register must be kept in a place within the domicile of the company.

Every such register must be open to inspection by any debenture-holder or shareholder without fee and to every other person on payment of a fee. Any debenture-holder or member may require a copy of the register or any part thereof on payment of a fee of 20p (S.87 as amended by S.52(1967)).

Trust Deed

An issue of debenture stock is normally secured by the appointment of trustees under a trust deed, which usually contains the following particulars:

(*a*) The terms of issue of the stock, including payment of interest, redemption, any conversion rights, etc.

(*b*) A mortgage on the secured assets, with particulars of the circumstances in which the security would be enforceable.

(*c*) Covenants by the company in respect of its business in general (e.g. to set a limit on its borrowings) and the charged assets in particular (e.g. to insure and maintain the property on agreed terms).

(*d*) The rights of the trustees to compromise or concur with the company in dealings concerning the charged assets.

(*e*) The remuneration of the trustees.

(*f*) The procedure for transfer and transmission.

(*g*) Regulations concerning meetings of the debenture-holders.

It will thus be seen that the single charge which provides security for many lenders is held by trustees on behalf of those lenders. A trust deed also has the effect of providing a central body which can look after the interests of the lenders, take instructions from them and, where necessary, act of their behalf.

Every debenture-holder is entitled to a copy of a trust deed on payment of 20p (S.87(3) as amended by S.52(1967)).

Any provision in a trust deed, or in a contract with debenture-holders secured by a trust deed, is void so far as it exempts a trustee from liability for breach of trust where he fails to show the degree of care and diligence required of him as a trustee. This does not, however, invalidate:

(*a*) any release otherwise validly given in respect of anything done or omitted to be done by a trustee before the giving of the release; or

(*b*) any provision enabling such a release to be given

(*i*) upon the agreement of not less than three fourths in value of the debenture-holders, voting personally or by proxy, at a meeting summoned for that purpose; and

(*ii*) either with respect to specific acts or omissions or on a trustee dying or ceasing to act (S.88).

Remedies Available to Debenture-Holders

When circumstances arise which give debenture-holders the right to take action, the remedies available to them will be those applicable to *any* creditor, *together with* any deriving from the conditions in the debenture or trust deed.

(*a*) Any debenture-holder, *secured or unsecured*, may
(*i*) sue on the promise to pay the interest and the principal;
(*ii*) issue execution if judgment is obtained;
(*iii*) petition for winding up.

(*b*) Holders of debentures, *secured by a charge*, may have the following additional remedies.

(*i*) To appoint a receiver and, where relevant, a manager.

(*ii*) To apply to the Court for appointment of a receiver and, where relevant, a manager.

(*iii*) To sell the charged assets if power of sale is contained in the debenture or trust deed (as it usually is). Any surplus from the sale after satisfaction of the debt must be returned to the company.

(*iv*) To foreclose. Application must be made to the Court for an order of foreclosure. This has the effect of depriving the company of ownership of the charged assets and the debenture-holders becoming the absolute owners. In any action for foreclosure, *all* the interested debenture-holders must join in the action (*Elias v. Continental Oxygen Co.* (1897)).

Receivers and Managers

The object of appointing a receiver is to protect the interests of the debenture-holders in respect of the charged assets. The appointment of a receiver is usually a prelude to liquidation, but if it is desired that the company continues in business a manager must be appointed. The period of continuing the business is normally merely long enough to facilitate the sale of the business as a going concern.

Appointment

There are two alternatives leading to the appointment of receivers and managers:

(1) Debenture-holders or their trustees may appoint a receiver or manager *only* if there is express power to do so in the debenture or trust deed.

(2) In any other case, a receiver or manager can be appointed only by the Court on application by the debenture-holders (see below).

Notice of the appointment of a receiver or manager must be given to the Registrar within seven days by the person appointing the receiver or manager or the person obtaining a Court order to do so. An entry to that effect must be made in the Registrar's Register of Charges (S. 102).

A receiver may not be a body corporate (S. 366), nor an undischarged bankrupt, unless appointed by the Court (S. 367).

Appointment by the Court

A receiver may be appointed by the Court when no express power to do so is contained in the debenture. A debenture-holder, on behalf of himself and other holders of the same class of debenture, may bring an action (known as a '*debenture-holders' action*'). His claim will be for:

(*a*) a declaration that the debentures are a charge on the assets;
(*b*) an account of the amount owed to the debenture-holders, what assets there are and particulars of any prior claims;
(*c*) the appointment of a receiver;
(*d*) an order of foreclosure or sale.

The right of action arises if:

(*a*) the principal has become payable; or
(*b*) there is unpaid interest or principal; or
(*c*) the company is being wound up; or
(*d*) the debenture-holders' security 'is in jeopardy', i.e. that there is the possibility of loss or diminution in value of the security or that the security will become unavailable to the debenture-holders or that the company is insolvent. Cases where the Court decided that the debenture-holders' security was in jeopardy include the following:

(*i*) Where the company's works had closed down and although the company was insolvent no condition of the debenture had given the right to appoint a receiver (*McMahon v. North Kent Ironworks* (1891)).
(*ii*) Where the directors proposed to distribute the reserves as dividends and leave the debenture-holders insufficiently secured (*Re Tilt Cove Copper Ltd* (1913)).
(*iii*) Where the business had closed down, funds and credit were exhausted and creditors were pressing for payment (*Re Braunstein & Marjolaine* (1914)).

Jeopardy may not be pleaded, however, merely because the security for the time being is inadequate, provided the creditors are not pressing for payment (*Re New York Taxi Cab Co.* (1913)).

A receiver appointed *by the Court* is an officer of the Court. He is therefore not an agent of the company nor of the debenture-holders. Consequently, as the Court cannot be liable, he is personally liable in respect of contracts entered into by him, although he is entitled to be indemnified out of the company's assets. Because of his position, he has less discretion of action than has a receiver 'appointed out of Court'. Thus, no action may be brought or continued by him without leave of the Court (*Viola v. Anglo-American Cold Storage Co.* (1912)), nor may action be brought against him except by the Court's leave.

Such a receiver is not compelled to carry out contracts made before his appointment. If, with the Court's consent, he repudiates a contract, the other party may have right of action against the company for damages. He may, however, carry out contracts such as may be necessary to maintain the company's goodwill. With the Court's consent, he may borrow and give security therefor in priority to the debenture-holders' security, if such action is reasonably necessary to preserve their security.

In respect of all his actions, the receiver is regarded as having been appointed for the benefit of all those interested in the assets and not only the debenture-holders.

The receiver may carry on the business only with the consent of the Court, and his remuneration is fixed by the Court.

Debenture-holders may forgo any right they have to appoint a receiver and apply to the Court for the appointment to be made.

Application may be made to the Court for a receiver to be appointed on behalf of the debenture-holders when the company is in the course of being wound up. In that case, the Official Receiver may be appointed (S. 368).

Appointment by the Debenture-Holders

The circumstances leading to the appointment of a receiver by the debenture-holders (i.e. 'out of Court') would be those prescribed in the conditions attached to the debentures.

The usual powers of such a receiver are to take possession of the assets forming the charge, to sell all or such of them as may be necessary and to pay the debenture-holders the amount due after discharge of preferential debts and charges. If expressly empowered to do so, he may carry on the company's business meanwhile.

A receiver appointed by the debenture-holders is, subject to any contrary provision, an agent of *the appointers*. It is usually provided, however, that he acts as agent of *the company*.

Such a receiver has the right to apply to the Court for direction in relation to any matter arising from the performance of his duties (S. 369 (1)). Should the company go into liquidation, the Court may fix the receiver's remuneration and, if necessary, may require him to refund remuneration he received prior to the Court order (S. 371).

Where there is a Floating Charge

In the event of the whole or substantially the whole of the company's property being charged to the debenture-holders by way of a floating charge and a receiver or manager is appointed, '*in Court*' or '*out of Court*', S. 372 (as amended) provides as follows:

(*a*) The receiver shall forthwith send to the company notice of his appointment in the prescribed form; and

(*b*) Within fourteen days thereafter the company shall submit a statement of affairs to the receiver; and

(*c*) Within two months of receipt of the statement, the receiver shall send:

(*i*) to the Registrar and the Court, a copy of the statement and any comments he wishes to make; and to the Registrar, also a summary of the statement and of his comments;

(*ii*) to the company, a copy of his comments or notice that he has made no comments;

(*iii*) to the trustees of the debenture-holders and to the debenture-holders (so far as he is aware of their addresses), a copy of the summary.

The Section goes on to require that within two months after each anniversary of his appointment and within two months after ceasing to act, the receiver must submit an abstract of his receipts and payments for the intervening period and for the cumulative period to date to the Registrar; the company; any trustees; and, so far as he is aware of their addresses, the debenture-holders.

The receiver has power to require verification of the statement of affairs from past and present officers of the company, anyone engaged in the formation of the company within a year before his appointment, and others who were employees and ex-employees within the same period. The statement of affairs must show, as at the date of the receiver's appointment, particulars of the company's assets and liabilities; its creditors, the securities held by them and when they were given; and such other information as may be prescribed (S. 373).

In a *debenture-holders' action*, where the debentures are secured by a floating charge and a trust deed, and action is taken to realise on the charged assets, the proceeds must be applied in the following order in the case of a deficiency:

(*a*) Costs of realisation.

(*b*) Costs and remuneration of the receiver.

(*c*) Costs, charges and expenses of the trust deed, including trustees' remuneration.

(*d*) Costs of the action.

(*e*) Preferential creditors as they would be in a winding up (see page 193).

(*f*) Claims of the debenture-holders (*Re Glyncorrwg Colliery Co.* (1926)).

Consequences of a Receiver being Appointed

The company is deprived of its ability to deal with the property which is subject to the charge, although the company continues as a legal person (*Moss Steamship Co. v. Whinney* (1912)).

Every invoice, order for goods and business letter containing the company's name must include a statement that a receiver or manager has been appointed (S. 370).

Directors' remuneration ceases, although if employed by the receiver they may claim remuneration from him.

Where the receiver is appointed out of Court and acts as agent for the company, employees' contracts continue in force (*Re Mack Trucks (Britain) Ltd* (1967)), but if a receiver is appointed by the Court or acts as agent for the debenture-holders, employee contracts are terminated (*Reid v. Explosives Co.* (1887)), although such employees may be re-employed by the receiver.

The receiver or manager is required to submit to the Registrar every six months an abstract of his receipts and payments (S. 374), unless there is a floating charge on substantially the whole of the undertaking (in which case, the provisions outlined above apply). Such a duty may be enforced by an order of the Court (S. 375).

11

DISTRIBUTION OF PROFITS

Distributable Profits

Except in the rare instances where permission is given for the payment of interest out of capital (see page 120), dividends can be paid only out of profits. Dividends may not be paid out of capital even if the Memorandum or Articles purport to permit it, as to do so would conflict with what may be inferred from the Companies Acts (*Verner v. General and Commercial Investment Trust* (1894)).

Difficulty has frequently been experienced, however, in deciding what constitutes 'profits' in respect of distributions to shareholders. The following principles are amongst those which have been established in the courts:

(*a*) **Increase in the value of assets.** If one compared the net asset value of a company for one year with that of the preceding year, any increase could be regarded as being the profit for the year (ignoring any introductions of capital, of course) (*Re Spanish Prospecting Co.* (1911)). In practice, however, it may be unsafe to accept this reasoning, because many valuations can only be arbitrary estimates.

The general accounting rule, and the one which would usually apply in law, is to ignore *unrealised* gains. Thus, the increase would not be available for distribution unless it derived from a sale of the asset. What may be construed as a contrary opinion, however, was given by the judge in *Dimbula Valley (Ceylon) Tea Co. v. Laurie* (1961). His view was that a surplus deriving from a *bona fide* valuation could be legally passed to the members in the form of *bonus shares*, even though the surplus was unrealised. It would also be necessary that such an increase represented an increase in the value of the assets as a whole, so that the single increase was not negatived by an overall fall (*Foster v. New Trinidad Lake Asphalte Co.* (1901)).

(*b*) **Maintaining the capital.** The capital of a company must remain intact, but in considering the consequences of losses of capital a distinction must first be made between the two types of capital.

(*i*) **Fixed capital** has been defined as 'property acquired and intended for retention and employment with a view to profit'.

(*ii*) **Circulating capital** has been defined as 'property acquired or produced with a view to resale or sale at a profit'. (*Ammonia Soda Co. v. Chamberlain* (1918)).

118

A series of Court of Appeal decisions concerning the availability of distributable profits following loss of *fixed* capital culminated in the decision in the above-quoted case. This was to the effect that it is not necessarily illegal to pay dividends out of current profits without making good deficiencies in the paid-up capital, even if such deficiencies were represented by a debit balance on the profit and loss account caused by losses in previous years.

Circulating capital, however, *must* be maintained.

The different treatment between the two types of capital may best be summed up by quoting the judgment in *Verner v. General and Commercial Investment Trust* (1894), which was as follows:

'Fixed capital may be sunk or lost, and yet the excess of current receipts over current payments may be divided; but floating or circulating capital must be kept up, as otherwise it will enter into and form part of such excess, in which case to divide such excess without deducting the capital which forms part of it will be contrary to law.'

(c) **Depreciation.** The law is somewhat unhelpful in providing guidance on the method of valuing assets. It has been stated, for example, that there can be instances where provision need not be made for depreciation. Thus, in *Lee v. Neuchatel Asphalte Co.* (1889) it was decided that where there was a wasting asset, such as a mine where the intention was to exhaust it, depreciation was not essential. However, such a ruling would not normally apply (*Bond v. Barrow Haematite Steel Co.* (1902)), and, in general, the law supports recognised accounting practice.

If, on a bona fide revaluation, it is apparent that an asset had been overdepreciated in the past, such overdepreciation may be brought back to the credit of the profit and loss account (*Ammonia Soda Co. v. Chamberlain* (1918)), as may goodwill previously written off (*Stapley v. Read Bros* (1924)). Such amounts would, of course, then be available for distribution.

(d) **Reserves.** The source of dividends need not be limited to profits of the current year, as dividends may be paid from reserves (*Re Hoare & Co.* (1904)).

(e) **Share premiums.** Sums received as premiums on the issue of shares cannot be distributed as dividends (S. 56(1)).

The Consequences of Distributing from Capital

Directors who pay dividends out of capital are jointly and severally liable to repay that amount to the company (*Re London and General Bank* (1895)), as this would amount to an illegal reduction of capital (*Re Sharpe* (1892)). An exception would be made in respect of a director who was not party to the distribution if he could take advantage of the general provisions of S. 448, which gives the Court power to grant relief to a director where it is of the opinion that he acted honestly and reasonably and that having regard to all the circumstances he ought fairly to be excused.

Any amount paid to shareholders *who were aware* of the illegal distribution may be recovered from them (*Moxham v. Grant* (1900)). Any such shareholder cannot, while retaining the proceeds, compel restitution by the directors (*Towers v. African Tug Co.* (1904)).

Share Interest Paid out of Capital

The one circumstance in which share interest may be paid out of capital is prescribed by S. 65. It applies where shares are issued to provide money to pay the cost of constructing works or buildings or of providing plant which is not capable of producing profit for some time. The interest may be paid for the period of unprofitability and the interest may be regarded as part of the cost. The conditions for so doing are as follows:

(*a*) The agreement must be authorised by the directors or by special resolution.

(*b*) The prior sanction of the Department of Trade must be obtained. The Department may appoint a person to investigate and report to the Department at the expense of the company. It may require the company to give security for payment of the enquiry costs.

(*c*) The period of paying interest will be determined by the Department. This must not extend beyond the close of the half-year next after the half-year during which the works or buildings are completed or the plant purchased.

(*d*) The rate of interest will be determined by the Department.

(*e*) Payment of the interest must not operate as a reduction of the amount paid up on the shares.

Details of the capital and the interest must be disclosed in the accounts.

Dividends

A trading company has implied power to pay dividends on its shares.

The invariable rule is that final dividends are declared by the company in general meeting. In practice, the amount of the dividend is decided by *the directors*, and the members in meeting merely endorse the decision. This is because most Articles include a clause similar to that in Table A, which states that 'the company in general meeting may declare dividends but no dividend shall exceed the amount recommended by the directors'. Clause 117 of Table A supports this by giving the directors power to set aside profits as a reserve before recommending a dividend. It would appear that this latter right of the directors exists even without power in the Articles (*Burland v. Earle* (1902)).

This principle may appear to be a denial of members' rights in that they have no effective control over the amount of return on their investments. The justification for the practice is that shareholders delegate to the directors the power and responsibility to preserve and improve the financial stability of the company—and allocating amounts to reserve is an important procedure in that respect. In carrying out this function, directors must pay regard to any provisions in the Articles as to the amounts and purposes of specific reserves. In exercising their discretion concerning dividends and reserves, directors must observe the general principle that whatever they do, must, in their view, be for the benefit of the company as a whole; they must not abuse their powers in order to provide advantage or disadvantage to any section of the members or creditors.

In *Bond v. Barrow Haematite Steel Co.* (1902) it was held that until a dividend had been declared the shareholders could not sue for it, and the Court would not override the discretion given by the Articles for directors to declare dividends. The action in this case was by the holders of fixed cumulative preference shares.

Subject to the Articles, the dividend is payable on the nominal value of the shares, irrespective of the amount paid up on them. Table A, however, states that the amount payable shall be in proportion to the amounts paid or credited as paid on the shares.

Declaration of Dividends

A dividend declared *by the company in general meeting* creates a debt by the company immediately it is declared (*Re Severn & Wye & Severn Bridge Rail Co.* (1896)), but if the dividend is declared payable on a specified date a shareholder may not demand payment until that date (*Potel v. Inland Revenue Commissioners* (1971)). Such a debt is a specialty debt and is not statute-barred until after 12 years (*Limitation Act, 1939*).

The directors may be given the discretion (as in Table A) to pay 'interim' dividends; that is, dividends paid between annual general meetings. Whereas a company '*declares*' a dividend in general meeting, directors '*resolve to pay*' interim dividends. The effect of this distinction is that directors may rescind their decision to pay, because such a decision does not impose a debt on the company (*Lagunas Nitrate Co. v. Schroeder & Co. and Schmidt* (1901)).

If a dividend has been declared but remains unpaid at the commencement of the winding up of the company, the debt created may not compete with any amount owing to a creditor who is not a member. Such amounts would, however, be taken into account in the final adjustment of the rights of the contributories between themselves (S. 212(1)).

The person to whom the dividend must be paid is the person whose name appears in the Register of Members at the time of the declaration or the date specified in the resolution. This conforms with the general rule that a company may recognise no other person. A contract to sell made about that time but before the transfer is effected in the company's books will usually have a price adjustment. Thus, if the transferee is to get the dividend, the contract is worded '*cum div*'; in the opposite case it would be '*ex div*'. If, however, there is no agreement as to who should have the dividend, the buyer is entitled to all dividends declared after the date of the contract (*Black v. Homersham* (1878)).

Capitalisation of Profits

Subject to any contrary ruling in the Articles, dividends may be paid only in cash (*Wood v. Odessa Waterworks Co.* (1889)). It is usual, however, to specify that the company in general meeting may authorise distribution of profits, wholly or in part, in some other form, such as paid-up shares. In such an instance, the company would declare a 'bonus' from its undistributed profits and simultaneously issue a corresponding number of new shares to which the bonus would be applied in paying up the shares in full and issuing them to the members in proportion to their current holdings. The justification is that undistributed profits 'belong' to the ordinary shareholders to the extent that they represent amounts which could have been issued to them in the past in the form of higher dividends. To issue bonus shares increases each ordinary shareholder's capital holding but does not alter the company's cash assets.

The share premium account and the capital redemption reserve fund may be drawn on for issuing paid-up bonus shares (Ss. 56, 58).

(The Act refers to '**bonus shares**' although the usual term used in financial circles is '**scrip**'. This is because the word 'bonus' implies the giving of something for nothing, whereas, as stated above, members would be receiving their entitlement in a form other than that of cash dividends. In fact, in *Re Eddystone Marine Insurance Co.* (1893) it was stated to be illegal if bonus shares were issued as a gift.)

12

THE ACCOUNTING RECORDS

The Accounts as Defined in the Acts

S. 1(5)(1976) states that references to documents required to be comprised in the accounts of a company in respect of any accounting reference period are references to:

(*a*) *The balance sheet* and *the profit and loss account* (see page 125).

(*b*) *The report of the auditors* required by S. 156(1)(as amended) to be attached to the balance sheet (see page 135).

(*c*) *The report of the directors* required by S. 157(1)(as amended) to be so attached (see page 132).

These documents must be (*a*) *prepared* in respect of each accounting reference period (see page 124); (*b*) *laid before the company in general meeting*; and (*c*) *delivered to the Registrar* (see page 126).

Accounting Periods

Because of the references in the 1976 Act to dates and periods relevant to the accounts, it is necessary to consider two terms which were introduced in that Act. But first, regard must be had to the alteration made to S. 455 of the 1948 Act (which interprets expressions in the Acts) for the definition of 'financial year'. S. 1(9)(1976) says that **financial year** is defined as 'any period in respect of which any profit and loss account prepared under that Section as it applies to that body is made up, whether that period is a year or not'.

S. 2(1976) refers to the two terms introduced by the 1976 Act as follows:

The Accounting Reference Date

A company may give notice in the prescribed form to the Registrar specifying a date as being the date on which in each successive calendar year the accounting reference period of the company is to be treated as coming to an end. (That is, the date to which the accounts are made up.) Unless such notice is given within six months of the incorporation of the company, the accounting reference date is 31st March; except that the Registrar may, with the consent of the company, determine some other date within two years of S. 1(1976) coming into operation. There is also provision for subsequent *alteration* (see below). Therefore, unless any action is initiated by the company, the date will automatically be 31st March.

The Accounting Reference Period

The *first* accounting reference period of a company begins on the day after the date to which the profit and loss account last laid before the company in general meeting before S. 1 (1976) came into force was made up. In the case of a company subsequently incorporated, it begins on the date of its incorporation. This first period must exceed six months and not exceed eighteen months.

The *subsequent* accounting reference periods are each successive period of twelve months beginning after the end of the first accounting reference period.

Alteration of the Accounting Reference Date

S. 3 (1976) makes provision for alteration of the accounting reference date upon notice by the company in the prescribed form to the Registrar:

(*a*) Such a notice may be given *during* an accounting reference period specifying a date ('the new accounting reference date') on which that and subsequent periods are to be treated as coming or having come to an end.

(*b*) If such a notice is given *after* the end of an accounting reference period, specifying the date on which that and subsequent periods are to be treated as having come to an end, it will not have effect:

(*i*) unless it is done in order to allow the accounting reference dates of a subsidiary and its holding company to coincide;

(*ii*) if the period for laying and delivering accounts for the previous accounting reference period has already expired.

The notice must state which period is to be treated as shortened or lengthened. Any extension of a period beyond eighteen months would not be sanctioned. Nor would an extension be permitted unless:

(*a*) No earlier extension had been made; or

(*b*) The notice is given not less than five years after the date any earlier extension had ended; or

(*c*) The change is to be made so that the accounting reference dates of a company and a subsidiary would coincide.

Preparation of Accounting Records

By S. 12 (1–5) (1976), every company must keep accounting records which meet the following requirements:

(*a*) They must be sufficient to show and explain the company's transactions.

(*b*) They must disclose, with reasonable accuracy, the financial position at any time, and enable the directors to ensure that any balance sheet or profit and loss account complies with the requirements of S. 149 (see below).

(*c*) In particular, they must contain:

(*i*) daily entries for all sums received and expended and the matters to which they relate;

(*ii*) a record of the assets and liabilities;

(*iii*) the statements mentioned at (*d*) below if the company's business involves dealing in goods.

(*d*) (*i*) Statements of stock held by the company at the end of each of its financial years.

(*ii*) Statements of stocktakings from which the year-end statements are prepared.

(*iii*) Statements of all goods sold and purchased, giving such sufficient detail as to facilitate identification of the goods and the buyers and sellers (except in the case of sales in the ordinary retail trade).

If records are maintained outside Great Britain, returns must be made to and kept in a place in Great Britain. They must be sufficient to disclose the financial position at intervals not exceeding six months and to enable the directors to prepare any balance sheet and profit and loss account complying with the Act (S. 12(7)(1976)).

S. 1(1–4)(1976) requires the directors, in respect of each accounting reference period, to prepare a profit and loss account and a balance sheet as at the date to which the profit and loss account is made up. There must be attached thereto the Auditors' Report and the Directors' Report.

Content and Form of the Accounts

S. 149 as amended by the 1976 Act states that every balance sheet shall give a true and fair view of the company's state of affairs and every profit and loss account shall give a true and fair view of its profit or loss for the financial year. The phrase 'true and fair' is important, because it may be possible to comply with the detailed legal requirements with exactness and yet nevertheless produce accounts which, overall, could not be strictly regarded as being 'true and fair'.

The balance sheet and profit and loss account must comply with the requirements of the Eighth Schedule of the 1948 Act as amended by the subsequent Acts (see Appendix 2). The Department of Trade has authority to modify the requirements as to the matters to be stated if it is necessary to adapt them to the circumstances of a company. This may be done at the request of or with the consent of the company.

Copies and Inspection of Accounting Records

Copies of the accounting records as defined in the Act must be sent, not less than twenty-one days before the meeting before which they are to be laid, to (*a*) every member, whether or not he is entitled to receive notice of the meeting; (*b*) every debenture-holder; and (*c*) all other persons entitled to receive notice of general meetings.

If the copies are sent less than twenty-one days before the date of the meeting, they may be deemed to have been sent if so agreed by all the members entitled to attend and vote at the meeting (S. 158).

The accounting records must be kept at the registered office of the company or such other place as the directors think fit. They must be open to inspection by the officers of the company at all times (S. 12(6) (1976)).

Preservation of Accounting Records

Subject to any direction given under the Winding-up Rules, accounting records must be preserved by the company (*a*) in the case of a private company, for three years, and (*b*) in the case of any other company, for six years from the date they are made (S. 12(9)(1976)).

Laying and Delivery of the Accounts

In respect of each accounting reference period, the directors must (*a*) lay before the company in general meeting, and (*b*) deliver to the Registrar a copy of every document required to be comprised in the accounts (S. 1(6)(7)(1976)). S. 155 as amended by the 1976 Act requires that every balance sheet and every copy thereof placed before the company or delivered to the Registrar must be signed on behalf of the board by two directors (or by a sole director).

The profit and loss account must be annexed to the balance sheet and the auditors' report attached thereto. The accounts annexed must be approved by the directors before the balance sheet is signed. Any balance sheet issued, circulated or published must have the above documents attached (S. 156 as amended by the 1976 Act).

S. 6(1976) states that the period allowed for laying and delivering the accounts is (*a*) in the case of a private company, ten months after the end of the accounting reference period, and (*b*) in the case of any other company, seven months after the end of the accounting reference period.

If the company carries on business or has interests outside the United Kingdom, the period will be extended by three months if the directors, before the end of the accounting reference period, give notice to the Registrar stating it has such interests and claiming the extension.

Where notice has been given which has the effect of shortening the accounting reference period (see page 124), the period allowed shall be the period allowed in relation to that accounting reference period or a period of three months beginning with the date of the notice, whichever last expires.

Penalties are prescribed in S.4(1976) for failure to comply with any of the above provisions. Every person who was a director immediately before the end of the accounting reference period to which the default refers is liable to a fine not exceeding the aggregate of £400 and £40 for each day of default. A defence is available to a director who can prove he took all reasonable steps to ensure compliance. Additionally, the company will be liable to a penalty, the rate of the penalty being on a rising scale according to the number of days in default.

S.5(1976) imposes a further control on any directors in default in delivery of the accounts. The Court may, on application by any member or creditor or the Registrar, make an order directing any directors who have failed to make good the default within fourteen days after notice requiring them to do so, to make good the default within a specified time. Such an order can lead to disqualification of a director under S.28 (1976) (see page 177).

Group Accounts

As special provisions apply where a company has subsidiaries, it is first necessary to define when a subsidiary company relationship exists.

Defining 'Subsidiary Company' and 'Holding Company'

Under S.154 a company is deemed to be a subsidiary of another company if, but only if:

(*a*) That other company
(*i*) is a member of it and controls the composition of its board of directors; or
(*ii*) it holds more than half in nominal value of its equity share capital; or
(*b*) The first-mentioned company is a subsidiary of any company which is that other's subsidiary (that is, it is a sub-subsidiary).

To control the composition of the board of directors means the power to appoint or remove all or a majority of the directors without requiring the consent of any other person. The Section states that the power to appoint exists if any of the following conditions apply:

(*a*) That a person cannot be appointed without the exercise in his favour of that other company's power.
(*b*) That a person's appointment follows necessarily as a consequence of his appointment as director of that other company.
(*c*) That the directorship is held by that other company itself or by a subsidiary of it.

If shares are held by a person as a nominee for the other company or a subsidiary of it (except in a fiduciary capacity), they will be treated as being held or exercisable by that other company. Thus, a company is deemed to control another company if all or part of the controlling shares are held by a person who is in fact acting on behalf of the first company.

A company is deemed to be a holding company of another if the latter company is a subsidiary of the former company.

Form of Group Accounts

The directors of a holding company are required to ensure that the financial year of each of its subsidiaries coincides with the company's financial year, except where in their opinion there are good reasons for not doing so (S. 153).

S. 151 provides that group accounts shall comprise (*a*) a consolidated balance sheet, dealing with the state of affairs of the company and its subsidiaries, and (*b*) a consolidated profit and loss account, dealing with the profit or loss of the company and its subsidiaries.

Provision is included for group accounts to be prepared in some other form if, in the opinion of the directors, it would be a better method of presenting the same information and in such a manner as to be readily appreciated by the members. In particular, the accounts may consist of more than one set of consolidated accounts dealing respectively with the company and one group of subsidiaries and with other subsidiaries; or separate accounts dealing with each of the subsidiaries; or of statements expanding the information regarding subsidiaries; or any combination of these forms.

The group accounts must give a true and fair view of the state of affairs and the profit or loss of the company and its subsidiaries, so far as concerns the members of the company (i.e. excluding minority interests) (S. 152).

Part II of the Eighth Schedule contains provisions specific to holding and subsidiary companies (see Appendix 2).

Presentation and Delivery of Group Accounts

S. 150 as amended by S. 8 (1976) states that in the case of a company which has a subsidiary at the end of its financial year, the rules in S. 1 (1976) concerning the laying and delivery of accounts will apply (see page 126). The following provisions are also made:

(*a*) Group accounts are not required where the company is the wholly-owned subsidiary of another body incorporated in Great Britain. This is, of course, because the accounts of the company would be included in the group accounts of its holding company.

(*b*) Group accounts need not include those of a subsidiary if the directors are of the opinion that:

(*i*) in view of the insignificant amounts involved, it would be impracticable or would be of no real value to the members, or it would involve expense and delay out of proportion to the value to the members; or

(*ii*) the result would be misleading or harmful to the business of the company or any subsidiary; or

(*iii*) the business of the holding company and the subsidiary company are so different that they cannot reasonably be treated as a single undertaking.

The approval of the Department of Trade is required in the last instance and where group accounts are regarded as being harmful.

Disclosure of Relationships with Other Companies

The 1967 Act requires information to be given in the accounts of relationships, as specified in the Act, with other companies. This applies where there is a subsidiary as defined by law and also where shares are held in a non-subsidiary.

(1) Particulars of Subsidiary Companies

S. 3 (1967) requires that a company with subsidiaries at the end of its financial year must state in its accounts, in a note on its accounts or as an annexed statement, in the case of each subsidiary:

(*a*) Its name.

(*b*) Its country of incorporation if that is outside Great Britain; if registered in Great Britain, the country of registration (England or Scotland) if different from that of the holding company.

(*c*) The identity of the class of shares held in the subsidiary and its proportion of the nominal value of the issued shares of that class. Information must be given of the extent to which the shares are held by another subsidiary of the company or its nominee, and by the company itself or its nominee.

The rules for determining if shares are held for the purpose of this Section are the same as those for deciding if one company is a subsidiary of another (see page 127). The Department of Trade offers two concessions:

(*a*) If the directors of the holding company are of the opinion that the number of subsidiaries would result in excessively lengthy particulars being given, they may confine themselves to giving particulars only in respect of those subsidiaries which principally affect the amount of profit or loss of the holding company or the amount of its assets. In such an instance, a reference to that effect must appear in the statement, and the *full* particulars must be annexed to the Annual Return made after the accounts have been laid before the company.

(*b*) Information concerning a subsidiary incorporated or carrying on business outside the United Kingdom need not be disclosed if the directors of the holding company consider that to do so would be harmful to the business or that of any subsidiary. To omit such information requires the consent of the Department of Trade.

(2) Particulars of Shares held in Non-Subsidiaries

S.4(1967) relates to any company (*not* being a subsidiary) in which equity shares are held to an amount exceeding in nominal value one tenth of the issued shares of that class or in which shares are held which exceed one tenth of the amount of the assets of the company. It prescribes that the requirements and concessions concerning a statement as set out in S.3(1967) above also apply where such investments in non-subsidiaries exist at the financial year-end.

(3) Particulars of Holding Company

S.5(1967) requires that a company which at the end of its financial year is a subsidiary of another company, must disclose in its accounts the name of the company regarded by the directors of the subsidiary company as its *ultimate* holding company. They must also state the country of incorporation of the holding company, if known to them. (Where there is a chain of subsidiaries, the *immediate* holding company may not be the *ultimate* holding company. Company A may be an immediate subsidiary of Company B, but if Company B is a subsidiary of Company C, then Company A's ultimate holding company is Company C.)

Disclosure of Directors' Emoluments and Emoluments Waived

Particulars of the information to be disclosed in any accounts or annexed statement laid before the company in general meeting of the amounts received by the directors by virtue of their directorships are given in the 1948 Act and the 1967 Act.

(1) The Aggregate of Directors' Remuneration

S.196 requires the following information to be given:

(*a*) The aggregate amount of the directors' emoluments. This figure includes fees and percentages, sums paid as expense allowances charged to income tax, contributions under pension schemes and the estimated value of any other benefits received other than in cash. It must also include any amounts paid for services as a director or otherwise in connection with management of the company or any subsidiary.

(*b*) The aggregate amount of pensions paid to directors and past directors. A distinction must be made as between pensions in respect of the company and of any subsidiary. The amount must include pensions paid to dependants or nominees of the directors. Any pension paid under a scheme which is substantially self-financed is ignored.

(*c*) The aggregate amount of any compensation to directors or past directors for loss of office as director or for loss of office in connection with management of the company, either in respect of the company or of any subsidiary.

(2) Analysis of Directors' Remuneration

S.6(1967) requires the following to be disclosed:

(*a*) The emoluments of the person who has been chairman throughout the financial year or, if there had been more than one chairman, the emoluments relevant to periods of chairmanship. This information is not required if the duties of the chairman were wholly or mainly discharged outside the United Kingdom.

(*b*) The number of directors in any of the following categories:

(*i*) Those receiving no emoluments;

(*ii*) Those receiving not more than £2,500;

(*iii*) Those receiving between £2,500 and £5,000;

(*iv*) Those receiving over £5,000, categorised in successive multiples of £2,500.

(*c*) The emoluments of the highest paid director where he is not also the chairman.

'Emoluments' include all those amounts as specified in (1)(*a*) above.
The provisions of this Section do not apply to a company which is neither a holding company or a subsidiary company if the aggregate of directors' emoluments does not exceed £15,000.

(3) Directors' Emoluments Waived

S.7(1967) requires disclosure of:

(*a*) The number of directors who have waived emoluments which would otherwise have been disclosed under S.196.

(*b*) The aggregate amount of emoluments waived.

(4) Directors' Duty to make Disclosures

S.198 imposes a duty on directors to give such notice to the company as may be necessary for the purposes of S.196, S.6(1967) and S.7(1967). Failure to do so would make a director liable to a default fine.

Disclosure of Loans to Officers

Accounts laid before members in general meeting must show:

(*a*) The amount of any loans made, guaranteed or secured by the company or a subsidiary during the year to any officer of the company or any person who became an officer after the making of the loan. This must include any loans made and repaid during the year.

(*b*) The amount of any loans made before the financial year to the extent they are outstanding at the end of the financial year.

Particulars are not required of loans made where the ordinary business includes the lending of money or of a loan up to £2,000 to an employee, certified by the directors to have been made in accordance with regular practice of the company in respect of loans to employees (S. 197).

Disclosure Concerning Employees' Salaries

S. 8 (1967) requires particulars to be given in the accounts concerning salaries of employees which exceed £10,000 per annum, except of those wholly or mainly employed outside the United Kingdom. There must be shown the number who received over £10,000 but not over £12,500, and those in categories of stages of £2,500 over £12,500.

'Emoluments' are those as defined in S. 196 (see page 130), but excluding contributions paid under pension schemes.

Directors are excluded from the requirements of this Section because their emoluments have to be declared under S. 196 and S. 6 (1967).

The Directors' Report

As mentioned at the beginning of this chapter, the documents comprising the accounting records include the Directors' Report. The *general* provisions are set out in S. 157 (as amended by the 1976 Act), which requires to be attached to every balance sheet a report by the directors with respect to:

(*a*) The state of the company's affairs.

(*b*) The amount, if any, recommended to be paid by way of dividend.

(*c*) The amount, if any, to be carried to 'reserve', within the meaning of that word in the Eighth Schedule.

In order to make the Directors' Report more meaningful, the 1967 Act requires *specific* information to be included, as shown below.

(1) Additional Matter of a General Nature (S.16 (1967))

(*a*) The names of persons who were directors *at any time* during the financial year.

(*b*) The principal activities of the company and its subsidiaries, and any significant changes thereof during the year.

(*c*) Any significant changes in the fixed assets. If some of those assets consist of interests in land and the market value differs significantly from the balance sheet valuation, particulars of the difference must be referred to by the directors with as much precision as is practicable.

(*d*) The number of each class of shares and the amount of any debentures issued during the year, the consideration received from each issue and the reason for making it.

(*e*) Particulars of any significant contract by the company in which, in the opinion of the directors, a director had a material interest, direct or indirect (other than a service contract). The names of the parties and the name of the director if not himself a party must be stated, as well as the nature of the contract and the director's interest.

(*f*) Particulars of any arrangement subsisting during the year enabling directors to acquire shares or debentures of the company or other body corporate, including an explanation of the arrangement and the names of the directors concerned.

(*g*) As regards each person who was a director at the end of the year, a statement of the number and amount of shares or debentures in the company, its subsidiary, holding company or fellow subsidiaries (stated separately) in which the director was interested at the beginning of the year (or on becoming a director) and at the end of the year. (This will accord with the register kept by the company as required by S.29(1967) (see page 90).)

(*h*) Particulars of any other matters, other than those required by the Act, so far as they are material for the appreciation of the company's state of affairs by the members.

(2) Distinction between Classes of Business (S.17(1967))

Where a company carries on two or more classes of business (other than banking or discounting) which in the opinion of the directors are substantially different, there must be shown:

(*a*) The proportions in which the turnover is divided amongst the classes.

(*b*) The extent (or approximate extent), in monetary terms, which in the opinion of the directors each class contributed to, or restricted, the profit or loss of the company for the year.

(3) Number and Wages of Employees (S.18(1967))

Relevant to the company and any subsidiaries, there must be stated:

(*a*) The average number of employees in each week under contracts of service. (This is the yearly total amount of those employed each week, divided by the number of weeks in the year.)

(*b*) The aggregate remuneration, including bonuses, of such employees in the year.

The Section does not apply if the average number is less than 100, nor to wholly-owned subsidiaries. Persons working wholly or mainly outside the United Kingdom are excluded.

(4) Political and Charitable Donations (S.19(1967))

If a company (other than a wholly-owned subisdiary) has, during the year, given money for political or charitable purposes or both, in excess of £50, a statement must be included of the amount donated for each purpose. In the case of donations for political purposes, there must also be stated, so far as applicable:

(*a*) The name of the person receiving the donation and the amount.

(*b*) The amount given as a donation to a political party and the identity of the party.

(5) Particulars of Exports (S. 20 (1967))

Where a company or its subsidiaries is in business supplying goods, the total value of goods exported must be stated if the turnover for the year exceeds £50,000. If no goods have been exported, there must be a statement to that effect. Any goods exported by the company as an agent are disregarded.

As an Alternative to Entries in the Accounts

S. 163 prescribes that information required to be given in the accounts may instead be shown in the Directors' Report, but S. 22 (1967) states that if this is done the Report must show the corresponding amounts for the immediately preceding year (as would be the case if the figures were given in the accounts).

Responsibility of the Directors

S. 23 (1967) as amended by the 1976 Act states that in respect of any failure to comply with the Act in regard to the Directors' Report, every person who was a director immediately before the end of the relevant period shall be liable to a fine. It may be a defence to prove that such a person took all reasonable steps for securing compliance.

13

THE AUDITORS

The Auditors' Report

S.156 (as amended) requires the auditors' report to be attached to the accounts prepared under S.1 (1976).

The members, having delegated to the directors the power to manage the financial affairs of the company and having no right to examine the books, must be afforded some safeguard of their interests. This is provided by the auditors, who are required to examine the books made available to them by the directors. It is a fundamental principle, therefore, that the auditors investigate and then report on their findings to the *members* and not to the directors. S.14(1)(1967) as amended by the 1976 Act, requires the auditors to report to the members on the accounts examined by them, and on every balance sheet, every profit and loss account and all group accounts prepared under S.1 (1976) of which a copy is laid before the company in general meeting during their tenure of office.

This does not mean the auditors must *send* a copy of their report to each member. They are required to report to the directors or the secretary, and it is the directors' responsibility to lay the auditors' report with the accounts before the members in general meeting. The auditors' responsibility does not end there, however, because they are required to ensure that the report placed before the members is exactly as submitted by them to the directors.

S.14(2)–(6)(1967) further prescribes as follows:

(*a*) The report must be read in general meeting and be open to inspection by any member.

(*b*) It must state whether, in the auditors' opinion, the company's balance sheet and profit and loss account (and group accounts where applicable) have been properly prepared in accordance with the Acts. It must also state whether, in their opinion, a true and fair view is given

(*i*) in the case of the balance sheet, of the state of the company's affairs at the end of the financial year;

(*ii*) in the case of the profit and loss account (not being a consolidated profit and loss account), of the company's profit or loss for the financial year;

(*iii*) in the case of group accounts submitted by a holding company, of

135

the state of affairs and profit or loss of the company and its subsidiaries so far as they concern the members of the company.

(c) In preparing their report, the auditors have the duty to carry out such investigations as will enable them to form an opinion as to whether

(i) proper accounting records have been kept by the company and adequate returns have been received from branches not visited by them;

(ii) the balance sheet and profit and loss account (unless it is a consolidated profit and loss account) are in agreement with the accounting records and returns.

If in the auditors' opinion these requirements have not been met, they must state that fact in their report.

(d) Every auditor has the right of access at all times to the books, accounts and vouchers of the company, and is entitled to require from the officers of the company such information and explanations as he thinks necessary to perform his duties as auditor. Should an auditor fail to obtain such cooperation, he must so state in his report.

Responsibility to provide Auditors with Information

Following the above requirement on the officers to provide information at the demand of the auditors, the 1976 Act sets out further responsibilities:

(a) The auditor of a holding company has the right of access only to the accounts of that company, but if his audit is to be effective he must have assurances concerning the accounts of each subsidiary, because these will form part of the group accounts published by the holding company.

S.18(1976) states that if the subsidiary is incorporated outside Great Britain it is the duty of *the subsidiary and its auditors* to provide the auditor of the holding company with such information and explanations as he may reasonably require to carry out his duties. If the auditors of the subsidiary fail to comply with this requirement they will be guilty of an offence.

If the subsidiary is incorporated in Great Britain it is the duty of *the holding company* to comply with its auditor's demand to take all reasonable steps to obtain the necessary information from the subsidiary.

In both instances there are penalties on the holding company and the subsidiary company and their officers for failure to comply.

(b) S.19(1976) makes general requirements concerning the provision of information to auditors to enable them to carry out their duties. An officer who knowingly or recklessly makes a statement (orally or in writing) to an auditor which is misleading, false or deceptive in a material particular which conveys (or purports to convey) any information or explanation which the auditor requires, is guilty of an offence. The penalty may be a fine or imprisonment or both.

Auditors' Right to Attend Meetings

Auditors are entitled to attend any general meeting of the company and to receive all notices and other communications relating to any general meeting which any member is entitled to receive. They may be heard at any general meeting on any part of the business which concerns them as auditors (S. 14(7)(1967)).

The right to attend meetings of an auditor who has been removed from office is set out on page 139. The rights of an auditor who has resigned are stated on page 141.

Judicial Statements Concerning the Position of Auditors

The duties and rights of auditors as specified in the Acts have been elaborated on in sundry legal decisions.

Extent of the Auditor's Duties

As an auditor, it is not part of his duty to advise the company or its shareholders as to the action they should take. His duty is to ascertain and state the true financial position of the company at the time of the audit (*Re London and General Bank* (*No. 2*) (1895)).

An auditor must be acquainted not only with the requirements of the Companies Acts but also with the special regulations contained in the company's Articles, but he is not bound to be a legal expert (*Re Republic of Bolivia Exploration Syndicate* (1914)).

Degree of Diligence

An auditor 'is only bound to be reasonably cautious and careful'. 'He is a watchdog, not a bloodhound. He is justified in believing tried servants of the company ... He is entitled to assume that they are honest and to rely upon their representations, provided he takes reasonable care. If there is anything calculated to excite suspicion he should probe it to the bottom.' (*Re Kingston Cotton Mill Co* (*No. 2*) (1896))

An auditor should ensure that moneys and securities of the company are actually in the company's possession or in proper custody. He should not accept a certificate by the company's brokers that they hold certain securities for the company without actually seeing the securities (*Re City Equitable Fire Insurance Co.* (1925))

Liability of Auditors

There have been apparently conflicting decisions concerning the liability of auditors to third parties, mainly because there is no contractual relationship between an auditor and a third party. The current ruling appears to be that if, as a result of failure to exercise reasonable skill and care in expressing an opinion, a third party suffers financial loss as a result of relying on that opinion, a right to damages will exist

(*Hedley Byrne & Co. v. Heller & Partners* (1964)). This principle was underlined by a House of Lords decision in *Arenson v. Casson Beckman Rutley & Co.* (1975). This was to the effect that a third party may succeed in an action for damages against an auditor who had negligently valued shares if it could be shown that the auditor should have known that the third party would rely on the auditor's skill and judgment.

Any provision in the Articles or any contract exempting an auditor from, or indemnifying him against, liability in respect of negligence, fraud, breach of duty or breach of trust, is void (S. 205). The Court may grant relief if it is satisfied that the auditor acted honestly and reasonably and ought fairly to be excused (S. 448).

The Auditor as Agent

To the extent that he acts as auditor within the meaning in the Acts, an auditor is an agent of the shareholders, even if he was not appointed by them. Where he acts as an *accountant* on behalf of the directors, however, he is not an agent of the shareholders. Although the auditor is an agent of the shareholders, the members are not prevented from exercising their rights in respect of wrongful acts by the directors where notice of certain facts had been available to their agent, because such notice is not necessarily notice to the principals (*Spackman v. Evans* (1868)).

An auditor is not an agent of the company for the purpose of acknowledging a debt within the *Limitation Act, 1939* (*Re Transplanters (Holding Company) Ltd* (1958)), but he *is* an agent of the company for the purposes of a Department of Trade investigation under S. 167 and in assisting a liquidator to prosecute delinquent officers and members under S. 334.

Appointment and Removal of Auditors

Because the auditors' responsibility is to guard the shareholders' interests in respect of the company's accounts, it is very necessary that the power to appoint and, if necessary, to remove them, rests with the shareholders. The 1976 Act introduced more stringent regulations in these respects.

Appointment

S. 14(1976) provides that an auditor or auditors must be appointed at the general meeting before which the directors lay copies of the accounts, and that such auditor(s) will hold office from the conclusion of that meeting until the conclusion of the next such meeting. The appointment must be *the specific resolve of the meeting*; prior to the 1976 Act an auditor willing to continue in office could be reappointed automatically if no contrary resolution was passed.

In the event of no auditor being appointed at the meeting, notice to that effect must be given by the company to the Secretary of State within one week. The Secretary of State may appoint a person to fill the vacancy.

The company's *first* auditors may be appointed by the directors before the first general meeting at which the accounts are laid, and such auditors will hold office until the conclusion of that meeting. If the directors fail to appoint the first auditors, the members in general meeting may do so.

Any casual vacancy may be filled by the directors or the company in general meeting.

Special Notice of a resolution to appoint an auditor other than for the reappointment of an auditor previously appointed by the members must be given (see below).

Removal

Irrespective of any agreement he may have with the company, the company may, by ordinary resolution, remove an auditor before the expiration of his term of office. Special Notice of such a resolution must be given (see below). Notice of the resolution must be given to the Registrar within fourteen days. Failure to do so will render the company and every officer guilty of an offence and liable to a fine (S.14(1976)).

S.15(6)(1976) prescribes that an auditor who has been removed is entitled:

(a) To attend the general meeting at which his term of office would otherwise have expired.

(b) To attend any general meeting at which it is proposed to fill the vacancy caused by his removal.

(c) To receive all notices and communications relating to such meetings and to be heard threat on business concerning him as former auditor.

Special Notice and Representations

As a further precaution against suspect appointments and removals, S.15(1)–(5)(1976) provides as follows. Special Notice (see page 149) is required for a resolution in general meeting to:

(a) Appoint as auditor a person other than a retiring auditor.

(b) Fill a casual vacancy in the office of auditor.

(c) Reappoint a retiring auditor who was appointed by the directors following a casual vacancy.

(d) Remove an auditor before the expiration of his term of office.

On receipt of such notice, the company must forthwith send a copy thereof:

(*i*) to the person proposed to be appointed or removed;
(*ii*) to the retiring auditor in (*a*) above;
(*iii*) to the resigning auditor if his resignation caused a casual vacancy.

The retiring auditor in (*a*) above or the auditor proposed to be removed in (*d*) above may make written representations, of a reasonable length, to the company and require their notification to the members. The company must then (unless received too late)

(*i*) state in any notice of the resolution to the members the fact that the representations have been made; and
(*ii*) include a copy of the representations.

If the representations are not sent out because of being received too late or because of default by the company, the auditor may require them to be read at the meeting. The representations need not be sent out or read if the court is satisfied, on application by the company or any other person claiming to be aggrieved, that the section would be abused to secure needless publicity for defamatory matter.

Resignation of Auditors

The resignation of auditors may be indicative of friction between them and the directors, and because this may be due (from the directors' point of view) to the auditors' overzealous investigation, the 1976 Act makes particular provision in this respect. The intention of the legislation is to ensure that if an auditor resigns under circumstances which he considers should be made known to the members, then he can compel the directors to put his views to the members. The resigning auditor also has the right to demand that the members be called to a meeting to hear his explanation of those circumstances.

Notice of Resignation

S.16(1976) prescribes as follows. An auditor may resign by a written notice to that effect being deposited at the registered office of the company. The date of termination would be the date the notice was deposited or such later date as may be specified therein. The notice *must* contain either:

(*a*) A statement that there are no circumstances connected with his resignation which the auditor considers should be brought to the notice of the company's members or creditors; or
(*b*) A statement of circumstances which he considers *should* be made known.

Within fourteen days of deposit of the notice

(*i*) a copy of it must be sent to the Registrar by the company; and
(*ii*) if the notice contained a statement as in (*b*) above, a copy of the

notice must be sent by the company to every person entitled to be sent copies of the accounts.

There is provision for the court to direct that copies need not be sent out if, within fourteen days, the company or other person claims to be aggrieved and the court is satisfied that needless publicity for defamatory matter is being sought. If the court makes an order to that effect a statement setting out the effect of the order must be sent, within fourteen days of the court order, to those entitled to copies of the accounts. If the court makes no such order, then the representations must be sent within fourteen days of the court's decision.

Auditors' Right to Requisition a Meeting and Circulate a Statement

If the auditor's notice of resignation contains a statement as mentioned above, S. 17(1976) prescribes as follows. The auditor may deposit with the notice a signed requisition calling on the directors forthwith to convene an extraordinary general meeting of the company to receive and consider such explanation of the circumstances connected with his resignation as he may wish to place before the meeting. Within twenty-one days from the depositing of the requisition, the directors must convene the meeting for a day not more than twenty-eight days after the notice convening the meeting is given. The auditor may also require a statement of the circumstances connected with his resignation to be circulated to the members:

(*a*) Before the general meeting at which his term of office would otherwise have expired; or

(*b*) Before any general meeting at which it is proposed to fill the vacancy caused by his resignation; or

(*c*) Before a meeting convened on his requisition.

Any notice of the meeting given to the members must state that the statement has been made and must include a copy of the statement. If this is not done because the statement was received too late or because of the company's default, the auditor may require it to be read out at the meeting.

An auditor who has resigned has the right to attend such meetings as are mentioned above, to receive notice and relevant communications thereof and to be heard at the meetings.

Remuneration of Auditors

The remuneration of auditors appointed by the directors or by the Secretary of State may be fixed by the directors or the Secretary of State as the case may be. Otherwise, it may be fixed by the company in general meeting or in such manner as the meeting may determine (S. 14(8) (1976)).

Qualification of Auditors

S. 161 as amended by S. 13(1976) prescribes that a person may not be qualified for appointment as auditor unless he is a member of one of the following recognised bodies:

The Institute of Chartered Accountants in England and Wales.
The Institute of Chartered Accountants of Scotland.
The Association of Certified Accountants.
The Institute of Chartered Accountants in Ireland.

An auditor may be eligible if he has obtained similar qualifications outside the United Kingdom, unless it appears to the Secretary of State that the relevant country does not confer corresponding privileges on persons qualified in the United Kingdom.

The following are not qualified:

(a) An officer or servant of the company, or a partner or employee of such an officer or servant.

(b) A body corporate.

A person may not act as an auditor at a time when he knows he is disqualified, and if an auditor becomes disqualified he must thereupon vacate office and notify the company accordingly.

14

MEETINGS

Extent of the Acts

The Acts prescribe numerous rules regarding meetings which are specific and which cannot be altered. Other provisions in the Acts allow a company to frame rules in its Articles, and provided these do not conflict with any requirement of the Act they have the force of law. There are also certain precepts which, although not part of statute law, are generally accepted principles which the law will apply. Examples of the last include the right of minorities to be heard at meetings and the necessity adequately to disclose the nature of the business in the notice of a meeting.

Types of Meetings

Meetings may be classified as follows:

(*a*) General meetings of the members:
    (*i*) The Statutory Meeting;
    (*ii*) The Annual General Meeting;
    (*iii*) Extraordinary General Meetings.
(*b*) Meetings of a class of member.
(*c*) Meetings of debenture-holders.
(*d*) Meetings of directors.
(*e*) Meetings relevant to winding up.

The Statutory Meeting

This meeting is held only once in the lifetime of a public company. Its purpose is to inform members of the state of affairs of the company following its formation and to allow them to discuss any relevant matters. S. 130 provides as follows:

Every *public* company (limited by shares or by guarantee and having a share capital) must hold a Statutory Meeting not less than one month nor more than three months from the date it was entitled to commence business (see page 56). (It is common practice first to form a private company and immediately thereafter to convert it into a public company. In such an instance, there is no requirement to hold a Statutory Meeting.)

The Statutory Report

At least fourteen days before the meeting is to be held, every member must be sent 'the statutory report'. If the report is sent later than that time it may be regarded as having been duly forwarded if all the members entitled to attend and vote so agree. The report must be certified by not less than two directors and a copy, so certified, must be delivered to the Registrar immediately after sending it to the members. It must state:

(a) The total number of shares allotted, distinguishing those allotted as fully or partly paid up otherwise than in cash; the extent to which any partly paid-up shares are paid up; and the consideration for which the shares have been allotted.

(b) The total amount of cash received in respect of allotted shares, distinguished as aforesaid.

(c) An abstract of the receipts and payments of the company, made up to a date within seven days of the date of the report and showing under distinctive headings receipts from shares and debentures and other sources, payments made, particulars of the balance in hand, and an account or estimate of the preliminary expenses.

(d) The names, addresses and descriptions of the directors, the auditors (if any) and the secretary.

(e) Particulars of any contract of which a modification is to be put to the meeting for approval, and particulars of the modification. (S.42 states that a company required to hold a statutory meeting may not vary the terms of a contract referred to in a prospectus or in a statement in lieu except subject to the approval of the statutory meeting.)

So far as the report relates to shares allotted and cash received therefor, and to receipts and payments on capital account, it must be certified as correct by the auditors (if any).

At the Meeting

A list showing the names, addresses and descriptions of members and the number of shares held by each must remain open and accessible to any member throughout the meeting.

Members present may *discuss* any matter relating to the formation or arising out of the report without previous notice, but no resolution may be passed of which notice has not been given in accordance with the Articles.

The meeting may adjourn from time to time. At an adjourned meeting a resolution may be passed if notice of it has been given before or *subsequent* to the former meeting. (This is contrary to the general rule that the business of an adjourned meeting is confined to that specified for the first meeting.)

Default

Failure to hold the statutory meeting or to submit the report renders every director knowingly in default (or every officer on default by the company) liable to a fine. Under S. 222 it is a ground for a compulsory winding up but only on the petition of a shareholder (S. 224), although the Court may direct the holding of the meeting or submission of the report instead of making a winding-up order (S. 225).

The Annual General Meeting

The only regular general meeting required by statute to be called is the annual general meeting. The Acts place no restriction on the matters which may be discussed at the annual meeting but certain items of business are *normally* dealt with thereat. For example, auditors must be appointed at each general meeting '*before which the accounts are laid*'. This need not be the annual general meeting if, for example, the accounts are not ready in time for that meeting. Matters generally dealt with at the annual meeting are referred to as **ordinary business** and most Articles follow Table A in defining the items as:

(*a*) The declaration of a dividend.
(*b*) The presentation of the accounts and the auditors' report.
(*c*) The submission of the directors' report.
(*d*) The election of directors.
(*e*) The appointment of auditors and the fixing of their remuneration.
(Details of action at the meeting relating to the above will be found in the relevant chapters of this book).

S. 131 provides as follows. The meeting must be held *in each calendar year*, with no more than fifteen months between any two meetings; except that provided the first annual general meeting is held within eighteen months of incorporation it need not be held in the year of incorporation or in the following year.

If there is default in holding the meeting, the Department of Trade, upon application by any member, may call or direct the calling of the meeting. It may give such directions as it considers expedient, including modifying or supplementing the operation of the company's Articles in relation to the calling, holding and conducting of the meeting. The Department may direct that one member present in person or by proxy shall be deemed to constitute the meeting. Any meeting so called and held shall be deemed to be the annual general meeting, but if the meeting is not held in the year of the default then it is not to be regarded as the annual meeting of the year in which it *is* held, unless the meeting so resolves. A copy of any such resolution must be sent to the Registrar within fifteen days.

It must be recognised that failure to call an annual general meeting can arise only from some unusual circumstances and it may consequently be impossible to call and hold the meeting in the manner prescribed in the Articles. The Court must therefore have some latitude in arranging for the meeting to be held.

Extraordinary General Meetings

These are any meetings of the general membership except the statutory meeting and the annual general meeting. They are held as circumstances make necessary, and Articles always give the directors power to call such meetings as they require. They are usually called by the directors to obtain the shareholders' consent to matters which are beyond the authority of the directors or to obtain the views of the members.

Convening upon Requisition by the Members

Obviously, there may be occasions when the *members* require certain matters to be discussed between annual meetings and some arrangement must be made for such meetings to be held if the directors refuse a *request* to call a meeting. Articles may make provision for the requisitioning of meetings by the members but any condition for doing so may not be more demanding than the terms of those available in the Acts.

S.132 gives power to requisition the convening of an extraordinary general meeting to the holders of at least one tenth of such paid-up capital as carries the right to vote at general meetings (or those representing one tenth of the total voting rights in the case of a company with no share capital). The requisition must state the objects of the meeting and be deposited at the registered office of the company. It may consist of several documents in like form, signed by all the requisitionists.

Within twenty-one days of the requisition being deposited, the directors must convene the meeting (though there is no requirement that they fix it within any particular limit of time). Should they fail to do so, the requisitionists or any of them representing more than one half of the total voting rights of all of them, may themselves convene the meeting. It must be convened as nearly as possible in the same manner as the directors convene meetings. Any meeting convened by the requisitionists must be held within three months of depositing the requisition.

Expenses incurred by the requistionists because of default by the directors must be repaid by the company and retained out of sums due to the defaulting directors by way of fees or other remuneration for directors' services.

Requisition by the Auditors (see page 141)

The Convening of General Meetings

In the unlikely event of the Articles making no provision for the calling of general meetings by the directors, S.134(*b*) states that two or more members holding not less than one tenth of the issued share capital may call a meeting.

Invariably, the directors have power to call general meetings and they should instruct the secretary to do so 'by order of the board'. A secretary has no power to convene a meeting without such authority (*Re Haycraft Gold Reduction and Mining Co.* (1900)), although his action could be ratified by the directors before the meeting (*Hooper v. Kerr, Stuart & Co.* (1900)).

If it is *impossible* to convene a meeting in the prescribed manner (for example, because of the non-availability of the directors), the Court, either on its own motion or on the application of any director or a member who would be entitled to vote at the meeting, may order the meeting to be called, held and conducted in such manner as it thinks fit. It has the right to direct that one member, present personally or by proxy, may constitute the meeting (S. 135).

Notice of General Meetings

The *manner* of giving notice will be as prescribed in the Articles (S. 134(a)). Table A provides that notice may be given personally or by post at the member's registered address. A notice convening an annual general meeting must specify it as such (S. 131(1)).

Indication of Business to be Transacted

A notice must be sufficiently detailed fairly and adequately to describe the nature of the business to be transacted, so as to provide members with enough knowledge of relevant facts to form an opinion. For example, if the directors are interested in a contract to be voted on at the meeting, the notice must give particulars of those interests (*Kaye v. Croydon Tramways Co.* (1898)). Again, if a resolution is to be put allowing additional remuneration to the directors, the amount must be stated if it is large (*Baillie v. Oriental Telephone and Electric Co.* (1915)).

This requirement for adequate disclosure applies to **special business**. This is defined as all business at the annual general meeting which is not 'ordinary business' (see page 145) and all business at extraordinary general meetings. Ordinary business does not require to be set out in such detail because its scope is defined in the Articles.

Where it is intended to put a special or an extraordinary resolution, the notice must identify the resolution as such (S. 141).

Length of Notice

The minimum amount of written notice which may be required by the Articles is as follows:

(*a*) *Twenty-one days*' notice must be given for the annual general meeting.

(*b*) *Fourteen days'* notice must be given for any other general meeting (S. 133); *but*

Twenty-one days' notice is required if a special resolution is to be put (S. 141).

Shorter notice is acceptable (*a*) for the annual general meeting, if *all* the members entitled to attend and vote so agree, and (*b*) for any other general meeting, by agreement by a majority in number of those entitled to attend and vote and holding not less than 95 per cent in nominal value of the shares giving the right to vote. A resolution confirming any such agreement to shorter notice should be minuted (*Re Pearce Duff & Co.* (1960)). This provision does not permit a company to *dispense* with notice.

Where Special Notice must be given, *twenty-one* days' notice must be given to the members (see page 149).

'Days' notice' means 'clear' days' notice—that is, excluding the day of service and the day of the meeting (*Re Hector Whaling Co.* (1936)). Table A states that a notice sent by post is deemed to be served twenty-four hours after posting.

Entitlement to Notice

S. 134 provides that, subject to any contrary provisions in the Articles, notice of a general meeting must be served on *every* member. Articles frequently withhold the entitlement to notice from those members without voting rights, but all members must, of course, be sent copies of the accounting records. It is also usual not to issue notices to members who have supplied no address in the United Kingdom for the service of notices. Even without such an Article, it has been established that it is not necessary to serve notice on a member resident outside the United Kingdom if this would involve unreasonable delay or difficulty (*Re Warden and Hotchkiss Ltd* (1945)). (The validity of such a ruling is doubtful in days of air travel.)

Table A extends the right to notice to the personal representatives of members who would have been entitled to notice.

A meeting would be invalid if notice was not given to even one entitled member (*Smyth v. Darley* (1849)). Most companies safeguard themselves by including an Article which states that *accidental* omission to give notice to a member will not invalidate the meeting.

Auditors are entitled to attend all general meetings and to receive notices thereof. (See Chapter 13 for the auditors' rights in special circumstances.)

Defective Notice

The proceedings of a meeting will be invalid if the notice of it is in-valid. If the defect in the notice referred to a resolution, the resolution will be invalid. If, however, *all* the members are present and so agree, the defect may be waived and the business validated (*Re Oxted Motor Co.* (1921)).

Special Notice

Certain resolutions require Special Notice. Notice of the intention to put the resolution must be given *to the company* not less than twenty-eight days before the meeting. The company must give *the members* twenty-one days' notice of a meeting at which such a resolution is to be put. If the company calls the meeting for twenty-eight days or less after receiving the Special Notice, the notice is nevertheless deemed to have been properly given (S. 142).

Special notice must be given in the following circumstances:

(*a*) To remove an auditor or to appoint an auditor in the circumstances stated on page 139.

(*b*) To remove a director or to appoint someone in place of a director so removed (see page 82).

(*c*) To appoint or reappoint an 'over-age' director (see page 83).

All these resolutions are *ordinary* resolutions.

Resolutions

A resolution is the decision of a meeting. A *proposed* resolution is a **motion**, although the Act and Articles frequently use the word 'resolution' for both terms.

Ordinary Resolutions

These are those passed by a simple majority. All resolutions are ordinary resolutions unless otherwise stated in the Act or the Articles. Thus, if a Section states that a certain matter must be dealt with by the company in general meeting, an ordinary resolution will suffice unless the Section states otherwise.

Extraordinary Resolutions

S. 141 (1) defines this as one to be passed by a majority of not less than three fourths of such members as vote, personally or by proxy.

Special Resolutions

These require the same majority as for extraordinary resolutions, but not less than twenty-one days' notice of the intention to propose it must be given. However, *less* than twenty-one days' notice will suffice where so agreed by a majority in number of members entitled to attend and vote, who hold not less than 95 per cent of the nominal value of shares giving voting rights (S. 141 (2)).

'The Majority'

In deciding if a resolution has been passed by the requisite majority, account must be taken only of the votes *cast*, for and against. The votes of absent members and those who abstain are ignored (S. 141 (4)).

Registration of Copies of Resolutions and Agreements

S. 143 as amended by S. 51 (2)(1967) requires that copies, printed or in some other form approved by the Registrar, of the following resolutions and agreements, must be forwarded to the Registrar within fifteen days of their passing or making:

(*a*) Special resolutions.

(*b*) Extraordinary resolutions.

(*c*) Resolutions agreed to by *all* members but which, if not so agreed to, would have been required to be passed as special or extraordinary resolutions.

(*d*) Resolutions agreed to by *all members of a class* of shareholder but which, if not so agreed to, would have been required to be passed by some particular majority or in some particular manner.

(*e*) Resolutions or agreements binding all members of a class of shareholder though not agreed to by all those members.

(*f*) Resolutions for voluntary winding up under S. 278 (1)(a).

A copy of every such resolution or agreement for the time being in force must be embodied in or annexed to every copy of the Articles issued thereafter.

S. 63 requires the filing of a resolution to increase the authorised share capital within fifteen days of it being passed.

Under the *European Communities Act, 1972*, the filing of a resolution which amends the Memorandum or the Articles does not become effective until the fifteenth day after the Registrar has acknowledged it in the *Official Gazette*.

Voting

Show of Hands

The common law rule is that voting must first be by show of hands, whereby each member personally present has one vote, irrespective of his holding. Thus, a proxy may not vote on a show of hands.

Poll

Immediately following the declaration of the result of a vote by show of hands, a poll may be demanded. A poll enables votes to be cast relative to the number and type of shares held, as prescribed in the Articles. The *demand* for a poll cancels the show of hands vote.

There is a common law right to demand a poll, and S. 137 gives the right under statute. It states that a company's Articles shall be void to the extent that:

(*a*) They exclude the right to demand a poll at general meetings (except to elect a chairman or adjourn the meeting).

(*b*) They require the demand to be made:

(*i*) by more than five members entitled to vote; or

(*ii*) by a member or members representing more than one tenth of the total voting rights of all members; or

(*iii*) by a member or members holding shares with a right to vote, on which the aggregate amount paid up is more than one tenth of the total sum paid on all such shares.

The Act therefore prevents Articles being framed so as to make difficult the right to demand a poll. Table A allows demands by those holding one tenth of the total voting rights or one tenth of the total paid on all shares. It also allows a demand to be made by at least *three* members present in person or by proxy. Additionally, it gives the chairman the right to demand a poll. S.137 also permits a proxy to demand or join in a demand for a poll within the set provisions.

Taking a poll may be a lengthy business and it may not be possible to do it at the meeting at which it is demanded. The time and place for taking a poll may be determined by the chairman, unless there are regulations in the Articles for doing so (*Re Chillington Iron Co.* (1885)). A poll is, however, regarded as being part of the meeting (*Shaw v. Tati Concessions Ltd* (1913)).

It is common practice to adjourn the meeting to a later date for the result to be announced. In this respect, the date when a resolution becomes effective is the date the result of the poll is *announced* and not the date when the votes were cast (*Holmes v. Keyes and Others* (1958)).

A member absent when a poll was demanded may nevertheless vote on the poll (*Campbell v. Maund* (1836)).

Voting Rights

S.134(e) states that so far as the Articles make no other provisions, every member has one vote for each share or each ten pounds of stock he has in the company. Invariably, however, the Articles specify the voting powers of shareholders, indicating any difference in voting rights as between classes of members. If there *are* differences, details of them must be given in the prospectus.

Table A provides that on a show of hands every member with voting rights is entitled to one vote and that on a poll every such member has one vote for each share. Further provisions are:

(*a*) The voting rights of a person of unsound mind rest in his legal representative.

(*b*) A member in arrear with calls or other sums due on his shares may not vote.

(*c*) Votes on a poll may be given personally or by proxy.

(*d*) Where shares are held jointly, the vote of the senior holder who tenders a vote will be accepted. It was decided in *Burns v. Siemens Bros* (1919) that joint holders may require their holding to be split, allowing each joint holder to be the senior in respect of one of the split holdings.

Determination as to who is entitled to vote is by reference to the register of members, an entry therein being *prima facie* evidence of the ownership of the shares. For example, a bankrupt member whose name remains on the register is entitled to vote, but in *Morgan v. Gray* (1953) it was decided he should vote on the instructions of the trustee in bankruptcy.

Table A states that any objection to the qualification of a voter must be raised at the meeting or adjourned meeting for a ruling by the chairman.

By S. 138, a member entitled to more than one vote may split them for and against the resolution. This may be done, for example, if the voter was, in fact, a trustee for more than one beneficiary and voted according to the different wishes of the beneficiaries.

Table A provides that the chairman has a casting vote in the event of equality of voting. There is no such right under the common law (*Nell v. Longbottom* (1894)).

Proxies

A proxy is a document whereby a person entitled to vote transfers that right to another person (known as 'the proxy'). The proxy need not be a member.

There is no common law right to vote by proxy but S. 136 specifically empowers any person with the right to vote at meetings to appoint another person as his proxy. This is subject to the following conditions (unless the Articles provide otherwise):

(*a*) It does not apply in the case of a company with no share capital.

(*b*) The proxy of a member of a *private* company has the same right to *speak* at the meeting as has the member.

(*c*) A member of a private company may not appoint more than one proxy for the same meeting.

(*d*) A proxy may not vote except on a poll.

S. 136 goes on to make more positive the right to vote by proxy. It requires that in every notice of a meeting there must appear with reasonable prominence a statement of a member's right to appoint a proxy and that such a proxy need not be a member.

By S. 137(2) a proxy may demand or join in the demand for a poll. Thus, although a proxy is not able to use the superior power a poll may give him until a poll is held, he can ensure that a poll will in fact be taken, provided he has or can enlist the necessary voting strength to demand a poll.

Proxies must be deposited with the company before the meeting, but S.136 does not allow the Articles to demand that the deposit be made more than forty-eight hours before the meeting. Table A states that proxies, signed by the member or his attorney or, in the case of a corporation, under seal or signed by a duly authorised officer, must be lodged at the registered office or other stipulated place not less than forty-eight hours before the time of the meeting or adjourned meeting, or not less than twenty-four hours before a poll.

Table A also states that revocation of a proxy or the previous death or insanity of the principal will not be effective unless written notice of the event has been received by the company before the meeting. (A principal may, however, effectively revoke his proxy by attending and voting at the meeting or by lodging a later proxy).

Voting by Corporation Representatives

If a corporation is a member of a company, it may appoint a representative to attend and vote at meetings of the company. The appointment would be by resolution of the appointing corporation (S.139). Such a representative is deemed to be not a proxy, as an 'artificial person' obviously cannot attend personally.

Adjournment

An adjourned meeting is merely a continuation of the first meeting and the business at the adjourned meeting is confined to business as set out in the notice of the first meeting. It follows that no notice of the adjourned meeting is necessary, although Table A says that a new notice shall be given if the adjournment is for thirty days or more. Such a notice must, of course, refer only to business uncompleted at the first meeting.

Under common law, a resolution passed at an adjourned meeting is deemed to have been passed at the original meeting because one is a continuation of the other, but this is overridden by S.144. This states that a resolution passed at an adjourned general meeting, class meeting or board meeting is deemed to be passed on the date on which it was *in fact* passed.

Further examples of company law being at variance with the common law are the right to give notice of resolutions between the statutory meeting and any adjournment thereof (see page 144) and the right to deposit proxies between a general meeting and an adjourned meeting (see above).

The Articles may give the chairman the power to adjourn on his own motion or he may be able to do so only with the consent of the members.

As regards the statutory meeting, however, the power to adjourn rests with the *meeting* (S. 130(8)). It is generally accepted that a chairman has power to adjourn on his own motion in the event of disorder at a meeting. If a chairman abuses his power to adjourn by doing so improperly and then vacates the chair, the remaining members may appoint a new chairman and continue the meeting (*National Dwellings Society v. Sykes* (1894)).

The Quorum

There must be a specified number of people, qualified to attend and vote, present in order to constitute a valid meeting. This minimum number is known as the 'quorum'. In the event of the Articles being silent on this point, two will constitute a quorum for a private company and three in the case of any other company (S. 134(c)).

Table A sets the quorum at three members present in person. If (as in Table A) the Articles state that a quorum must be present 'at the time the meeting proceeds to business', the meeting may continue after the quorum has been lost during the course of the meeting (*Re Hartley Baird Ltd* (1954)). (Most Articles now read so that no business may be transacted after a meeting becomes inquorate.)

A representative of a corporation is a member 'personally present' and may be counted for the purpose of the quorum (*Re Kelantan Coconut Estates Ltd* (1920)).

There are exceptions to the general rule, stated in *Sharp v. Dawes* (1876), that one person cannot constitute a meeting. If the Court orders the calling of a meeting because it is impossible to call it as provided in the Articles (S. 135, see page 147), or the Department of Trade calls an annual meeting (S. 131, see page 145), it may be directed that one member may constitute the meeting. Where there is only one member of a class of shareholders, a resolution signed by the member will indicate the 'consent of a meeting of the class' (*East v. Bennett Bros* (1911)). The sole holder of ordinary shares validly constituted a meeting which passed a special resolution to reduce the capital (*Re X.L. Laundries* (1969)).

'Disinterested Quorum' (see page 86)

The Chairman

Election

By Table A, the chairman of the board is to preside at general meetings. If he does not appear within fifteen minutes of the appointed time or refuses to preside, another director appointed by the board will preside. If no director is then present within fifteen minutes or is willing to act, the members present may appoint one of their number as chairman.

If no provision is made in the Articles, a member may be appointed from those present (S. 134(d)).

Authority under Table A

(*a*) The chairman *may* adjourn the meeting with the *consent* of the members, and *shall* do so if *directed* by the members.

(*b*) The chairman may demand a poll.

(*c*) He may direct the manner, time and place of a poll, except in connection with the election of a chairman or the adjournment of the meeting. (These must be voted on immediately.)

(*d*) His declaration of a vote by show of hands and an entry thereof in the minutes book is conclusive evidence, unless a poll is demanded.

(*e*) He has a casting vote in the event of an equality of votes.

Other Authority

(*a*) A chairman is responsible for maintaining order at a meeting and its conduct (*Re Indian Zoedone Co.* (1884)).

(*b*) A declaration by the chairman that an extraordinary or special resolution is carried is conclusive evidence thereof without proof of the number of votes for and against, unless a poll is demanded (S. 141(3)).

(*c*) A chairman's decision on points of order or the result of voting must be accepted as correct unless it is shown to be fraudulent (*Re Caratel (New) Mines Ltd* (1902)).

Minutes

As Evidence of the Proceedings

S. 145 prescribes as follows:

(*a*) Minutes must be kept of all general meetings and meetings of directors.

(*b*) Minutes signed by the chairman of that meeting or of the next succeeding meeting shall be evidence of the proceedings.

(*c*) Where minutes have been so made, then, until the contrary is proved, the meeting shall be deemed to have been duly held and all proceedings thereat and appointments to be valid.

(*d*) If minutes are not kept, the company and every officer in default shall be liable to a fine.

Thus, the onus of disproving the accuracy of minutes duly signed rests with the person disputing it. If, however, the Articles stipulate that such minutes are *conclusive* evidence, then apparently their accuracy cannot be challenged (*Kerr v. Mottram* (1940)).

Inspection and Copies

Minutes of *general* meetings must be kept at the registered office of the company and be open to inspection during business hours to any member without charge. Every member may be furnished with a copy of any such minutes within seven days of demand at a charge not exceeding $2\frac{1}{2}$p per every 100 words.

In the event of refusal to inspect or to provide copies, the company and every officer in default is liable to a fine. The Court may order immediate inspection or the provision of copies (S. 146).

There is no right of members to inspect minutes of board meetings.

Form of Minutes

Minutes may be kept in bound books or by recording them in any other manner, provided adequate precautions are taken against falsification and for facilitating its discovery (S. 436).

Circulation of Members' Resolutions and Statements

S. 140 gives members facilities to bring certain matters to the attention of the members generally at a forthcoming meeting. The procedure is to requisition the company and there are two separate demands which can be made:

(1) To give notice to the members of the intention to move a *resolution* at the next *annual* general meeting which may be properly moved at that meeting.

(2) To circulate to the members a *statement* of not more than 1,000 words regarding any matter referred to in any proposed resolution or the business of *any* general meeting.

The following conditions apply:

(*a*) Any number of members may make the requisition, provided they represent not less than one twentieth of the total voting rights of all members entitled to vote at the meeting, or it may be made by not less than 100 members holding shares on which an average of not less than £100 each has been paid.

(*b*) All the requisitionists must sign the requisition (which may consist of one or more documents) and it must be deposited at the company's registered office:

(*i*) in the case of a resolution, not less than six weeks before the meeting;

(*ii*) in the case of a statement, not less than one week before the meeting.

(*c*) The requisitionists must deposit or tender with the requisition a reasonable sum sufficient to cover the company's expenses.

(*d*) The notice of the resolution or the statement must be circulated with the notice of the meeting.

(*e*) If, after a requisition requiring notice of a resolution has been deposited, the company calls an annual general meeting for a date six weeks or less after the deposit, the requisition will be deemed to have been deposited within the stipulated time.

(*f*) The Court may grant relief from the requirement to circulate a statement if, on the application of the company or other person claiming to be aggrieved, it is satisfied that the circulation is intended to be used to secure needless publicity of defamatory matter. The Court may also order the company's costs in making the application to be paid wholly or in part by the requisitionists.

Class Meetings

Provision is usually made in the Articles for the variation of the rights of a class of shareholders at a meeting of such members (see page 172).

'The Majority Rule'

Although it may appear that members holding a majority of the voting rights can dominate the making of decisions at meetings, it must be remembered that certain matters require the agreement of a proportion other than a simple majority. Various forms of protection are also available to minority shareholders and these are discussed in Chapter 17.

The Conduct of Debate

There are certain generally accepted rules of procedure which in themselves do not have the force of law but which in practice may form the basis of a legal decision. For example, it is unreasonable for a large number of members all to claim the right to speak at a meeting but the opportunity should be given for every shade of opinion to be expressed. Certainly minorities, no matter how small, must be allowed a voice and if this is denied it may give rise to a claim in law that the minority was subject to oppression or unfairness.

The seconding of a motion is not essential unless the Articles so demand. If, however, the mover of a motion was unable to obtain a seconder, a chairman would be justified in refusing to put the motion to the meeting.

Any member may propose an amendment to a motion before it is put to the vote of the meeting. The amendment must be within the scope of the notice of the meeting and of the original motion, and it may not be a negative of the motion. Upon an amendment being validly proposed it must be debated and voted on. If the amendment is passed, the original motion is reworded accordingly and becomes a 'substantive motion'. It is then discussed and voted on, unless a further amendment to it is put.

15

IDENTIFYING INTERESTS IN SECURITIES

In the past, there have been many suspect circumstances where it was not possible by referring to public and company records to establish who in fact had interests in the financial affairs of a company. It was possible to hide the true identity of those financially interested by registering company securities in the names of nominees, which could be persons, companies, trusts, etc. For example, on a takeover bid it was not always possible to discover who actually controlled or had a large stake in the bidding company or, sometimes, in the 'victim' company. Where the identity of a person with a certain interest in a company is disguised there obviously must exist the possibility of fraud or deceit. There have also been abuses whereby the registered owner of shares voted at the direction of another party, who thereby had an undisclosed influence on the company's affairs.

The Acts of 1967 and 1976 attempt to eliminate such practices by requiring declarations to be made by those with defined 'interests'. The 1948 Act merely gave power to investigate the true interests only *after* events had shown there had been use of hidden power.

Disclosure of Directors' Interests in Company Securities

The legal provisions requiring directors to declare their interests in the company's shares and debentures are quoted on page 87. The provisions concerning options (see page 93) may also be relevant.

Disclosure of Interests in Voting Shares

Although it is obviously necessary to establish the interests of directors because of their privileged position, it may also be useful to know the extent of the voting powers of non-directors. A non-director or a combination of such persons may well have a controlling interest or, at least, a strong influence by reason of the votes attaching to the shares held.

Unlike the disclosures required of directors, this part of the legislation requires disclosure by *any* person with an interest in *a proportion* of the *voting shares*. It does *not* require disclosure of the consideration and it relates only to *listed* companies.

The provisions of S.33(1967) as amended by S.26(1976) may be summarised as follows.

Application of the Section

(*a*) The provisions only apply in respect of a company which has been granted a listing by a recognised stock exchange as respects the whole or any portion of its share capital.

(*b*) The interests mentioned in the section refer only to a class of issued shares which carry rights to vote in all circumstances at general meetings.

Disclosing an Interest

A person must disclose an interest in shares as defined above on:

(*a*) Becoming interested in the prescribed percentage of the nominal value of that share capital; or

(*b*) Increasing an interest to the prescribed percentage; or

(*c*) Increasing an existing interest of the prescribed percentage or reducing it whilst still retaining the prescribed percentage; or

(*d*) Reducing his interest below the prescribed percentage or becoming uninterested.

The *prescribed percentage* means 5 per cent or such percentage as may be prescribed from time to time by the Secretary of State.

The disclosure must be in the form of a written notice to the company, specifying the event and the date it occurred. It must state the number of shares in which the person is then interested in or, where relevant, that he is no longer interested. The notification must be made within five days of the person becoming aware of the occurrence imposing the obligation. The notice must identify the person making it and quote his address.

A *director* must state he is making the disclosure in fulfilment of his obligation under the Section. (He must also make a disclosure, in respect of the *same* event, of his interest in the company's securities as required by S.27(1967) (see page 87), stating that it is made in fulfilment of his obligation under *that* Section.)

Defining 'Interest'

The rules set out in S.28(1967) (see page 88) apply (so far as they relate to shares) in defining a declarable interest. In addition to those there specified to be *disregarded* are the following:

(*a*) An interest, for the life of the person or another, under a settlement which includes shares, which is irrevocable or where the settlor has no interest in any income or property of the settlement.

(*b*) An interest of a person holding shares as security in the ordinary course of his business as a lender of money.

(*c*) The interest of the High Court by virtue of S.9 of the *Administration of Estates Act, 1925*.

(*d*) The interest of the Accountant General of the Supreme Court.

(*e*) Any interest as prescribed by the Department of Trade.

(*f*) An interest as holder of shares by a member of the Stock Exchange, carrying on business as a jobber and holding the shares for the purpose of his business.

Register of Interests in Voting Shares

S.34(1967) requires every company to which S.33(1967) applies to keep a register to record disclosures made to the company. The information must be inscribed against the name of the person providing it, with the date of the inscription. The entries against each name must be in chronological order and must be made within three days of the notification being received. Entry in the register does not affect the company with notice of the rights of any person in relation to the shares.

The register must be kept where the Register of Directors' Interests is kept. It must be available during business hours for inspection by any member without charge and by any other person for a fee. A copy of the register or any part of it must be supplied, for a fee, within ten days of a person requesting it. The Court has power to compel inspection or the supply of copies where it is refused, and the company and its officers may be liable to a fine.

There may be a separate part of the register for entries as required by S.27(1976) (see below).

Power of the Company to Require Disclosure of Beneficial Interests

Responsibility for declaring an interest rests with the person having it and a company may not make an entry in the register, even if it knows that an event qualifies for entry, unless it receives notification of the event. However, S.27(1976) allows a company to serve written notice on a member to require him, within such reasonable time as is stated in the notice:

(*a*) To indicate in writing the capacity in which he holds any shares as defined in S.33(1967); and

(*b*) If he holds them *otherwise* than as beneficial owner, to indicate in writing (so far as is known to him) the persons who have an interest in them and the nature of the interest.

If, as a result of this demand, the company is informed that another person *has* an interest in the shares, it may, by notice in writing, require that person:

(*a*) To indicate in writing the capacity in which he holds that interest; and (*b*) If he holds it otherwise than as beneficial owner, to indicate the identity and nature of the interest of the persons who have an interest.

The section also empowers a company to serve a written notice on a member to indicate in writing, within a specified time, whether any of the voting shares held by him are subject to an agreement or arrangement whereby another person is entitled to control the member's exercise of his rights (that is, the member votes at the direction of another). The member must identify any such party and give particulars of the agreement or arrangement.

Where a company receives any information as a consequence of the operation of this section (i.e. as to beneficial ownership or the control of voting rights), it must inscribe in a *separate part* of the Register of Interests in Voting Shares (*a*) the fact that the requirement was imposed and the date it was imposed and (*b*) the information received as a consequence.

The rights as to inspection and copies of these entries are those appertaining to the main register.

Any person failing to comply with a notice from the company requiring the above information, or in purporting to comply with it knowingly making a false or reckless statement in a material particular, is liable to a fine or imprisonment or both.

Investigation of Ownership of a Company

Appointment of Inspectors

The 1948 Act gives the Department of Trade extensive powers to investigate the effective ownership of a company. Under S.172, if the Department is satisfied that there is good reason for doing so, it may appoint inspectors to investigate and report on the membership of the company to determine the 'true persons' who are or have been financially interested in the company's success or failure (real or apparent), or who are or were able to control or materially influence the policy of the company.

Unless the application is vexatious, the Department *must* appoint inspectors on an application by members entitled to do so as prescribed in S.164—that is, by (*a*) at least 200 members or members holding at least one tenth of the issued shares, or (*b*) at least one fifth of the members of a company with no share capital.

An inspector has the same powers as are set out in Ss.166 and 167 (see page 165), but the scope of the investigation may be expressly restricted, e.g. to matters relating to a particular class of share or for a specified period. However, the terms of the appointment may allow investigation of any arrangements or understandings which, even though not legally binding, are relevant. The inspector may include in his investigation those whom he has reasonable cause to believe to be or have been financially interested, including persons acting on behalf of others and agents and officers of the company.

The Department is under no obligation to furnish the company or any person with a copy of the inspector's report if it is of the opinion that there is good reason for not divulging the report or part of it. Any report or part not divulged must, however, be kept by the Registrar.

Investigation without Appointing an Inspector

If the Department of Trade decides that good reason exists for investigating the ownership of shares or debentures of a company but that it is unnecessary to appoint an inspector for that purpose, it may, under S.173, require any person believed to be or to have been interested in them (or their solicitors or agents) to provide any information which he can be reasonably expected to have or could obtain as to past and present interests and the names and addresses of persons so interested. An 'interest' is deemed to be held by a person:

(*a*) If he has any right to acquire or dispose of a share or debenture or to vote in respect thereof; or

(*b*) If his consent is necessary for the exercise of any rights of another person interested; or

(*c*) If other persons interested can be required or are accustomed to exercise their rights on his instructions.

Power of the Department in Cases of Difficulty

Where, in the case of an investigation under S.172 or S.173 as described above, the Department of Trade experiences difficulty in discovering the relevant facts about any shares (issued or to be issued) because of the unwillingness of persons to assist in the investigation, S.174 states that the Department may order that until further order the following restrictions will apply:

(*a*) Any transfer of shares and, in the case of unissued shares, any transfer of the right to be issued and any issue thereof, is void.

(*b*) No voting rights may be exercised in respect of the shares.

(*c*) No further shares may be issued in right of those shares or in pursuance of any offer made to the holder.

(*d*) No payment may be made in respect of sums due from the company on the shares, whether in respect of capital or otherwise (except in a liquidation).

If such an order is made or the Department refuses to cancel an order it has made, a person claiming to be aggrieved may appeal to the Court. If the Court sees fit, it may lift the restriction. An order by the Department or the Court which permits transfer of the shares may continue the other restrictions.

Any person who disposes of shares subject to a restriction order or who votes on them or who fails to communicate the restriction to any person entitled to vote on the shares (as holder or by proxy), is liable to a fine or imprisonment or both. If shares are issued in contravention of an order, the company and every officer is liable to a fine.

16

INVESTIGATIONS

There must be procedures, designed and supported by the law, to allow authorities to enquire into matters concerning a company when circumstances appear to make it necessary. There may be suspicions of fraud, misappropriation, oppression or contravention of statutes or official regulations. As part of such an enquiry, it may be necessary to establish who were the persons nominally responsible for the company's activities, who effectively controlled those activities and who profited thereby. These three categories may well be composed of different persons.

The Acts require that certain returns be made to the Registrar. These are referred to specifically in the relevant chapters of this book and are discussed generally in Chapter 18. Apart from the fact that such returns cannot necessarily provide sufficient information to bring certain irregularities to light, however, there is always the possibility that a required return was not made at all.

The records which the law requires companies to maintain in the form of registers are, in general, available for inspection, but this right is limited in its effect to the extent that they are not available as 'public records'. Again, the information they provide would be likely to be inadequate for the required purpose.

The law therefore prescribes the circumstances in which special powers may be given to conduct an enquiry, the procedure for doing so and the consequent actions which may be taken.

Investigation of Ownership of a Company

Ss. 172–174 lay down the procedure for establishing who in fact are or were the effective owners of a company. It may be carried out at the instigation of the Department of Trade or on the demand of members of the company. As this procedure is one of the measures available to establish who has interests in a company, it is dealt with in Chapter 15, but it is, of course, a form of investigation.

Investigation of a Company's Affairs

The Department of Trade has authority to appoint inspectors to investigate and report on the affairs of a company, upon application by members (S. 164) or in other circumstances (S. 165), as shown below.

Appointment of Inspectors on Application by Members

S.164 provides for the appointment of one or more inspectors to investigate and report on the affairs of a company, upon application by (*a*) not less than 200 members or members holding not less than one tenth of the shares issued, or (*b*) at least one fifth of the members of a company with no share capital.

The applicants must provide such evidence as may be demanded in order to show they have good reason for requiring the investigation. If the Department agrees to the application, it may be conditional upon the applicants giving security, to an amount not exceeding £100, for payment of the costs of the investigation.

Appointment of Inspectors in other Circumstances

S.165 as amended by S.38(1967) provides that the Department of Trade *must* appoint inspectors to investigate the affairs of a company and report thereon if (*a*) the company by special resolution or (*b*) the Court by order declares that its affairs ought to be investigated by an inspector appointed by the Department.

The Department *may* appoint inspectors, even if the company is in the course of being wound up voluntarily, if there appear to be circumstances suggesting:

(*a*) That its business is being or has been conducted with intent to defraud its creditors or the creditors of any other person; or otherwise for a fraudulent or unlawful purpose; or in a manner oppressive to any part of its members; or that it was formed for any fraudulent or unlawful purpose; or

(*b*) That persons concerned with its formation or management have in connection therewith been guilty of fraud, misfeasance or other misconduct toward it or its members; or

(*c*) That its members have not been given all the information with respect to its affairs as they might reasonably expect.

Power to Investigate Related Companies

An inspector appointed in any of the above circumstances may, if he thinks it necessary, investigate the affairs of any body corporate which is or has been at any relevant time the company's subsidiary, holding company, fellow subsidiary or holding company of its subsidiary. The inspector's report must include the result of any such investigation so far as it is relevant to the investigation of the first company (S.166).

Power to Demand Attendance and Production of Documents

S.167 as amended by S.39(1967) states that it is the duty of all officers and agents, past and present, of the company or of an associated company as defined above, to produce to the inspectors all books and documents in their custody or power, and to give the inspectors all the assistance they are reasonably able to give. It also states that such officers and agents may be required to attend before the inspectors when so required.

Any officer or agent may be examined on oath by the inspector. If the inspector wishes to examine on oath a person whom he has no power to so examine, he may apply to the Court. If the Court sees fit, it may order that person to attend and be examined on oath. The person examined must answer all such questions as the Court may put or allow to be put. Notes of the examination must be made, read over to or by the person examined, and signed by him.

If any officer or agent refuses to attend when required to do so, or refuses to produce any book or document it is his duty to produce, or refuses to answer any question put to him by the inspector, the inspector may certify the refusal in writing to the Court. The Court, after hearing any witnesses for or against the alleged offender and after hearing any statement offered in his defence, may punish the offender as if he had been guilty of contempt of the Court.

The term 'agent' above includes auditors, bankers and solicitors. By S.175, however, a solicitor need not disclose any privileged communication made to him (except the name and address of his client) and a banker need not disclose any information as to the affairs of any of his customers other than the company.

Inspector's Power to Inform the Department of Trade of a Suspected Offence

At any time during the course of the investigation, an inspector may inform the Department of Trade, without making an interim report, if his investigations tend to show that an offence has been committed (S.41 (1967)).

The Inspector's Report

The inspector may, and if so directed must, make interim reports to the Department of Trade. A final report must be made at the conclusion of the investigation. The Department must:

(*a*) Forward a copy to the registered office of the company;

(*b*) If it thinks fit, furnish a copy on request and on payment of a fee to any member of the company, to any body corporate dealt with in the report or whose interests as a creditor or any such body corporate as appears to the Department to be affected;

(*c*) Furnish a copy to members if they requested the investigation;

(*d*) Furnish a copy to the Court if the inspector was appointed following an order of the Court.

It may also order the report to be printed and published (S.168).

Further Action by the Department of Trade

As a consequence of the inspector's report, the Department of Trade may be empowered to take action under S.35(1967) for the compulsory winding up of the company or to bring proceedings on behalf of a body corporate under S.37(1967) (see page 168).

Inspection of a Company's Books and Papers

The Demand to Produce Documents

The Department of Trade has power to enquire into the affairs of a company even if no order for an investigation has been made. This power is limited to a compulsory examination of documents relevant to the company but it has the advantage of discovering facts expeditiously. It may also lead to further action by the Department. The provisions are contained in Part III of the 1967 Act.

S.109(1967) enables the Department to require a company *at any time* to produce specified books or papers if the Department considers there is good reason to do so. Authority for the demand (which may be produced as evidence on request) may be given by the Department to any of its officers. These provisions apply to any company registered in Great Britain, and to bodies incorporated outside Great Britain and carrying on business in Great Britain.

Additionally, the Department may:

(*a*) Require the production of documents from any person who appears to be in possession of them, but without prejudice to any lien that person may claim.

(*b*) Take copies or extracts from documents produced.

(*c*) Require the person producing them, or any other person who is a present or past officer, to provide an explanation of them.

(*d*) Compel the person in (*a*) above to disclose the whereabouts of the documents if they are not produced.

Failure to comply with any of the above requirements may make the company or any person so required liable to a fine or imprisonment or both. It would be a defence to prove that the documents were not in the person's possession or control and that it was not reasonably practical for him to comply.

Entry and Search of Premises

If the documents are not produced as required under the above section, the Department of Trade may apply to a Justice of the Peace for a search warrant to enable the police to find and take possession of them. A warrant would not be granted unless the information laid gave reasonable ground for suspecting that the documents would be found on certain premises. Any documents taken as a result may be retained for three months, but if criminal proceedings are commenced as mentioned in the circumstances (*a*) or (*b*) below, the documents may be retained until the conclusion of those proceedings (S.110(1967)).

Security of Documents Produced

The provisions of S.111(1967) are as follows. No information obtained under Ss.109 or 110 of the 1967 Act may be published or disclosed without the written consent of the company, except by the Department of Trade or an officer of the Department, an inspector appointed by the Department, or the Treasury or an officer of the Treasury. Publication or disclosure may be made *without consent*, however, where it is required for:

(*a*) Criminal proceedings arising out of the Companies Acts or for misconduct in management of the company's affairs or misapplication of the company's property.

(*b*) Criminal proceedings arising out of the *Exchange Control Act, 1947*.

(*c*) Complying with any requirement or exercising any powers with regard to inspectors' reports.

(*d*) Instituting proceedings under S.37(1967) (see page 169).

(*e*) Instituting proceedings by the Department of Trade for winding up the company.

(*f*) The purposes of proceedings under S.110(1967) (see above).

It is an offence for any person to publish or disclose any information or document in contravention of the above provisions.

Investigation of Share Dealings

S.32(1967) provides that if it appears to the Department of Trade that there has been contravention of Ss.25, 27 or 31 of the 1967 Act (relating to share options purchased by a director or his family (see page 94) or to a director's obligation to disclose interests of himself and his family in securities of the company (see page 87)), the Department may appoint an inspector to investigate and report.

The provisions of S.167 concerning the duty of officers and agents to assist the inspector will apply (see page 165). The inspector may also investigate any associated company and require information or the production of documents from members of a stock exchange and from licensed dealers in securities.

Powers of the Department of Trade Following an Investigation

S.35(1967) provides as follows:

(*a*) If the Department of Trade considers that in the public interest a company should be wound up, it may petition for it to be wound up by the Court if the Court considers it would be just and equitable to do so. This decision may arise from:

(*i*) an inspector's report made under S.168 (see page 166); or

(*ii*) any information or document obtained under Part III of the 1967 Act (see page 167).

(*b*) If it appears to the Department of Trade, from any report or document mentioned above, that the business of the company is being carried on in a manner which is oppressive to any part of its members, it may petition for an order under S.210 (see page 173), additionally or alternatively to a petition for winding up.

S.37(1967) states that if, based on reports or documents mentioned above, the Department of Trade considers that civil proceedings ought in the public interest to be brought by a body corporate, the Department itself may bring the proceedings in the name of and on behalf of the body corporate.

17

MAJORITY RULE AND MINORITY RIGHTS

The Principles of Majority Rule and Minority Rights

Management of the company's affairs is in the hands of the directors, subject only to any limitation on those powers as set out in the Articles. Members may not, therefore, interfere with the day-to-day management of the company. Directors may be removed and others appointed only with the consent of those holding a majority of the voting shares.

To a considerable extent, therefore, the right to make decisions concerning the company's affairs rests with those holding the majority voting power. If the majority support the directors, generally speaking there is nothing the minority can do about it (*Hogg v. Cramphorn Ltd* (1966)). Basically, this principle is upheld by the law but provision is made for the protection of minorities where the majority rule operates against them unfairly.

The Rule in *Foss v. Harbottle*

The leading case of *Foss v. Harbottle* (1843) underlines the general principle of majority rule. Two shareholders sought to bring an action against the directors, alleging that they had been guilty of mismanagement and responsible for losses by the company. It was held that an action could not be brought by the minority shareholders for the following reasons:

(*a*) It was within the power of the majority to ratify the action of the directors. The Court could not take away the company's right to manage its affairs in accordance with its own constitution.

(*b*) As it was the *company* which suffered loss and not the members as individuals, it was for the *company* to seek redress if it so wished. This underlines the principle of the 'corporate personality' of the company (see page 3).

Thus, in *Edwards v. Halliwell* (1950) it was stated that:

'The Rule in *Foss v. Harbottle* comes to no more than this. First, the proper plaintiff in an action in respect of a wrong alleged to be done to a company is *prima facie* the company. Secondly, where the alleged wrong is a transaction which might be made binding on the company and on all its members by a simple majority of the members, no individual member is allowed to maintain an action in respect of that matter for the simple reason that, if a mere majority of the members is in favour of what has been done, then *cadit quaestio*.'

(*c*) The Courts are reluctant to interfere with the management of a company or even to give opinions on it.

(*d*) To allow it would open the floodgates to a succession of such actions.

Exceptions to the Rule in *Foss v. Harbottle*

The Rule cannot be inflexible because there could be situations where its implementation would result in unfairness towards the minority. Thus, a minority may bring an action in the following circumstances:

(*a*) To prevent the company from committing an act which is illegal or *ultra vires*, because such an action could not be ratified by a majority.

(*b*) To prevent the company from taking an action for which a special resolution is required, when such a resolution was not in fact passed (*Edwards v. Halliwell* (1950)).

(*c*) To prevent a fraud on a minority. If the minority shareholders were denied the right to bring an action on behalf of themselves and all the others, the wrongdoers, because they were in control, could ensure the *company* would not bring the action (*Menier v. Hooper's Telegraph Works* (1874)). Thus, the wrong would have been against the company, but the minority may bring an action for enforcement of the company's rights if the majority refuse to do so.

(*d*) To restrain the company from doing an act which is contrary to the Articles (*Salmon v. Quinn & Axtens* (1909)).

(*e*) To enable a shareholder to exercise rights attaching to his holding, such as having his vote recorded (*Pender v. Lushington* (1877)).

(*f*) To bring an action for breach of a director's fiduciary duties. In *Wallersteiner v. Moir* (1974) the defendant, who had applied for an enquiry into the activities of a director and major shareholder of two companies, was sued for libel. The law did not at first regard the defendant's counterclaim as being an exception to the Rule, but eventually damages were awarded against the plaintiff. As the counterclaim was on behalf of the companies concerned, however, the damages belonged to *them* and the costs were borne by the *plaintiff*. The Court of Appeal (*Wallersteiner v. Moir (No. 2)* (1975)) then held that the circumstances justified a minority action on behalf of the company and that it should indemnify Mr Moir against the costs of the action. Lord Denning stated:

'The rule is easy enough to apply when the company is defrauded by outsiders; the company itself is the only person who can sue. But suppose it is defrauded by insiders who control its affairs—by directors who hold a majority of the shares—who then can sue for damages? If a board meeting is held, they will not authorise proceedings by the company against themselves. If a general meeting is called, they will vote down any suggestion that the company should sue them themselves. Yet the company is the one person who is damnified. In one way or another, some means must be found for the company to sue.'

Minority Rights under the Acts

Specific provisions to protect the rights of a minority are made under the Acts as follows:

(*a*) For cancellation of a variation of class rights under S. 72 (see below).

(*b*) Those relevant to reconstructions and amalgamations under Ss. 206, 209 and 287 (see Chapter 19).

(*c*) To petition under S. 210 or S. 222 (see pages 173 and 174).

(*d*) Relevant to investigation of a company's affairs under S. 164 or S. 165 (see page 164).

(*e*) Relevant to investigation of ownership of a company under Ss. 172–174 (see page 161).

(*f*) For cancellation of an alteration to the objects clause under S. 5 (see page 27).

Variation of Class Rights

Class rights are those rights which are specific to a particular class of share. They do not relate to those rights which accrue to *all* shareholders.

Almost invariably, the Articles prescribe the procedure whereby any class rights may be altered, but if no provision is made then the necessary consents to an alteration must be obtained as part of a scheme of arrangement under S. 206 (see page 182).

S. 72 states that where provision *is* made, either in the Memorandum or the Articles, for authorisation of a variation in class rights, any such variation may be conditional only upon:

(*a*) The *consent* of any specified proportion of the holders of that class; or

(*b*) The *sanction of a resolution* passed at a *separate meeting* of the holders of that class.

Thus, Table A requires the *consent in writing* of the holders of three fourths of the issued shares of the class or the sanction of an Extraordinary *resolution* passed at a separate meeting of the class.

The Courts have had to decide what constitutes a variation of class rights, by distinguishing between class *rights* and the conditions necessary for the full *enjoyment* of those rights. For example, if there is an increase in the number of shares issued which has the effect of decreasing the proportion of the total share issue held by preference shareholders, it would not constitute a variation of the *rights* of those shares, although it might alter their *value* (*White v. Bristol Aeroplane Co. Ltd* (1953)). (Table A, in fact, states that preferential rights of a class of shares shall not be deemed to be varied by the issue of further shares ranking *pari passu* with them.)

Application for Cancellation of a Variation

Although the general rule of company law is that a decision made in accordance with a company's Articles is binding upon the company and every member (provided there has not been oppression or fraud), S.72 contains a procedure whereby class members may apply for the cancellation of any agreement to vary their rights.

If rights have been varied, then the holders of not less than 15 per cent of the issued shares of that class may apply to the Court to have the variation cancelled. Such holders may not include those who had consented to or voted for the variation. Application must be made within twenty-one days after the consent was given or the resolution passed. It may be made by one or more objectors appointed in writing by the others.

Upon such an application being made, the implementation of the variation may not be proceeded with. The Court will then hear the applicants and any other interested parties. The Court will disallow the variation if it is satisfied that, having regard to all the circumstances, it would unfairly prejudice the holders of *that class*. The equity of the scheme as regards the company *generally* would not concern the Court, neither would it take account of the effect on the objectors *personally*. If not so satisfied, the Court will permit the variation.

Within fifteen days of the Court order, a copy of it must be sent by the company to the Registrar.

The Court's decision is final.

Oppression of a Minority

A member or members who consider that as a minority they are subject to oppression may have recourse to one of two sections of the 1948 Act.

Application for Winding up by the Court

One of the circumstances in which, under S.222, a company may be wound up by the Court (see page 199), is that the Court is of the opinion that it is 'just and equitable' that the company be wound up. Oppression by a majority may be accepted as being within such a circumstance. Thus, in *Loch v. John Blackwood Ltd* (1924) a petition was granted because a director with a majority shareholding refused to call meetings, submit accounts, appoint auditors or give any information concerning the company's plans. This was done in an attempt to obtain the minority shares at a low price.

Alternative to Winding up

If there are circumstances where winding up could be regarded as being just and equitable, an oppressed minority shareholder has an alternative action open to him. This would apply if a winding-up order would *unfairly prejudice the minority holders*. For example, dissolution may result in a loss of shareholder capital, whereas it may be possible to remedy the situation of the minority by some other means.

S. 210 provides that if the affairs of a company are being conducted so as to be oppressive on some part of the members such as to justify winding up but that to do so would unfairly prejudice those members, then the following will apply:

(*a*) Any member complaining of oppression of some part of the members may apply to the Court. An applicant must show he is being oppressed in his capacity as a *member* and not as one holding office in the company (*Elder v. Elder and Watson* (1952)).

(*b*) The Court may, in order to bring to an end the matters complained of, 'make such order as it thinks fit'. This may be for regulating the company's affairs in the future; or for the purchase of the shares of any member by other members; or, for the purpose of reducing the company's capital, the purchase of the shares by the company. Thus, the Court may order some rearrangement of the company's internal affairs so that the minority is no longer treated unfairly or it may arrange for the objector to be 'bought out'.

(*c*) In the event of a Court order altering the Memorandum or the Articles, then, subject to the terms of the order, no further alteration may be made by the company which is inconsistent with the order without leave of the Court.

(*d*) A copy of the order must be delivered by the company to the Registrar within fourteen days of its making.

Defining 'Oppression'

In claiming to be oppressed, an applicant is not necessarily required to prove dishonesty by the majority. His rights depend upon the principle that members are entitled to have the business of the company conducted fairly and in accordance with its constitution and the law (*Re H. R. Harmer Ltd* (1959)).

In *Scottish Co-operative Wholesale Society v. Meyer and Another* (1959) the Court accepted 'oppressively' in relation to the treatment of the minority as meaning 'burdensome, harsh and wrongful'. To prove mere negligence, inefficiency or carelessness in the management of a company is not sufficient ground for a petition. It is not oppressive conduct if there is no suggestion of unscrupulous or overbearing behaviour or lack of probity towards any member (*Re Five Minute Car Wash Ltd* (1966)).

In claiming oppression it must be shown that the majority shareholders either exercise their power to procure that something is done or not done in the conduct of the company's affairs, or procure by an express or implied threat of an exercise of that power that something is not done. To qualify, any such conduct must be unfair to other members and lacking in the degree of probity members are entitled to expect (*Re Jermyn Street Turkish Baths Ltd* (1971)).

A petition will fail if its real object is to exert pressure on the company to achieve a collateral purpose, e.g. to force repayment of a loan owed to the petitioner. Such an application would be regarded as an abuse of the process of the Court (*Re Bellador Silk Ltd* (1965)).

If the Articles have been changed so as to alter the voting rights to the detriment of a minority, a claim that the minority is being oppressed will fail, because it must be assumed until the contrary is proved that the members voting for the alteration were of the honest opinion that such a change would benefit the company *as a whole* (*Rights and Issues Investment Trust Ltd v. Stylo Shoes Ltd* (1964)).

18

STATUTORY RECORDS AND RETURNS

Records to be Kept by a Company

The Acts are specific as to the information which must be recorded within a company. They also stipulate where such records are to be kept (often with a requirement to notify the Registrar of their location), within what periods of time entries must be made, and, where appropriate, the rights of inspection and the provision of copies. The documents are listed below, the Sections quoted being those which give the right to inspect and/or receive copies where applicable:

(*a*) Copies of directors' service contracts (S.26(1967)) (see page 80).

(*b*) The Articles and the Memorandum, including a copy of every resolution or agreement then in force to which S.143 applies (Ss.24 and 25) (see pages 35 and 150).

(*c*) Copies of every instrument creating a charge requiring registration (S.105) (see page 111).

(*d*) The statutory books:

(*i*) The register of members (S.113) (see page 65).

(*ii*) The accounting records (S.158; S.12(1976)) (see page 126).

(*iii*) The register of charges (S.105) (see page 111).

(*iv*) The register of directors and secretaries (S.200) (see page 96).

(*v*) The register of interests in voting shares of a listed company (S.34 (1967)) (see page 160).

(*vi*) The register of directors' interests in company securities (S.29 (1967)) (see page 90).

(*vii*) Minute books of general meetings proceedings (S.146) (see page 155).

(*viii*) Minute books of board meetings proceedings.

(*ix*) The register of debenture-holders, if kept (S.87 as amended) (see page 112).

The auditors have the right of access at all times to the books, accounts and vouchers of the company (S.14(8)(1967)).

Form of Records

Any books required to be kept by a company may be kept by making entries in bound books or recording the matters in any other manner.

176

When a bound book is not used, adequate precautions must be taken to guard against falsification and to facilitate its discovery (S. 436).

Returns to the Registrar of Companies

Inspection and Copies

Any person may inspect documents kept by the Registrar of Companies, and may require a certificate of incorporation or a copy or extract of any other document to be certified by the Registrar (S. 426 as amended).

The Secretary of State has power to fix fees payable to the Registrar in respect of the receipt of documents required to be delivered to him and for inspection of documents kept by him (S. 37(1976)).

Penalisation for Default

One of the reasons for requiring sundry returns to be made by companies to the Registrar is to enable information to be available on public record, as prescribed by the Act above. The effectiveness of such facilities is considerably reduced if the returns are not made within the stipulated periods. S. 428 states that following default in complying with any provision concerning the filing of returns, if the default is not made good within fourteen days of a notice requiring compliance, the Court may, on application by any member or creditor of the company or the Registrar, make an order directing the company and every officer to comply within a specified time.

Because of a general laxity in making returns, S. 28(1976) introduced more stringent measures. It states that a person persistently in default in relation to the delivery of any return, account or other document or the giving of notice to the Registrar, may be subject to a Court order disqualifying him from being a director or in any way concerned with the management of a company for a specified period not exceeding five years. It may be conclusively proved that a person has been 'persistently in default' by showing that in the five years ending when an application is made to the Court by the Secretary of State a person had been adjudged guilty on three or more defaults. A person shall be so adjudged guilty if:

(*a*) He is convicted of any offence of contravening or failing to comply with any requirement of the Acts as specified above; or

(*b*) An order is made against him under S. 428 (enforcement of a company's duty to make returns, see above) or S. 5(1)(1976) (failure to lay accounting records before a general meeting or deliver to the Registrar (see page 127)).

The Secretary of State must give not less than ten days' notice to the person concerned of his intention to apply for an order, and at the hearing of the application that person may appear and give evidence or call witnesses.

Under S.29(1976) the Secretary of State is required to maintain a *Register of Disqualification Orders* containing particulars of orders made by the Court (and any leaves granted in relation to orders) and notified to the Secretary of State. The particulars must be deleted on expiration of an order. The register must be open to inspection of payment of a fee. The orders to be registered are those made under S.188 (see page 82), S.9 of the *Insolvency Act, 1976*, and S.28(1976) above.

Penalisation for False Statements

If a person wilfully makes a statement false in any material particular, knowing it to be false, in any return, report, certificate, balance sheet or other document required to be submitted under the Act, he shall be guilty of a misdemeanour (S.438).

Form of Return

S.34(1976) states that references in the Acts to sundry notices, declarations, etc., are to be regarded as being requirements to make such returns by the use of 'prescribed forms'. This is to ensure uniformity in the manner of presentation.

S.35(1976) allows the Secretary of State to prescribe as he considers appropriate the size, weight, quality and colour of paper and the style, etc., of print, so that documents delivered to the Registrar are of standard size, durable and easily legible.

The Registrar may accept any material other than a document, provided it gives the required information and is of a kind approved by him (S.36(1976)). Thus, information may be acceptable if it is on microfilm.

Operative Date of a Return

Under S.9 of the *European Communities Act, 1972*, the Registrar is required to notify receipt in the *Official Gazette* of any document relevant to changes in the constitution of a company. A company may not rely on the effect of any such document, as against any other person who cannot be shown to have known the facts or events of which the document is evidence, until the fifteenth day after publication. The filing of a resolution altering the Memorandum or the Articles, the filing of the Annual Return, notice of a change in the directors and notice of a winding-up order will not, therefore, be effective upon the *filing* of the evidence.

The Annual Return

Every company is required to make a Return containing specified information once at least in every calendar year. The Return must be completed within forty-two days after the annual general meeting and the company must forthwith forward to the Registrar a copy signed by a director and the secretary (S. 126).

Company having a Share Capital

S. 124 requires that a company with a share capital must provide the information prescribed in the Sixth Schedule of the 1948 Act, which is as follows:

(1) The address of the registered office of the company.

(2)—(*i*) If the register of members is, under the provisions of this Act, kept elsewhere than at the registered office of the company, the address of the place where it is kept.

(*ii*) If any register of holders of debentures of the company or any duplicate of any such register or part of any such register is, under the provisions of this Act, kept, in England in the case of a company registered in England or in Scotland in the case of a company registered in Scotland, elsewhere than at the registered office of the company, the address of the place where it is kept.

(3) A summary, distinguishing between shares issued for cash and shares issued as fully or partly paid up otherwise than in cash, specifying the following particulars:

(*a*) The amount of the share capital of the company and the number of shares into which it is divided.

(*b*) The number of shares taken from the commencement of the company up to the date of the return.

(*c*) The amount called up on each share.

(*d*) The total amount of calls received.

(*e*) The total amount of calls unpaid.

(*f*) The total amount of the sums (if any) paid by way of commission in respect of any shares or debentures.

(*g*) The discount allowed on the issue of any shares issued at a discount or so much of that discount as has not been written off at the date on which the return is made.

(*h*) The total amount of the sums (if any) allowed by way of discount in respect of any debentures since the date of the last return.

(*i*) The total number of shares forfeited.

(*j*) The total amount of shares for which share warrants are outstanding at the date of the return and of share warrants issued and surrendered respectively since the date of the last return, and the number of shares comprised in each warrant.

(4) Particulars of the total amount of the indebtedness of the company in respect of all mortgages and charges which are required (or, in the case of a company registered in Scotland, which, if the company had

been registered in England, would be required) to be registered with the registrar of companies under this Act, or which would have been required so to be registered if created after the first day of July, 1908.

(5) A list:

(*a*) Containing the names and addresses of all persons who, on the fourteenth day after the company's annual general meeting for the year, are members of the company, and of persons who have ceased to be members since the date of the last return or, in the case of the first return, since the incorporation of the company.

(*b*) Stating the number of shares held by each of the existing members at the date of the return, specifying shares transferred since the date of the last return (or, in the case of the first return, since the incorporation of the company) by persons who are still members and have ceased to be members respectively and the dates of registration of the transfers.

(*c*) If the names aforesaid are not arranged in alphabetical order, having annexed thereto an index sufficient to enable the name of any person therein to be easily found.

(6) All such particulars with respect to the persons who at the date of the return are the directors of the company and any person who at that date is the secretary of the company as are by this Act required to be contained with respect to directors and the secretary respectively in the register of the directors and secretaries of a company.

It should be noted that the particulars of members as required in paragraph (5) refers to those who were members on the fourteenth day after the annual general meeting. If the company so wishes, the *full* particulars required by paragraph (5) need be given only once in any three years, provided that particulars of those becoming or ceasing to be members and of transfers since the last Return are given in the other years.

The Return need not be made either in the year of the company's incorporation or, if it is not required by S. 131 to hold an annual general meeting in the following year, in that year.

The Return is required to be submitted on a prescribed form.

Company not having a Share Capital

A company with no share capital must provide the above information except that required under paragraph (5) of the Sixth Schedule (S. 125).

Private Company

S. 128 states that a private company must submit with the Return a statement or statements that it continues to qualify for the status of a private company.

(*a*) A certificate, signed by a director and the secretary, must be presented to the effect that since the date of incorporation (in the case of a first Return) or since the date of the last Return, the company has not issued any invitation to the public to subscribe for any shares or debentures of the company.

(*b*) Should the number of members exceed fifty, there must be another statement, similarly signed, to the effect that the excess of the number of members over fifty consists wholly of the persons who, under S.28, are not to be included in reckoning the number of fifty.

19

RECONSTRUCTIONS AND AMALGAMATIONS

Radical changes in the structure or control of a company may take one of several forms or a combination of forms, as follows:

(a) By a reduction of capital to make the accounts more realistic as a preliminary to reconstruction.

(b) By a scheme of arrangement under S. 206, whereby a compromise is made between the company and its creditors or its members.

(c) By a scheme of arrangement with its creditors under S. 306 when a company is in the process of being wound up.

(d) By a sale of the undertaking under a power in the Memorandum.

(e) By a sale of the undertaking to a new company in exchange for shares under S. 287.

(f) By a sale of shares by the holders to another company in order to facilitate an amalgamation, where S. 209 may be applicable.

The terms 'reconstruction' and 'amalgamation' are not defined in the Acts but the interpretations generally accepted are as follows.

Reconstruction means the transfer of the undertaking of a company to a new company, whereby the shareholders of the old company are entitled to receive shares or other interests in the new company.

Amalgamation means the combination of two or more companies into a new company or the acquisition of control of one company by another.

Scheme of Arrangement under S. 206

A scheme under the Act may be used to enable the rights of a class of shareholders to be varied where no provision to do so is contained in the Articles (see page 172). The term 'arrangement' (to quote the Act) includes a reorganisation of the share capital by the consolidation of shares of different classes or by the division of shares into shares of different classes or by both methods. Its other purpose is to effect a compromise with creditors of the company. A scheme of arrangement may be part of a reconstruction and provisions to facilitate this are contained in S. 208 (see below). The essential ingredients of a scheme are:

(a) A proposed 'arrangement' in specific terms between the company and the other parties.

182

(*b*) The ordering by the Court of the convening of a meeting of the parties affected.

(*c*) The approval of the scheme by specified majorities.

(*d*) The Court's sanction of the scheme.

(*e*) The binding of all parties to the terms of the scheme.

The Procedure

The procedure, as prescribed by Ss. 206 and 207, is as follows:

(1) Application must be made to the Court for permission to hold a meeting of such creditors or members or any class thereof as are affected by the scheme. The application may be made by the company or any of the affected parties. If the company is in the process of winding up, the application may be made by the liquidator.

(2) The Court will then order the calling of the meeting. With the notice must be sent a statement:

(*a*) Explaining the effect of the proposed arrangement; and

(*b*) In particular, detailing any material interests of the directors, whether as directors or members or creditors or otherwise, and the effect thereon of the compromise in so far as it is different from the effect on the like interests of other persons. The obvious purpose of such a clause is to prevent the directors (who usually propose the scheme) from concealing any advantage they may have over other parties to the scheme. It is the duty of a director to give notice to the directors of such particulars as may be necessary for inclusion in the notice of the meeting. If debenture-holders are affected by the scheme, a similar statement must be made in respect of any trustees for the debenture-holders.

(3) A resolution must be passed at the meeting in favour of the scheme by a *majority in number* of those affected, present and voting personally or by proxy, *representing three fourths in value*. For example, 20 creditors owed £10 each would not be able to outvote 8 creditors owed £100 each. Also, the majorities are of those *voting* (which differs from the ruling in a S. 306 scheme).

(4) If the Court grants approval of the compromise it becomes binding on the company and on those who are party to the arrangement, or, in the case of a company being wound up, on the liquidator and the contributories. The Court is not bound to sanction the scheme even if the requisite majorities vote in favour of it. The Court acknowledges that those affected by the scheme are likely to be the best judges, however, and it would be slow to differ from their view (*Re English, Scottish and Australian Chartered Bank* (1893)). Nevertheless, the Court will consider the scheme as to its likely effect on the interests of the class as a whole. In *British American Nickel Corporation v. M. J. O'Brien* (1927) it was stated that:

'The power to approve a scheme must be exercised for the purpose of benefiting the class as a whole and not merely individual members only. ... While usually a holder of shares or debentures may vote as his interests direct, he is subject to the further principle that where his vote is conferred on him as a member of a class he must conform to the interests of the class itself.'

(5) A copy of the Court order must be delivered to the Registrar, and an order sanctioning a scheme has no effect until it is so delivered. A copy of an approving order must be annexed to every copy of the Memorandum of the company issued after the order is made.

The Scheme as Part of a Reconstruction or Amalgamation

S. 208 enables the Court to make such ancillary orders as may be necessary to facilitate a reconstruction or amalgamation of which a scheme under S. 206 is a part. If, under the scheme, the whole or part of the undertaking or property of the company is to be transferred to another company, the Court may make an order providing for all or any of the following matters:

(*a*) The transfer to the transferee company of the whole or part of the undertaking and the property or liabilities of the transferor company. (This would be effected by vesting orders, which merely require registration.)

(*b*) The allotting by the transferee company of shares, debentures or other like interests in that company.

(*c*) The continuation by or against the transferee company of any legal proceedings pending for or against the transferor company.

(*d*) The dissolution, without winding up, of the transferor company.

(*e*) The provision to be made in respect of persons who dissent from the scheme.

(*f*) Such incidental, consequential or supplemental matters as may be necessary to effect the reconstruction or amalgamation.

A copy of such an order must be filed with the Registrar within seven days.

The Court cannot order the transfer of *personal* contracts, such as service contracts (*Nokes v. Doncaster Amalgamated Collieries Ltd* (1940)) or rights and duties of personal representatives (*Re Skinner* (1958)).

Scheme of Arrangement in winding up under S. 306

There is provision under S. 306 for a compromise with *creditors* when a company is in the course of being wound up or is about to wind up. To be effective, the scheme must be sanctioned by an extraordinary resolution of the company, and three fourths of the creditors in number *and* value must agree (that is, any creditor not voting at all would be counted as being *against* the agreement). Any creditor or contributory may appeal to the Court against the arrangement within three weeks of the agreement.

This method is rarely used because the requirements of S. 206 regarding the proportion of the creditors to be in agreement is less demanding.

A Sale of the Undertaking under S. 287

The principle of a reconstruction under S. 287 is that a company winds up voluntarily, in the course of which its assets and undertaking are transferred to another company. The members of the transferor company receive shares or other interests in the transferee company.

A special resolution must be passed by members of the transferor company to authorise the sale and to empower its liquidator either to:

(*a*) Receive in compensation or part-compensation, shares or other like interests in the transferee company for distribution among the members of the transferor company; or

(*b*) Enter into another arrangement whereby the members may, in lieu of receiving cash, shares or other like interests in the transferee company or in addition thereto, participate in the profits or receive any other benefits from the transferee company.

If the above conditions are complied with, the sale or arrangement is binding upon the members (subject to the rights of dissentient shareholders as indicated below). The special resolution will not be invalid by reason of it being passed before or concurrently with the resolution to voluntarily wind up, but if an order by the Court for winding up the company is made within a year it *will* be invalid unless sanctioned by the Court.

The shares must be distributed to the members in strict accordance with their rights to share in the assets on a winding up (*Griffith v. Paget* (1877)).

Dissentient Shareholders

Although the approval of only a three quarters' majority is required to approve the scheme, the section does allow a dissentient shareholder to avoid being bound by the agreement. If a member did not vote in favour of the special resolution he may express his dissent by a written notice to that effect, addressed to the liquidator and left at the registered office of the company within seven days after the passing of the resolution. He may require the liquidator either to (*a*) abstain from carrying the resolution into effect, or (*b*) purchase his interest at a price to be determined by agreement or arbitration. Any such purchase money must be paid before the company is dissolved. (The option is available to the liquidator, not the member.)

The Articles cannot be framed so as to deprive a dissentient member of his rights under S. 287 (*Payne v. Cork Co. Ltd* (1900)).

A scheme need not be invalid even if the shares to be issued are to be partly paid, thereby putting a liability on a member to pay the balance when called to do so.

A member's protection is his right to express his dissent. If, however, he neither approves the scheme *nor* formally dissents from it, he cannot be compelled to participate. In that case he will abandon his interests in the company, although the scheme may provide for the sale of his interests and for the consideration to be paid to him by the liquidator.

The Creditors

The section does not allow for any objection by creditors of the company because they must be paid their debts in a winding up, unless they have agreed to look to the transferee company for payment. Should they not be paid they may obtain an order for compulsory winding up or winding up under supervision. If this was done within a year of the resolution approving the scheme, the scheme could not be put into operation without the sanction of the Court.

In a *creditors'* voluntary winding up, the liquidator's powers under S. 287 are subject to the sanction of the Court or the Committee of Inspection (S. 298).

Amalgamation by Purchase of Shares

The Takeover Bid

Effective control of a company is in the hands of those holding a majority of voting shares because of their power to appoint and remove directors. If one company wishes to amalgamate with another company, it can do so if it persuades a sufficient number of the latter's shareholders to sell their voting shares. This is the principle of the 'takeover bid'. If the offers are accepted, the bidding company becomes the holding company of the other. A member of a listed public company has an unfettered right to sell his shares to whomsoever he wishes. Accordingly, the directors of a 'victim company' may not thwart that right if they disapprove of the proposed merger. The law will not interfere and, in fact, the Act facilitates such a merger.

In practice, most bids are not contested, because they result from an agreement between the two boards of directors which is supported by the other shareholders. And, of course, a bid cannot succeed against the wishes of directors holding the controlling shares.

A bid is subject to certain constraints, however:

The *Prevention of Fraud (Investments) Act, 1958*. Those provisions relevant to false or misleading statements in circulars have relevance to documents circulated in the course of a bid.

The *Fair Trading Act, 1973*. A proposed merger may become impossible if it is referred to the Monopolies and Mergers Commission and as a result of which the Secretary of State declares that a monopoly situation would exist that would be against the public interest.

The City Code on Takeovers and Mergers. This is not part of the law and therefore has no 'legal teeth'. It is, however, effective in that it lays down an extensive code of practice which is adhered to by financial bodies. It is a method whereby the City 'keeps its own house in order' by voluntarily subscribing to a set of rules so as to prevent the perpetration of questionable practices which might otherwise occur. The terms of the code are made more stringent from time to time as events appear to make necessary.

The Legal Provisions

S.209 allows the transferee company compulsorily to acquire the shares of a dissenting minority if the following conditions are met:

(*a*) There must be a scheme or contract involving the transfer of shares (or any class of shares) to the transferee company. That is, there must be an offer on specific terms made to all the holders of the shares which the bidding company wishes to acquire. It would not refer to 'piecemeal' purchases whereby the proposed transferee company made different offers to certain shareholders at various times.

(*b*) The offer must be accepted by the holders of not less than nine tenths in value of the shares involved, excluding any already held by the bidder, its subsidiary or a nominee of either.

(*c*) The acceptances must have been made within four months of the offer being made.

(*d*) The transferee company may, at any time within two months after the expiration of the above four months, give notice in the prescribed form to any dissenting shareholder that it wishes to acquire his shares on the same terms as had been accepted by the other holders.

(*e*) Within one month of the notice being served on him, a dissenting member may make application to the Court expressing his dissent. The attitude of the Court, however, would be to deem the offer to be a fair one unless the dissenting shareholder could prove otherwise (*Re Grierson, Oldham and Adams Ltd* (1967)). The onus of proof would therefore be on the dissenting member, but the Court would not approve a scheme which is intended to enable the majority shareholders to expropriate the shares of a minority (*Re Bugle Press Ltd* (1960)).

(*f*) Unless the Court has ordered to the contrary, the transferee company must then:

(*i*) send a copy of the notice to acquire the shares to the transferor company, together with a transfer executed *on behalf of the shareholder* by any person appointed by the transferee company and *on its own behalf*; and (*ii*) pay or transfer to the transferor company the consideration for the dissenting member's shares. The transferor company must then register the transferee company as the holder of those shares. The consideration received by the transferor company must be paid into a separate bank account and held in trust by the company for the person entitled to the shares for which the consideration was received.

The transferee company has the option of exercising or not exercising its power of compulsory purchase (*Re Carlton Holdings Ltd* (1971)). The section states, however, that *if* it has given notice to a dissenting shareholder, the transferee company is entitled *and bound* to acquire his shares on the terms accepted by the majority holders.

Where the transferee company already holds more than one tenth of the shares involved before the offer is made, the provisions of S.209 will *not* apply unless (*a*) the same terms are offered to all other holders of the shares and (*b*) those accepting the offer, besides holding nine tenths in value, are also not less than three fourths in number of those holders.

As previously stated, the transferee company need not serve notice on a dissentient member of its intention to acquire his shares. However, if, as a result of a scheme under S.209, a company has nine tenths of the relevant shares (including any it had before the scheme), it must, within one month from the date the shares were acquired, inform any dissenting shareholders of that fact. A dissentient shareholder may then, within a further three months, give notice in the prescribed form requiring the transferee company to acquire his shares. The company would then be entitled *and bound* to acquire the shares on the same terms as applied to the earlier transactions or on otherwise agreed terms. Alternatively, the terms may be decided by the Court on application by the company or the shareholder.

Compensation for Loss of Office

It is often a condition in a takeover scheme that some or all of the directors of the company being taken over should resign. In addition to the requirements of the City Code as to disclosures of the effect of a bid on directors, the Act makes specific provisions.

S.192 states that if, in connection with the transfer of the whole or part of the undertaking of a company, a payment is to be made to any director as compensation for loss of office, particulars of the proposed payment must be disclosed to the members and approved by the company. Any payment made which is not so disclosed and approved must be held by him in trust for the company.

Under S.193, a director has a duty to take all reasonable steps to ensure that particulars of any such payment are included in or sent with any notice given to the shareholders of an offer for their shares. This applies in connection with:

(*a*) An offer made to the general body of shareholders.

(*b*) An offer made by or on behalf of another body corporate with a view to the company becoming that body's subsidiary.

(*c*) An offer made by or on behalf of an individual with a view to his obtaining the right to exercise control of not less than one third of the voting power at any general meeting of the company.

(*d*) Any other offer which is conditional upon acceptance to a given extent.

Thus, although a director may not be a party to a circular concerning a bid, he must ensure that anyone else issuing a statement includes in it particulars of any compensation which would be due to the director under the arrangement.

If, under any of the above circumstances, a director is paid more for his shares than could at that time have been obtained by other shareholders, or any valuable consideration is given to the director, the excess or the money valuation of the consideration is deemed to have been paid as compensation.

Any of the payments referred to above which are *bona fide* payments of damages for breach of contract or by way of pension for past services, are not included in the payments envisaged in the above sections (S. 194).

By Sale under a Power in the Memorandum

Power may be (and usually is) contained in the objects clause of the Memorandum to sell the undertaking of a company to another company in exchange for shares in that company. The transferor company would be wound up and shares in the transferee company distributed to members of the old company.

Because the company is 'proposed to be or is in the course of being wound up', the provisions of S. 287 will apply in respect of the distribution of the shares (*Bisgood v. Henderson's Transvaal Estates* (1908)), thus giving dissentient members specified rights (see below).

20

DISSOLUTION

The Processes

The legal existence of a company can be terminated only as a result of a positive action; a company cannot simply die. The processes leading to dissolution may be summarised as follows:

(*a*) *By an order of the Court without winding up* under S. 208 where a reconstruction or amalgamation is being undertaken (see page 184).

(*b*) By striking a '*defunct company*' off the register. If the Registrar has reasonable cause to believe that a company is not carrying on business, he may write to the company to enquire if that is in fact the case. If no reply is received within a month he must within fourteen days thereafter send a further letter stating that no reply was received to the first letter and that if no reply is received to the second letter within one month a notice would be published in the *Official Gazette* with a view to striking the company's name off the register. If no reply is received within that time or a reply confirms that the company is not carrying on business, a notice would be published in the *Official Gazette* and a copy of it sent to the company. The notice will state that, unless cause is shown to the contrary, the company will be dissolved and its name struck off at the expiration of three months from the date of the notice.

If winding up of a company has commenced and the Registrar has cause to believe that no liquidator is acting, or that the affairs of the company are fully wound up but returns have not been made by the liquidator for a period of six successive months, a similar notice as above will be published and a copy sent to the company or the liquidator as the case may be. Notice of dissolution will be published in the *Official Gazette* but (*a*) any liability of a director or member will continue and may be enforced, and (*b*) the Court will still have power to wind up the company.

If the company or any member or creditor feels aggrieved by the striking off, application may be made to the Court within twenty years of the dissolution. If the Court is then satisfied that the company was carrying on business at the time of being struck off or otherwise that it is just that the company be restored to the register, it may order the name to be restored (S. 353).

(*c*) *By winding up* under Part V of the 1948 Act and subject to the *Winding up Rules* (see below).

Dissolution Declared Void

At any time within two years of the date of dissolution, the Court may, on application of the liquidator or any other interested party, make an order declaring the dissolution to have been void. Proceedings may then be taken as if the company had not been dissolved. The person who makes the application must, within seven days after the making of the order, deliver to the Registrar a copy of the order (S. 352).

Winding Up

S. 211 specifies that winding up may be:

(*a*) By the Court ('compulsory winding up') (see Chapter 21); or
(*b*) Voluntary (see Chapter 22); or
(*c*) Subject to the supervision of the Court (see Chapter 22).

The provisions of the Act relevant to winding up apply to all the above modes except where the contrary is stated. *Those provisions which are common to all modes are given in this chapter; those specific to any one mode are given in the chapter devoted to that mode.*

The process of winding (which is also known as **liquidation**) entails:

(*a*) The surrender of control of the company's affairs by the directors to a liquidator.
(*b*) Applying the assets of the company in satisfaction of its debts and the costs of the liquidation.
(*c*) Returning any surplus assets to those entitled to them.

Liability of Past and Present Members

S. 213 defines a **contributory** as a person liable to contribute to the assets of a company in the event of its winding up. S. 212 establishes the liability of contributories as follows:

(*a*) Every past and present member is liable to contribute to the assets of the company to an amount sufficient for payment of its debts and the costs of winding up, and for the adjustment of the rights of the contributories among themselves.
(*b*)(*i*) The liability is limited to the amount unpaid on the shares in the case of a company limited by shares. (*ii*) The liability in the case of a guarantee company is the amount undertaken to be contributed in the event of winding up, but additional to any amount unpaid on the shares.
(*c*) A past member is not liable if he ceased to be a member for one year or upward before commencement of the winding up.

(*d*) A past member is not liable to contribute in respect of any debt contracted by the company after he ceased to be a member.

(*e*) A past member is not liable to contribute if it appears that the present members are able to satisfy the contributions required of them.

(*f*) Any sum due to a member in his capacity as a member may not compete with the claims of creditors who are not members. His claim on the company would be taken into account in the final adjustment of the rights of the contributories among themselves.

(*g*) A past or present director with unlimited liability is liable, in addition to his liability as a member, as though he were a member of an unlimited company, except:

(*i*) he is not liable if he ceased to be a director for a year or upward before winding up;

(*ii*) he is not liable for company debts contracted after he ceased to hold office;

(*iii*) he is not liable (subject to the Articles) unless the Court deems it necessary for him to contribute.

The liability of a contributory is in the nature of a specialty debt (S. 214).

The personal representative of a contributory who has died is liable to contribute in due course of administration (S. 215). The trustee of a contributory who is bankrupt becomes a contributor and the company may prove in the bankruptcy in respect of present and future calls (S. 216).

Possible exceptions to the above general provisions are as follows:

(*a*) Upon the winding up of an unlimited company re-registered as a limited company (S. 44 (1967)) (see page 10).

(*b*) Where directors have been party to fraudulent trading (S. 332) (see page 195).

Debts of the Company

Proof of Debts

If the company is solvent at the time of winding up, all debts and claims against it, whether present or future, certain or contingent, ascertained or sounding only in damages, may be admitted to proof; where necessary, a just estimate of the value is made. If the company is insolvent, the rules of bankruptcy apply as to such matters as proof by secured creditors, rights of set-off, etc. (Ss. 316, 317).

Order of Payment

The assets must first be applied in payment of all fees and costs incurred in the process of winding up. Then follow preferential debts, ordinary debts and deferred debts.

Preferential Payments

S.319 states that the following debts must be paid in priority of all other debts:

(*a*) All local rates due and payable during the previous twelve months; one year's taxes (i.e. the Inland Revenue is not restricted to any particular year).

(*b*) Wages for services rendered during the previous four months. Under S.63 of the *Employment Protection Act, 1975*, certain other payments are to be treated as wages.

(*c*) Accrued holiday remuneration payable to an employee on the termination of his employment.

The limit per claimant under (*b*) and (*c*) has been increased to £800 by the *Insolvency Act, 1976*.

(*d*) Employers' contributions in respect of National Insurance benefits payable within the preceding twelve months.

(*e*) Sums due by the company on account of tax deductions under PAYE for the preceding twelve months.

These debts rank equally among themselves. If they cannot be paid in full they must abate in equal proportions. They have priority over claims in respect of debentures secured by a floating charge and may be paid out of any property subject to such a charge. The priority is lost, however, if the floating charge crystallizes before the winding up (see page 108) (*Re Griffin Hotel Ltd* (1940)).

Fraudulent Preference

If those controlling a company were aware that it was insolvent and that liquidation must ensue, they could so arrange the company's affairs that when winding up commenced some creditors would be in a deliberately created secure or preferential position. S.320 provides that the rule in bankruptcy must apply so as to make illegal any such manipulation. Any conveyance, mortgage, delivery of goods, payment, execution or other act relating to property made or done by or against the company within six months before commencement of winding up, which would have been invalid in a personal bankruptcy, would likewise be invalid in the event of winding up. Any such action would be deemed a 'fraudulent preference'.

It would be so regarded only, however, if it could be shown that there was *intention* improperly to favour a creditor. Thus, the execution of a charge on company property in favour of a bank was not regarded as being fraudulent, because it was accepted that the purpose was to keep on good terms with the bank in the expectation of future help (*Re F.L.E. Holdings Ltd* (1967)).

Effect of a Floating Charge

If a floating charge on the undertaking or property of a company is created within twelve months before commencement of winding up it is invalid (unless it can be proved the company was solvent immediately after creation of the charge), except as to the amount of cash paid together with interest at 5 per cent or such other rate as prescribed by order of the Treasury (S. 322). In other words, if the company was insolvent when the floating charge was created it will not cover past indebtedness, but a creditor (particularly a bank) is assisted by the Rule in *Clayton's Case* (1816) as applied by the Court of Appeal in *Re Yeovil Glove Co., Ltd* (1965) whereby credits paid in to an overdrawn account will reduce the old (uncovered) debt, and subsequent withdrawals will be covered by the floating charge. In this way, turnover on the account may make the charge fully effective before the 'hardening period' of one year has passed.

Disclaimer of Onerous Property

S. 323 prescribes that the liquidator may disclaim any part of the property of the company which consists of:

(*a*) Land burdened with onerous covenants.
(*b*) Shares or stock in companies.
(*c*) Unprofitable contracts.
(*d*) Property which is unsaleable or not readily saleable because of the binding of the possessor to the performance of any onerous act or the payment of money.

Disclaimer must be made within twelve months of commencement of winding up and with leave of the Court. However, the party interested in any disclaimed property may serve notice on the liquidator requiring him to decide whether he will disclaim or not. If the liquidator does not, within twenty-eight days, give notice of his intention to apply for leave to disclaim, the company will be deemed to have adopted the contract.

Offences by Officers of Companies in Liquidation

Ss. 328 to 330 and the *Theft Act, 1968*, provide a lengthy list of offences which could make a past or present officer of a company being wound up guilty of a misdemeanour. They include failure to disclose to the liquidator all property, books of accounts and papers of the company and failure to deliver those in his custody or control; failure to make full and true statements concerning the company's affairs; concealing or removing property of the company; failing to disclose a false debt; concealing, destroying, mutilating or falsifying company documents; obtaining goods on credit for the company by fraud; carrying on business for a fraudulent purpose or to defraud creditors.

S. 332 makes a person personally liable for all or any of the debts of the company as the Court directs, if in the course of winding up it appears that any business of the company has been conducted with intent to defraud creditors or for any fraudulent purpose.

S. 333 states that if it appears that any person who has taken part in the formation or promotion of the company, or any past or present directors or officers, who has misapplied or retained any property of the company or been guilty of any misfeasance or breach of trust, the Court may examine into his conduct and order him to repay or restore the property or contribute to the assets by way of compensation as the Court thinks fit.

S. 334 contains provisions for referring the matter to the Director of Public Prosecutions where it appears in the course of winding up that any past or present officer or any member has been guilty of an offence for which he is criminally liable.

Notification of Liquidation in Business Letters, etc.

If a company is in the course of being wound up, every invoice, order or business letter on which the company's name appears must contain a statement that the company is being wound up (S. 338).

Company Books as Evidence

All books and papers of the company and of the liquidator are, as between the contributories, *prima facie* evidence of the truth of all matters to be recorded therein (S. 340).

Disposal of Books and Papers

Books and papers of a liquidated company may be disposed of:

(*a*) As the Court directs, in the case of a winding up by or under the supervision of the Court.

(*b*) As the company directs by extraordinary resolution, in the case of a members' voluntary winding up.

(*c*) As the Committee of Inspection (or the creditors if there is no Committee) directs, in the case of a creditors' voluntary winding up.

After five years from the dissolution of the company, no responsibility will rest on the company, the liquidator or any person to whom custody of the books and papers was committed, by reason of any books or papers not being forthcoming (S. 341).

Pending Liquidations

In the event of a winding up not being concluded within a year, the liquidator must submit to the Registrar at such intervals as are prescribed statements containing prescribed particulars regarding the progress of the liquidation (S. 342).

Unclaimed Assets

All money representing assets which is unclaimed for six months after becoming payable must, in the case of a company registered in England, be paid into the Insolvency Services Account at the Bank of England. Any person claiming entitlement to such sums may apply for an order for repayment (S. 343 as amended by the *Insolvency Act, 1976*).

The provisions concerning companies registered in Scotland are contained in S. 344.

Meetings to Ascertain Wishes of Creditors or Contributories

As to all matters relating to a winding up, the Court may have regard to the wishes of the creditors or contributories. For the purpose of ascertaining those wishes it may direct the calling of meetings of the creditors or contributories. Regard would be had of the value of each creditor's debts. In the case of contributories, regard would be had of the number of votes conferred by the Act or the Articles (S. 346).

The Liquidator

The rules concerning the appointment of the liquidator and those powers and duties of a liquidator which are specific to any one mode of winding up are given in Chapter 21 or Chapter 22 as relevant.

Appointment

A body corporate is not qualified for appointment as liquidator and any such appointment would be void (S. 335).

It is an offence for a person to offer any financial inducement to a member or a creditor to secure his own appointment as liquidator or to prevent the appointment of some other person (S. 336).

The person appointed as liquidator should not be someone closely associated with the directors, particularly if it appears that the board's conduct may require investigation (*Re Charterland Goldfields Ltd* (1909)).

Powers and Duties

In general, the duties of a liquidator are to bring into his control all the property of the company (including any calls due from members); ascertain, agree and pay the company's debts; and, if necessary, adjust the rights of the contributories as between themselves. Finally, he must distribute any surplus assets among those entitled to them.

Upon liquidation, the board of directors becomes *functus officio* and the liquidator assumes its powers. Accordingly, the liquidator may be regarded as being a fiduciary agent of the company, in the same way that the directors were. As a company continues to exist as a legal entity during winding up, its property does not vest in the liquidator (as is the case in a personal bankruptcy), so that contracts made by the liquidator are made on behalf of the company. The extent of any *control* on a liquidator is as specified in relation to a particular mode of winding up.

It follows, therefore, that the liquidator is not a trustee in the full sense of the word. He is not liable for his negligence, although action may be brought against him for 'statutory negligence' if a member or creditor suffers financial loss by the liquidator's breach of statutory duty, such as paying creditors in the wrong order (*Pulsford v. Devenish* (1903)).

If a liquidator defaults in filing, delivering or making any return or in giving any notice as required of him by law and fails to make good the default within fourteen days of a notice requiring him to do so, the Court may, on application by any contributory or creditor or the Registrar, order the liquidator to make good the default within a specified time (S. 337).

21

WINDING UP BY THE COURT

The Compulsion to Wind up

A winding up by the Court is otherwise known as a **compulsory winding up,** so called because it derives from a Court order following a petition to the Court. Although a company may petition, it is unlikely to do so because it would obviously prefer a voluntary liquidation.

Reasons for Winding up

S. 222 states that a company may be wound up by the Court in the following circumstances:

(1) *If the company so resolves by special resolution.*

(2) *Upon default in delivering the Statutory Report or in holding the Statutory Meeting.* Only a contributory may petition if the Statutory Report has not been delivered or the Statutory Meeting has not been held. Any such petition may not be made before the expiration of fourteen days after the last day on which the meeting ought to have been held (S. 224(1)(b)). As an alternative to making an order, the Court may direct that the Report be delivered or the Meeting held (S. 225(3)).

(3) *If the company does not commence business within a year of incorporation or it suspends business for a whole year.* The Court has only *discretionary* power to order a winding up in either of these instances. It would normally do so only if it appeared that the company had no intention of carrying on business (*Re Capital Fire Insurance Association* (1882)).

(4) *If the membership falls below the statutory minimum.* In such a circumstance, the usual procedure would be for the company to wind up voluntarily. Because so few members would be involved, the Court would normally refuse to order a winding up.

(5) *If the company is unable to pay its debts.* S. 223 (as amended by the *Insolvency Act, 1976*) defines inability to pay debts as follows:

(*a*) If a creditor owed £200 by the company has served on the company a written demand for payment and the company has for three weeks thereafter failed to pay the sum or to secure or compound it to the reasonable satisfaction of the creditor; or

(*b*) If an execution or a judgment, decree or court order in favour of a creditor is returned unsatisfied; or

(c) If the Court is satisfied that the company is unable to pay its debts.

(6) *If the Court is of the opinion that it is just and equitable that the company be wound up.* What is 'just and equitable' is not defined in the Act, but examples of orders made under this rule are as follows:

(a) Where the main object of the company has ceased to exist or become impossible to achieve (*Re German Date Coffee Co.* (1882)).

(b) Where the company was formed for a fraudulent purpose (*Re T. E. Brinsmead & Sons* (1897)).

(c) Where the company is merely a 'bubble'; that is, there was no intention of carrying on business in a proper manner (*Re Anglo Greek Steam Co.* (1866)).

(d) Where there is deadlock, such as two members, each holding half the shares, in continuous disagreement (*Re Yenidje Tobacco Co. Ltd* (1916)).

(e) Where the directors, holding a majority of voting shares, refuse to give information to the members, or to hold meetings, etc. (*Loch v. John Blackwood Ltd* (1924)).

(f) Where a director is prevented from exercising his functions (*Re Davis and Collett Ltd* (1935)).

S.225(2) states that a petition by the members on this ground will succeed if the Court is of the opinion that the petitioners are entitled to relief and that, although some other remedy is available, it would be just and equitable to wind up the company. If some other remedy is available to the members and they are acting *unreasonably* in petitioning, however, they must pursue that other remedy. A minority of members complaining of oppression have an alternative to compulsory winding up in that they may apply to the Court for relief under S.210 (see page 174).

The Right to Petition

S.224 prescribes that the following may petition the Court for the winding up of a company:

(a) **The company**, by passing a special resolution.
(b) **Any contributory**, except that no petition may be made unless:
    (i) the number of members is reduced below the statutory minimum; or
    (ii) some of the contributory's shares have been held by him for at least six months during the preceding eighteen months or were devolved on him through the death of a former member or he was an original allottee.

It is unusual for a contributory to petition, and no order would be granted unless the petitioner could maintain that the rights of the contributories would be prejudiced by a *voluntary* winding up (S.310). Also, no order would be granted unless it could be shown that assets would be available to the shareholders after payment of the creditors; if there are to be no surplus assets the contributory would have no interest in the winding up (*Re Expanded Plugs Ltd* (1966)).

(*c*) **Any creditor.** There is no requirement that the debt must be £200 or over, but the Court is unlikely to grant an order if the debt is less than that sum. Where the debt is contingent or prospective, the creditor must present a *prima facie* case for winding up and give security for the costs. If the debt is disputed by the company the Court would not normally grant an order and it may even grant an injunction to prevent the creditor from petitioning (*Niger Merchants Co. v. Capper* (1877)). Alternatively, the Court may decide the validity of the debt (*Re Imperial Silver Quarries* (1868)).

(*d*) **The Official Receiver.** A petition may be made by the Official Receiver after a voluntary winding up has commenced, but the Court must be satisfied that the voluntary winding up cannot be continued with due regard to the interests of the creditors and the contributories.

The Department of Trade may petition under S. 35 (1967) if it appears from any report made by its inspectors that it is in the public interest the company be wound up (see page 168).

The Procedure in Outline

(1) The petition is presented.

(2) The Court hears the petition.

(3) A winding up order is made and the Official Receiver becomes the provisional liquidator.

(4) A Statement of Affairs is submitted to the Official Receiver.

(5) The Official Receiver submits a preliminary report to the Court.

(6) Meetings of the creditors and the contributories are convened by the Official Receiver to decide about the appointment of a liquidator and a Committee of Inspection.

(7) The liquidator (and, where so agreed, a Committee of Inspection) is appointed.

(8) The liquidator settles the list of contributories and proceeds with the liquidation.

(9) The liquidator calls further meetings as necessary or as requested.

(10) On completion of the winding up, the liquidator applies to the Court for an order dissolving the company.

(Some of the provisions given below derive from the Act where so stated; the others are prescribed in the *Winding up Rules*.)

The Petition

Presentation of the Petition

The petition must be presented to the Registrar of the appropriate Court and supported by an affidavit. It must give the date of incorporation of the company; the address of its registered office; its capital; its objects; and the grounds for petitioning. It must be advertised seven clear days before the date fixed by the Court Registrar for the hearing. The advertisement must contain the name and address of the petitioner and of his solicitor, and include an invitation to persons wishing to appear at the hearing to certify their intention to do so.

A copy of the petition must be served on the company (unless the company is the petitioner) or on the liquidator if the company is already in voluntary liquidation.

The Court may restrain the presentation where it considers it would cause irreparable damage to innocent shareholders or would injure the goodwill of the company (*Mann v. Goldstein* (1968)). It would take similar action if it considered the presentation was vexatious or an abuse of the Court (*Charles Forte Investments Ltd. v. Amanda* (1964)).

At any time after presenting the petition and before the hearing, the company, any creditor or any contributory may apply to the Court (*a*) to stay any action against the company (S. 226), or (*b*) to appoint a provisional liquidator (S. 238). This may be in order to safeguard the assets of the company. Such an appointment automatically serves as a stay of action against the company.

A petition may not be withdrawn except with leave of the Court.

Hearing the Petition

S. 225 prescribes that the Court may:

(*a*) Dismiss the petition; or
(*b*) Adjourn the hearing, conditionally or unconditionally; or
(*c*) Make an interim order; or
(*d*) Make any other such order as it thinks fit (see page 199, *Just and Equitable*, and page 198, *Statutory Report and Meeting*); or
(*e*) Make an order for winding up.

An order may not be refused on the ground only that the assets have been mortgaged to an amount equal to or in excess of those assets or that the company has no assets.

Commencement of Winding up

The winding up commences (*a*) at the time of presentation of the petition, except that (*b*) if there has been a resolution to wind up voluntarily it dates from that resolution (S. 229).

Any disposition by the company of its assets after commencement is void, unless the Court orders otherwise. The same prohibition applies in respect of share transfers and any alteration in the status of the members (S. 227).

Any attachment, sequestration, distress or execution enforced against the estate or effects of the company after commencement of winding up is void to all intents (S. 228).

(The commencement date is referred to as 'the relevant date'.)

Consequences of a Winding-up Order

(*a*) A copy of the order must forthwith be forwarded by the company to the Registrar (S. 230). The order does not become effective, as against any person who cannot be shown to have knowledge of the fact, until the fifteenth day after the Registrar has notified receipt of the document in the *Official Gazette* (S. 9, *European Communities Act, 1972*).

(*b*) The order operates in favour of all creditors and contributories as if made on the joint petition of a creditor and a contributory (S. 232).

(*c*) The Official Receiver becomes the provisional liquidator (S. 239).

(*d*) No action may be taken against the company without leave of the Court (S. 231).

(*e*) All servants of the company are discharged and a servant is released from any restrictive clause in his service contract (*Measures Bros Ltd v. Measures* (1910)).

The Court has power to stay the proceedings after the order has been made, on application by the liquidator or Official Receiver or any contributory or creditor, on such conditions as it thinks fit (S. 256).

The Statement of Affairs

S. 235 states that within fourteen days of the relevant date there must be submitted to the Official Receiver a statement of affairs, verified by affidavit, setting out:

(*a*) Particulars as to the company's assets, debts and liabilities.

(*b*) The names, addresses and occupations of its creditors, the securities held by them respectively and when they were given.

(*c*) Any other information the Official Receiver may require.

Those liable to submit the Statement of Affairs are:

(*a*) One or more of the directors and the secretary at the relevant date; or

(*b*) Such of the following as the Official Receiver, subject to direction by the Court, may require:

(*i*) Past or present officers of the company.

(*ii*) Persons who took part in the formation of the company within a year before the relevant date.

(*iii*) Persons who are or within the previous year were employees of the company.

(*iv*) Officers or servants of a company which was an officer of the company in liquidation.

Such persons may claim for any costs and expenses incurred in making the statement. Creditors and contributories may inspect the statement and be supplied with a copy or extract.

Preliminary Report by the Official Receiver

As soon as practical after receiving the Statement of Affairs, the Official Receiver must submit a preliminary report to the Court, stating:

(*a*) The amount of capital issued, subscribed and paid up, and an estimate of the assets and liabilities.

(*b*) The causes of the failure.

(*c*) Whether he considers that further investigation is desirable as to the promotion, formation or failure of the company or the conduct of its business (S. 236(1)).

Further Report by the Official Receiver

The Official Receiver may make a further report if he considers that fraud has been committed or if there is any other matter he considers should be brought to the notice of the Court (S. 236(2)). The making of such a report gives the Court the powers provided by S. 270 to order the public examination, under oath, of those suspected of fraud in relation to the promotion of the company or in relation to the conduct of the company's affairs, or any officer of the company.

The Liquidator

(*See also the general provisions set out on page* 196.)

Appointment

The Court may appoint a liquidator to wind up and perform such duties thereto as the Court may impose (S. 237). S. 239 and the *Winding Up Rules* prescribe as follows:

(*a*) The Official Receiver becomes the provisional liquidator and acts until he or another person becomes the liquidator.

(*b*) The Official Receiver must summon separate meetings of creditors and contributories to decide whether or not to apply to the Court for the appointment of a liquidator other than the Official Receiver. The meetings must be held within a month of the winding-up order or within six weeks if a Committee of Inspection is to be appointed (see page 205). It must be advertised and at least seven days' written notice must be given to each creditor and contributory. With the notice must be sent a summary of the Statement of Affairs with the Official Receiver's observations. Notice must also be served on any officer required to attend and give evidence.

If the creditors and the contributories disagree as to who is to be the liquidator, a decision will be made by the Court.

By S.240 a liquidator must notify his appointment to the Registrar and give such security as is required.

The remuneration of the liquidator is determined by the Court (S. 242), except that it is fixed by the Committee of Inspection if one is appointed.

Resignation, Removal and Release

A liquidator appointed by the Court may resign or, on cause shown, be removed by the Court (S.242(1)). If he wishes to resign, he must summon separate meetings of the creditors and contributories. If they agree to accept his resignation, he must file a memorandum of resignation with the Court and notify the Official Receiver, and his resignation thereupon becomes effective. If the meetings do not accept his resignation the Court will make the decision.

A creditor or contributory may call for the removal of the liquidator. 'Cause shown' generally means unfitness for the office, failure to carry out statutory duties, bias in relation to certain parties, etc. If a Receiving Order in bankruptcy is made against a liquidator he is thereupon deemed to be removed.

If a liquidator has resigned or been removed or has completed the winding up, he may apply for his release. He must submit his final account for audit and report thereon by the Department of Trade (S. 251). Previously, he must notify his intention to the creditors and contributories and send them a summary of his receipts and payments.

Powers of the Liquidator

S.245(1) states that in a winding up by the Court, the liquidator may, *with the sanction of the Court or a Committee of Inspection*:

(*a*) Bring or defend actions in the name of the company.

(*b*) Carry on the business so far as is necessary for its beneficial winding up.

(*c*) Appoint a solicitor to assist him in his duties.

(*d*) Pay any class of creditors in full.

(*e*) Make compromises with creditors, debtors and contributories.

S.245(2) states that the liquidator may, *without sanction*:

(*a*) Sell property and things in action of the company.

(*b*) Execute deeds, receipts and other documents on behalf of the company, and use the company's seal for that purpose.

(*c*) Draw, accept, and endorse bills of exchange and promissory notes in the name of the company.

(*d*) Prove in the bankruptcy of a contributory.

(*e*) Raise money on the security of the assets.

(*f*) Take out in his own name letters of administration to any deceased contributory.

(*g*) Appoint an agent to do any business he is unable to do himself.

(*h*) Do all other things necessary for the winding up and distribution of the assets.

In exercising his powers, S.246 states that, subject to the provisions of the Act, the liquidator:

(*a*) *May* summon meetings of creditors and contributories in order to ascertain their wishes.

(*b*) *Must* summon meetings:

(*i*) if the creditors or contributories so direct by resolution; or

(*ii*) on the written request of one tenth in value of the creditors or contributories.

(*c*) Must have regard to any directions given:

(*i*) by resolution of the creditors or contributories in general meeting; or

(*ii*) by the Committee of Inspection. (In case of conflict, the former will override the latter.)

The liquidator may apply to the Court for direction on any particular matter, and a person aggrieved by an act or decision of the liquidator may also apply.

Books and Accounts of the Liquidator

S.247 requires the liquidator to keep records of meetings, etc., as are prescribed.

S.248 makes regulations concerning sums to be paid into an account with the Bank of England.

S.249 requires the liquidator to submit accounts of his receipts and payments, and provides for their audit.

Committee of Inspection

At the first separate meetings of creditors and contributories after a winding-up order is made, a decision must be made as to whether application should be made to the Court for the appointment of a Committee of Inspection, and who would be the members of the committee. The function of such a committee is to act with the liquidator (S.252).

S.253 prescribes that the committee members will be creditors and contributories or persons holding general powers of attorney for them, in such proportions as are agreed in meeting or determined by the

Court. The committee must meet at least once a month. The liquidator or any committee member may call a meeting. A quorum is a majority of the members and decisions are made by a majority present at the meeting.

A member may resign upon written notice to the liquidator. A member must vacate office if he absents himself from five consecutive meetings without leave of its members, or if he becomes bankrupt or compounds with his creditors. A member may be removed by an ordinary resolution of those he represents, i.e. creditors or contributories. The liquidator must summon a meeting of creditors or contributories to fill any vacancy, but he may, if he considers it unnecessary to fill the vacancy, apply for a Court order to that effect.

If no Committee of Inspection is appointed, the Department of Trade may exercise its functions (S. 254).

List of Contributories

Following a winding-up order, the liquidator must settle a list of contributories, rectify the register of members where so required by the Act, collect the assets of the company and apply them in discharge of its debts. Where it appears to the Court that it will be unnecessary to make calls and adjust the rights of contributories, the Court may dispense with settlement of a list of contributories (S. 257).

A 'contributory' is defined in S. 213 and their liabilities are set out in S. 212 (see page 191). In preparing the list, those who were members at the time of commencement of the winding up will appear in the 'A' list. Past members as defined will be shown in the 'B' list.

The Court will adjust the rights of the contributories among themselves and distribute any surplus to the persons entitled thereto (S. 265).

Bringing in the Assets

The liquidator must take into his custody or under his control all the property and choses in action to which the company is entitled (S. 243). The Court, on the liquidator's application, may order that such property shall be vested in the liquidator in his official name and that he may thereafter bring or defend any actions in respect thereof in his official name (S. 244).

The Court may order any contributory to deliver to the liquidator any money, property or documents to which the company is *prima facie* entitled (S. 258). The Court may order any contributory to pay any money due from him to the company (S. 259). The Court may make calls on all or any of the contributories on the list to meet the company's debts (including the costs of the winding up) and to adjust the rights of contributories between themselves (S. 260).

Under S. 268 the Court has power to summon before it, for examination on oath, any officer of the company, any person known or suspected to have property of the company or to owe it money, or any person who may be able to give information about the company's promotion, formation, trade, dealings or property. It may also order production of any books or documents relating to the company.

S. 271 gives the Court power to order the arrest of any absconding contributory and the seizure of his books, papers and movable personal property if there is cause to believe he is attempting to leave the United Kingdom to avoid payment of calls or to avoid examination.

Debts of the Company

The Court may fix the time within which creditors are to prove their claims, failing which they would be excluded from any distribution (S. 264).

Payment of the company's debts is by way of declaration of dividends by the liquidator. Not more than two months before doing so, he must notify his intention to the Department of Trade. He must also notify any creditors mentioned in the Statement of Affairs who have not yet proved their debts, stating the final date for lodging proof. Notice of payment of the dividend must be given to the Department of Trade and to every creditor whose proof has been admitted.

22

VOLUNTARY WINDING UP AND WINDING UP SUBJECT TO SUPERVISION

A voluntary winding up is any liquidation instigated by the company. That is, it is not *imposed* on a company as is a winding up by the Court.

A **creditors' voluntary winding up** is a dissolution caused by the insolvency of the company.

A **members' voluntary winding up** is any other voluntary winding up.

Circumstances Leading to a Voluntary Winding up

A company may be wound up voluntarily:

(*a*) If it passes an **ordinary resolution** to do so. This would apply if an event had occurred which, by the Articles, calls for the liquidation of the company. Alternatively, if the duration of the life of the company as prescribed in the Articles has expired, then it must be wound up. Thus, the intention when such a company was formed would have been to limit its existence by specified circumstances, e.g. it may have been formed to complete a particular project and then wind up.

(*b*) If it passes a **special resolution** to do so; that is, there are other reasons than those stated above and the company is solvent.

(*c*) If it passes an **extraordinary resolution** to do so because it cannot continue its business by reason of its liabilities (S. 278).

Any of the above resolutions is referred to in the Act as 'a resolution for voluntary winding up'. Notice of it having been passed must be advertised in the *Official Gazette* within fourteen days (S. 279). The commencement of the winding up dates from the time of passing the resolution (S. 280).

Provisions Specific to all Forms of Voluntary Winding up

(*a*) The company ceases to carry on business, except so far as is required for its beneficial winding up (S. 281).

(*b*) Any transfer of shares and any alteration in the status of the members is void, unless sanctioned by the liquidator (S. 282).

(*c*) The servants of the company are not *ipso facto* dismissed (*Midland Counties Bank Ltd v. Attwood* (1905)), unless the liquidation is on the ground of insolvency (*Fowler v. Commercial Timber Co.* (1930)).

(*d*) After making preferential payments (see page 193) and the costs of the winding up, the assets of the company must be applied in satisfaction of its liabilities *pari passu*. Any surplus, subject to any contrary Article, must be distributed to the members according to their rights and interests in the company (Ss. 302 and 309).

(*e*) The liquidator or any creditor or contributory may ask the Court to determine any question concerning the winding up, or to exercise any of the powers the Court could exercise in a compulsory winding up (S. 307).

(*f*) A creditor or contributory is not barred from petitioning for the company to be wound up by the Court, but in the case of an application by a contributory the Court must be satisfied that the rights of the contributories would be prejudiced by a voluntary winding up (S. 310).

The Liquidator in any Form of Voluntary Winding up

Within fourteen days of his appointment, the liquidator must publish in the *Official Gazette* and deliver to the Registrar a notice of his appointment (S. 305). The Court has power to remove a liquidator and appoint another (S. 304).

By S. 303 a liquidator may exercise the following powers given under S. 245 to a liquidator of a company being wound up by the Court:

(*a*) To pay any class of creditor in full.

(*b*) To compromise with creditors.

(*c*) To compromise all calls, debts, liabilities and claims, taking security therefor and giving complete discharges.

Any exercise of such powers must be with the sanction of an extraordinary resolution in the case of a *members'* voluntary winding up, or with the sanction of the Court or Committee of Inspection (or the creditors if there is no such committee) in the case of a *creditors'* voluntary winding up.

The liquidator may also:

(*a*) Exercise any other power of a liquidator in a compulsory winding up, *without sanction* (see page 204).

(*b*) Settle the list of contributories.

(*c*) Make calls.

(*d*) Summon general meetings of the company in order to obtain its sanction by special or extraordinary resolution or for any other purpose he thinks fit.

He must pay the company's debts and adjust the rights of the contributories among themselves.

Members' Voluntary Winding up

The distinguishing feature of a members' voluntary winding up is that it commences with the assumption that the company is solvent. The procedure for such a winding up starts in the board room before the members' resolution to wind up is passed, as shown below.

The Statutory Declaration of Solvency

S. 283 prescribes as follows:

(a) At a meeting of the directors (or the majority of them if there are more than two directors), the directors must make a statutory declaration that having made a full enquiry into the affairs of the company they are of the opinion that the company will be able to pay its debts in full within a stated period (not exceeding twelve months) from the commencement of the winding up.

(b) The declaration must:

(i) be made within five weeks preceding the date of the winding-up resolution and be registered with the Registrar before that date; and

(ii) embody a statement of the company's assets and liabilities as at the latest practical date before the making of the declaration.

(c) Any director making such a declaration without having reasonable grounds for his opinion is liable to a fine and imprisonment. If a company is subsequently shown to be unable to pay its debts within the stated period it would be presumed that the director did not have reasonable grounds for his opinion, unless the contrary is proved.

The Liquidator

(*See also the provisions set out on page* 196 *and page* 209).

The liquidator is appointed by the members in general meeting and they may also fix his remuneration. The powers of the directors then cease, except so far as the company in general meeting or the liquidator sanctions otherwise (S. 285). Any vacancy in the office of liquidator may be filled by the company in general meeting (S. 286).

If the business or the property of the company is to be transferred or sold to another company, the powers of the liquidator are as prescribed by S. 287 (see page 185).

In the event of the winding up continuing for more than a year, the liquidator must call a general meeting of the company on the first (and, if necessary, subsequent) anniversary of the commencement of the winding up, or at the first convenient date within three months thereafter (S. 289).

If during the winding up the liquidator comes to the conclusion that the company will *not*, in fact, be able to pay its debts within the period stated in the directors' declaration, he must forthwith call a meeting of the creditors and lay before it a statement of the company's assets and liabilities (S. 288). From that time, the winding up would continue as a creditors' voluntary winding up and the provisions of Ss. 299 and 300, relevant to meetings and dissolution (see below), would apply (S. 291).

Dissolution

As soon as the company's affairs are fully wound up, the liquidator must lay before a general meeting of the company an account of the winding up, showing how it had been conducted and how the company's assets had been disposed of. This meeting must be called by advertisement in the *Official Gazette* at least one month before the meeting. Within a week after the meeting the liquidator must send a copy of the account to the Registrar and make a return of the holding of the meeting. On the expiration of three weeks from registration of the return the company would be deemed to be dissolved, although the Court may, on the application of the liquidator or any interested party, defer the date of dissolution (S. 290).

Creditors' Voluntary Winding up

S. 283 (4) states that a winding up where a declaration of solvency has *not* been made is referred to as 'a creditors' voluntary winding up'. As, therefore, the assumption is that the company is insolvent, the proceedings of a creditors' voluntary winding up give powers to the creditors. This contrasts with a members' voluntary winding up where it is assumed that the creditors' interests are not in jeopardy.

The First Meeting of Creditors

S. 293 prescribes that on the day the company in general meeting resolves to wind up (or on the day following), a meeting of the creditors must be held. The notices for both meetings must be sent on the same day. The notice of the creditors' meeting must also be advertised in the *Official Gazette* and in two local papers. At the creditors' meeting the directors must (*a*) submit a full statement of the company's affairs, a list of the creditors and an estimate of the amount of their claims, and (*b*) appoint a director to preside.

Should the members' meeting be adjourned without resolving to wind up, any resolution passed by the creditors will be deemed to have been passed immediately after the resolution to wind up *was* passed. Thus, the creditors' meeting does not have to be adjourned if the members' meeting is adjourned.

The Liquidator

(*See also the provisions set out on page* 196 *and page* 209).

The members and the creditors may each nominate a liquidator at their respective meetings. If they nominate different persons the creditors' nomination will prevail, but any director, member or creditor may, within seven days after the nomination, apply to the Court for an order directing that the members' nominee be appointed instead of or jointly with the creditors' nominee or for an order appointing some other person (S.294).

The remuneration of the liquidator may be fixed by the Committee of Inspection (see below) or by the creditors if there is no committee (S. 296(1)).

All powers of the directors cease on the appointment of the liquidator, except so far as the Committee of Inspection or the creditors sanction otherwise (S.296(2)).

The creditors may fill any vacancy in the office of liquidator (S.297).

Should the winding up continue for more than a year, the liquidator must summon meetings of the members and the creditors on the first anniversary of the commencement of the winding up (and on subsequent anniversaries, if necessary) or within three months thereafter. He must lay before the meeting an account of his conduct of the winding up during the preceding year (S.299).

Dissolution

The provisions relevant to members' voluntary winding up contained in S.290 (see page 211) also apply to creditors' voluntary winding up, except that separate meetings of creditors and members must be called (S.300).

Committee of Inspection

The creditors in meeting may appoint a Committee of Inspection of not more than five members. If the creditors do so, then the members may also appoint up to five members, but the creditors have the right to reject such nominees unless the Court directs otherwise.

The provisions of S.253 relevant to Committees of Inspection in compulsory windings up (see page 205) also apply to this committee (S.295).

Winding up Subject to Supervision of the Court

S.311 prescribes that when a company has passed a resolution for voluntary winding up, the Court may make an order that the winding up will continue but under such supervision of the Court as the Court thinks fit. A petition for such a winding up is deemed to be a petition for winding up by the Court to the extent that the Court may stay actions pending against the company (S.312).

The petition may be made by the liquidator, the company, a creditor or a contributory. This right is rarely exercised, however, because S.307 allows the liquidator or any dissatisfied contributory or creditor to ask the Court to decide any question relating to the winding up (see page 209).

The effects of a supervision order are as follows:

(*a*) The liquidator must report on a specified date the present position of the winding up and the realisation of the assets, and any other matter as the Court directs. Similar reports must be made thereafter at three-monthly intervals.

(*b*) The winding up is deemed to commence on the date of the resolution for voluntary winding up (S. 229(1)).

(*c*) For the purposes of Ss. 227 and 228 (see page 202), the winding up is regarded as being a winding up by the Court (S. 313).

(*d*) The Court has power to appoint and remove a liquidator and to fill any vacancy (S. 314).

(*e*) The liquidator may, subject to the terms of the Court order, exercise his powers in a voluntary winding up without sanction of the Court, except that he may not pay classes of creditors in full or make compromises with creditors, debtors or contributories without the Court's approval. In the case of a previous creditors' voluntary winding up, the sanction of the Court or the Committee of Inspection or the creditors would be required (S. 315).

23

OTHER CONSTRAINTS ON COMPANIES

References are made in relevant parts of the book to regulations other than those contained in the Companies Acts which may affect companies. Not all of these are in the form of statutes, some of them being directives (e.g. by the Stock Exchange) which do not have the force of law, though failure to follow them may mean loss of advantages. A summary of the constraints imposed by the more important of these provisions are given below.

European Communities Act, 1972

This Act became operative on 1st January, 1973, and S.9 became the first measure for bringing United Kingdom company law into line with practice in the rest of the Community.

Some of the most fundamental changes were those relevant to contracts made on behalf of companies. The principle in *Turquand's case* was extended and underlined by decreeing that a contract may not be set aside on the ground that it is *ultra vires* the company's capacity or beyond the directors' powers, provided it is one 'decided upon by the directors'. Until the scope of this rule is interpreted in the Courts it is uncertain whether this would relate only to transactions authorised or ratified by the board *collectively* or if it would also be applicable to acts by a single director. Certainly, the Act is clear that a *promoter* contracting on behalf of a company yet to be formed would be personally liable.

Another important change was in respect of returns made to the Registrar which affect the constitution of the company. The Act requires the Registrar to publish in the *Official Gazette* notification of receipt by him of the following documents:

(*a*) Any which makes or evidences an alteration in the Memorandum or the Articles. (The company is required also to send a printed copy of the Memorandum or Articles as altered.)

(*b*) Any return relating to the Register of Directors and of any change of directors.

(*c*) An Annual Return.

(*d*) Notification of the situation of the company's registered office and of any change in its situation.

(*e*) A copy of a winding-up order.

(*f*) Any order for dissolution of the company on winding up.

(*g*) A liquidator's return of a final meeting in winding up.

A company may not rely on the effect of any of the documents (*a*), (*b*), (*e*) or (*f*) above, as against any person who cannot be shown to have known the facts or events of which the document is evidence, until the fifteenth day after publication in the *Official Gazette*. A company may not also rely on the filing of item (*d*) above in respect of documents served on it at its registered office.

The Act extended the requirements of S. 201 of the *Companies Act, 1948*, in that letterheads, etc., must show the company's place of registration, the address of its registered office and its company number. If the document states the company's capital (there is no requirement to do so), then the figure must be of its *paid-up* capital. There must be given an indication that the company is a limited company if it has been permitted to dispense with the word 'Limited' in its name. A concession is given in that the nationality of a director is not required to be stated in the Register of Directors and on company literature if he is a national of one of the Community member-states.

Protection of Depositors Act, 1963

Certain companies invite the public to make *deposits* with them, with the promise of a fixed rate of interest and redemption at a fixed date or upon notice by the depositor. Such investments do not participate in the profits of the company and, accordingly, are not shares; they contain promises in respect of interest and redemption but they are not debentures. On both counts, therefore, the various forms of protection afforded by the Companies Acts are not available and the aim of the Act is to provide for those who are induced by advertisement to deposit sums of money.

Any such advertisement must comply with Department of Trade regulations, as set out in the Act and as amended by the *Companies Act, 1967*, as to disclosures to be made. Thus, such an advertisement would be controlled so as to provide protection in the same way as does a prospectus issued under the Companies Acts. Audited accounts must be lodged with the Registrar before the advertisement is published and at annual intervals thereafter (unless the company has issued no advertisement for fifteen months and is retaining no deposits). Copies of the audited annual accounts must be sent to every depositor.

Penalties are prescribed for making statements which are misleading, false or deceptive or which are made (dishonestly or otherwise), whereby a person is induced to invest money on deposit.

Prevention of Fraud (Investments) Act, 1958

A person applying for securities on the basis of a prospectus or making deposits in response to an advertisement has protection under the relevant statutes. The above Act (as amended by the *Protection of Depositors Act, 1963*) aims to protect persons who are induced by other means to invest in companies.

It prohibits any person from carrying on business as a dealer in securities unless he has been licensed to do so by the Department of Trade—that is, he holds a 'principal's licence'. Exempted from this prohibition are members of the Stock Exchange, the Bank of England, statutory and municipal corporations, and managers and trustees of authorised unit trusts, but the Act imposes control over brokers and dealers and those concerned with unit trusts to prevent the evils of 'share hawking'. For example, it is provided that a licensed dealer may only call on a person at his residence at the person's request. ('Call' includes a telephone call.) If a call is made on request then the dealer must give the person a written statement of the basic elements of the proposal.

Under the Act it is an offence for any person to make a statement, promise or forecast, which he knows to be misleading, false or deceptive, or which makes a dishonest concealment of material facts, or which is made recklessly (dishonestly or otherwise), to induce a person to enter into an agreement to acquire or dispose of securities.

Theft Act, 1968

By S.19(1) of this Act an officer of a company may be liable to imprisonment for a term not exceeding seven years if, with intent to deceive members or creditors of the company about its affairs, he publishes or concurs in publishing a written statement or account which he knows to be or may be misleading, false or deceptive in a material particular. Such a person would be guilty even though neither he nor the company obtained property as a result of the false statement. For example, he would be liable if the result of his statement was to induce members to retain their shares and they thereby suffered financial loss. The section refers to *any* statement and need not be one in a prospectus.

S.15(1) provides the offence of obtaining property by deception. This would cover a false statement dishonestly made in a prospectus or statement in lieu of prospectus which induced the payment of money to the company. The maximum penalty is ten years' imprisonment.

S.17(1) provides that where a person dishonestly, with a view to gain for himself or another or to cause loss by another, destroys, defaces, conceals or falsifies any account, record or document made or required for any accounting purpose or in furnishing information for any purpose, produces or makes use of any account or such record or document which to his knowledge is or may be misleading, false or deceptive in a material particular, is liable to imprisonment for a period not exceeding seven years.

S.18(1) provides that where an offence committed by a company under Sections 15 or 17 is proved to have been committed with the consent or connivance of any director, manager, secretary or other similar officer, or any person purporting to act in such capacity, such person as well as the company is guilty of that offence.

Fair Trading Act, 1973

Reference is made in Chapter 19 to the fact that a merger may be thwarted because it would result in an 'unacceptable' monopoly. The above Act continued the functions of the Monopolies Commission (now known as the **Monopolies and Mergers Commission**) which was set up under the *Monopolies and Mergers Act, 1965*. The Commission is required to investigate any circumstance referred to it by the Director General of Fair Trading which may indicate the existence, or possible existence, of a monopoly. The Commission would then report to the Secretary of State if it considered a monopoly did or may exist which is against the public interest. An order may then be made providing such powers as may be necessary to remedy or prevent the unacceptable situation.

The Secretary of State may himself make a reference to the Commission where a *contemplated* merger appears to qualify for investigation, such a circumstance possibly existing, of course, when a takeover bid is mooted.

A monopoly situation is regarded as existing when at least one quarter of the goods or services of any description are supplied by or to one person; or by or to members of related bodies; or by or to two or more persons who are not members of interconnected bodies. It would also exist when at least one quarter of all the exports of any description are produced by one person or by interconnected bodies.

The Admission of Securities to Listing

The only securities which can be dealt in on the Stock Exchange are those which have been 'admitted to listing'. Almost invariably, the directors of a public company will wish its securities to be listed because investors would be reluctant to subscribe for them unless the facilities of the Stock Exchange were available. There are obvious difficulties if a security cannot be sold on the open market and where daily valuations are not published.

To obtain admission, the company must apply to the Stock Exchange through the offices of its broker and by so doing it will bind itself to regulations which go beyond those prescribed by law. To be considered, the anticipated market valuation of the listed securities must be at least £500,000 and each class of share must have an anticipated value of at least £200,000. In the case of a first application, there would follow an extensive investigation of the antecedents of the company and those connected with it. The Stock Exchange would also require to approve the prospectus and may well insist on the inclusion of information not demanded under the law. Similarly, the Articles would have to include clauses beyond those required by the Companies Acts.

The directors must personally subscribe to a document known as the **Listing Agreement** and their concurrence must be evidenced in the minutes of a board meeting. This agreement consists of a lengthy series of undertakings. They include promises immediately to notify the Stock Exchange of any changes in the directorate; any proposed changes in the general nature of the business; any alteration in voting control; and any other information necessary to avoid the creation of a 'false market' in the securities. Immediate notification following a board meeting must be made of the profit figures (yearly or half-yearly), any exceptional factors in the period and the dividends to be recommended. The directors are also required to forward copies of all notices, circulars, etc., sent to members (other than those relevant to routine matters at the annual meeting).

The Stock Exchange will also regulate the content of various documents, such as share certificates, proxy forms, trust deeds, etc.

The City Code on Takeovers and Mergers

'This code is issued on the authority of the City Working Party, a body originally set up by the Governor of the Bank of England in 1959, for the purpose of considering good business practice in the conduct of takeovers and mergers. It does not have the force of law but represents the collective opinion of those professionally concerned in the field of takeovers and mergers on a range of business standards. Those who wish to have the facilities of the securities market in the United Kingdom available to them should conduct themselves in matters relating to takeovers and mergers according to the City Code; those who do not so conduct themselves cannot expect to enjoy those facilities and will find that they are withheld.'

The above quotation from the preamble to the Code explains its philosophy. It is a standard of conduct subscribed to by financial interests and which has proved to be effective without having 'legal teeth'. The very extensive set of rules has been amended from time to time as circumstances indicated the necessity to do so.

The administrative body is the **Panel on Takeovers and Mergers**, headed by a Director General. If there appears to have been a breach of the code, the person(s) concerned are invited to appear before the Panel for a hearing. There is provision for appeal against rulings by the Panel. If necessary, the Panel may have recourse to a private reprimand or public censure. In extreme cases it may deprive an offender of his ability to enjoy the facilities of the securities market. Where necessary, aspects of a case may be referred to the Department of Trade, the Stock Exchange or some other appropriate body.

The Panel and its secretariat are continuously available and interested parties are invited to consult with it from the earliest stages of a prospective bid. Its success has achieved its purpose in that the City has shown it can impose its own discipline and that extensive government control on the US pattern is unnecessary.

Appendix 1

REVISION QUESTIONS

Listed below are subject areas which could form the basis of examination questions. The items are not necessarily in examination form and, where appropriate, include guidance to what the answer should contain.

Chapter/question

2/1 Itemise the distinctive features as they differ between private companies and public companies as regards: (*a*) transferability of shares (may a public company restrict transfer; what usual rules apply in private companies?); (*b*) the minimum and maximum number of members (are there exceptions?); (*c*) commencement of business; (*d*) number of directors.

2/2 What is the position of a private company if it acts contrary to those provisions relevant to private companies? How can a private company change its status to public company? If it does change, what alternative forms must be filed?

2/3 Define an overseas company. What information must it display at its places of business and in its literature in this country?

3/1 List the rights a company may have against its promoter in respect of profits he makes.

3/2 Explain 'promotion services', 'preliminary expenses' and 'pre-incorporation contracts'. In respect of the last, explain the position of a person contracting in respect of the company's affairs before the company is incorporated. (Consider the *European Communities Act*.)

3/3 Who must sign the following documents upon registration of a company: (*a*) The Memorandum and Articles; (*b*) The declaration of compliance; (*c*) Particulars of Directors and Secretaries?

3/4 What is the effect of a Certificate of Incorporation being issued?

3/5 By what methods may a company bind itself to contracts? (Include companies operating outside the UK.)

4/1 Recite the contents of the Memorandum.

4/2 What power has the Registrar to refuse to register a proposed name of a company? (The 'guidelines' are not part of the law.) What special provisions apply in respect of overseas companies?

4/3 Name the two circumstances in which a company may be *directed* to change its name, and the two circumstances in which a company may *request* to change its name. What rules apply in each case? Give examples of 'passing off'.

4/4 What provisions apply concerning use of 'Limited' in a company's name? How are the provisions of the Companies Act concerning dispensation from use of the word amended by the *European Communities Act*?

4/5 What relevance may the *Registration of Business Names Act* have to limited companies?

4/6 When must the situation of the registered office be notified? (Amended in the 1976 Act.)

4/7 The law establishes the principle of the substratum in the objects clause. What is the effect of this principle and how has it been avoided to some extent?

221

4/8 What limitations are there to a company's ability to alter its objects? Outline the procedure to do so, assuming that an unsuccessful objection to the alteration was made. (Include references to the periods of time involved.)

4/9 What regulations concerning alteration of the Memorandum and the Articles were introduced by the *European Communities Act*?

4/10 Would an alteration of the Articles be permitted if it adversely affected a section of the members? (Would it constitute 'oppression'? Consider the general attitude of the Court to objections.)

4/11 Consider the following relationships which are established when the Memorandum and Articles are registered: (*a*) each member/the company; (*b*) the company/each member; (*c*) members/members (consider the position of a member *as* a member). Can such relationships have any reference to outside parties?

4/12 Relate the 'doctrine of constructive notice' to 'Turquand's Rule'. (Explain 'public documents'.)

4/13 Under what circumstances may a contracting party not successfully plead 'Turquand's Rule'?

4/14 Consider the relevance of the following references in S. 9 of the *European Communities Act* to 'Turquand's Rule': (*a*) 'good faith' of the party dealing with the company; (*b*) the transaction being one 'decided upon by the directors'; (*c*) 'within the capacity of the company'; (*d*) the directors' powers being 'free of any limitation' in the Memorandum or Articles.

5/1 Explain the legal significance of a prospectus being regarded as an advertisement. (Consider the principle of offer and acceptance.)

5/2 Is an invitation made 'to the public' in the following circumstances? (*a*) When a rights issue is made (is it renounceable?). (*b*) When it is limited to business acquaintances (is it a 'domestic' concern?). (*c*) When an exchange of shares was offered in a merger proposal. (Explain 'issued generally'.)

5/3 What is the broad difference between Part I and Part II of the Fourth Schedule?

5/4 When is a full prospectus not required?

5/5 The report of an expert was contained in a draft prospectus. How does he indicate his consent to its inclusion? What can he do if he wishes to withdraw his consent (*i*) before the prospectus is registered, (*ii*) after it is registered? (Ss. 40, 41, 43.)

5/6 What authority does the law give the Stock Exchange in respect of 'abridged prospectuses'?

5/7 Is an offer for sale a prospectus? What additional information must the former contain?

5/8 What principles apply in determining if a misstatement has been made in a prospectus?

5/9 An investor refuses to take up shares he has been allotted and claims repayment of the amount paid. What must he prove if he is claiming that a misrepresentation had been made in the prospectus?

5/10 What right exists for damages against a company if a misrepresentation in a prospectus was made (*a*) innocently, (*b*) fraudulently? (Refer to the *Misrepresentation Act*.)

5/11 What rights are there against *persons* where there has been misrepresentation in a prospectus? (Damages in tort for deceit under 1948 Act.)

5/12 What *criminal* proceedings can be taken in respect of misrepresentation in a prospectus? (The 1948 Act and the *Theft Act* are relevant.)

5/13 Concerning statements in lieu of prospectus, when would (*a*) the Third Schedule and (*b*) the Fifth Schedule be applicable? What is the purpose of filing such a statement?

6/1 What time-scale in respect of the opening of the subscription lists is applicable in respect of (*a*) revocation of applications and (*b*) allotment?

6/2 What is the minimum subscription? What is the reason for determining it? What relevance has it to the allotting of shares?

6/3 Explain 'admission of securities to listing'. What is the responsibility of directors concerning application moneys if admission is not granted? (Quote the relevant time-scales.)

6/4 When is an allotment (*a*) void, (*b*) voidable, (*c*) not void?

6/5 When must a return of allotments be made and what must it contain? (Explain 'consideration other than cash'. The 1976 Act requires particulars of premiums.)

6/6 When may (*a*) a private company and (*b*) a public company commence business? In the case of a public company, what statutory declaration must first be made? (Requirements for a Trading Certificate.) What would be the position if a company entered into a contract before it received its Trading Certificate?

6/7 What can the Share Premium Account be used for?

6/8 What restrictions apply to payment of commission in respect of an issue of shares? Do they apply to an issue of debentures? What disclosures must be made?

6/9 What are the exceptions to the general principle that no financial assistance may be given by a company towards the purchase of its shares?

7/1 When is membership deemed to commence in respect of (*a*) the subscribers, (*b*) the first directors and (*c*) other members? Explain the significance of the entry date and the date membership ceased as shown in the Register of Members.

7/2 What conditions apply in respect of the following becoming members? (*a*) A limited company. (*b*) An infant. (*c*) A partnership. (The law differs as between England and Scotland.) (*d*) Joint holders.

7/3 List the rights to inspect the Register of Members and to receive copies, and the limitations on those rights.

7/4 When should a person demand rectification of the Register of Members and what is the procedure for doing so?

7/5 What does a share certificate indicate? To what extent may a company be estopped from denying the validity of a certificate? (Consider the validity of a certificate issued following submission of a forged transfer.)

7/6 Has a member complete freedom to transfer his shares and to whoever he pleases? (Consider private companies, pre-emption and expropriation; public companies, listed or unlisted.)

7/7 In what respects does the instrument of transfer as prescribed in the *Stock Transfer Act* differ from 'the common form of transfer'? (Articles still requiring use of the latter are not operative.)

7/8 Explain the use of blank transfers.

7/9 *A* sells his shares to *B* on 10th January. The latter is entered in the Register of Members on 17th January. Concerning the intervening period, what is the position regarding any dividends paid, meetings held and calls made?

7/10 What action must follow the issue of a share certificate based on a transfer which was forged? What rights have the 'transferee', the true owner and the company?

7/11 What is meant by 'certification of transfer' and why is it done? What responsibilities does it impose on the company?

7/12 Explain (*a*) charging order, (*b*) garnishee order, (*c*) injunction or restraining order as regards company securities.

7/13 What liability may attach to a person whose shares have been forfeited? Has a company direct authority by law to forfeit shares?

7/14 Discuss the priority of any lien a company may have in respect of its shares. (S. 117 may be relevant.)

7/15 What rights has the personal representative of a deceased shareholder? Would the position be different if the deceased was a joint holder of the shares?

8/1 Define a 'director' as understood in law. Give an example of a person so regarded, although not registered as a director.

8/2 What provisions apply concerning consents by persons to act as directors? (Those named before incorporation; the first directors; subsequent directors.)

8/3 *X*, acting as a director, made contracts on behalf of a company. Would those contracts be enforceable if it was subsequently found that the director did not have the necessary qualification shares when he was 'appointed'?

8/4 What are the rules concerning directors' service contracts?

8/5 Compare 'appointment of an alternate director' and 'assignment of office' by a director.

8/6 To what companies does S. 185 (concerning 'over-age' directors) apply?

8/7 In a company to which S. 185 applies, when must an over-age director retire and how may he be reappointed?

8/8 Under what circumstances may a director be disqualified by Court Order? (S. 188, S. 28 (1976).)

8/9 *X* is not due to retire by rotation at the next annual general meeting, but *A* wishes to propose at that meeting that *X* be removed from office. Timetable the events up to the voting at the meeting, assuming that *X* takes measures to resist dismissal.

8/10 The directors of *A* Ltd committed an act which was a breach of trust. At that time, *F* was the secretary. *F* subsequently became a director. At his first board meeting a decision was taken which effectively confirmed and continued the earlier breach. To what extent, if any, would *F* be liable in respect of the breach?

8/11 At the January board meeting of a company a proposed contract with a firm was discussed. At that time, director *A* was a member of the firm. Director *B* became a partner in the firm in February. The contract was confirmed at the March board meeting. In April, director *C* became an agent of the firm, being paid commission on sales. How would those directors be affected by the rule concerning disclosure of interests in contracts?

8/12 Could the directors in question 8/11 vote on the contract in board meetings? How could advantage be taken of the legal provisions concerning 'general notice'?

8/13 *S* holds 1,000 ordinary shares and £2,000 in debentures in *T* Ltd. He then joins the board of directors and at the same time receives the right to subscribe for debentures in *T* Ltd. Two months later he sells his debentures in *T* Ltd, and uses the proceeds to buy more ordinary shares in *T* Ltd and to take up his right to subscribe for debentures in the subsidiary. What information must he pass to *T* Ltd in respect of these transactions and within what periods of time?

8/14 Would *S* (above) have to declare interests in shares of *T* Ltd held by the following? (*a*) *AB* Ltd, in which *S* holds one quarter of the voting shares. (*b*) A trust set up for his family, (*c*) his adopted infant daughter, (*d*) himself jointly with *V* on behalf of a golf club.

8/15 State the information to be recorded by *T* Ltd, the style of recording and when it must be made, in respect of *S* as outlined in questions 8/13 and 8/14. Must this information be passed to the Stock Exchange and, if so, when?

8/16 A director is removed from office by the members in general meeting. Under what conditions could he (*a*) be *granted* compensation for loss of office and (*b*) *claim* compensation?

8/17 Discuss the importance of *Panorama Developments (Guildford) Ltd v. Fidelis Furnishing Fabrics* as regards the status of the office of secretary.

8/18 Would it be illegal for a director (*a*) to receive a loan from a finance company of which he is a director and (*b*) to buy debentures in the company which give him the option to convert them into shares?

9/1 At the last annual general meeting of a company before it was wound up solvent, no dividend was declared on the preference shares. Have the holders any right to the arrears? What right, if any, would the preference shareholders have if, after payment of all debts, there were insufficient resources to repay all the share capital in full? What would be their position if there were surplus funds after all the share capital had been fully repaid?

9/2 What are the permitted resources for repaying redeemable preference shares and any premium then payable?

9/3 In what ways does the procedure following a resolution to increase capital differ from that relevant to other alterations of capital?

9/4 Outline the stages for effecting a reduction of capital.

9/5 A particular capital reduction scheme involves repayment of part of the share capital because the cash resources of the company are beyond its requirements. What action may the Court take if creditors object to the reduction?

9/6 If the Court gives its consent to the above reduction of capital, what conditions may it impose?

9/7 On what principles would the Court act if a capital reduction scheme did not involve creditors?

10/1 What would be the position of a lender if the money was borrowed (*a*) *ultra vires* the objects clause, (*b*) beyond the directors' powers? Under what circumstances would the lender have the right (*c*) to 'trace', (*d*) of subrogation and (*e*) to sue the directors?

10/2 The directors borrow money from *X* on behalf of the company, such action being within their authority, but the money is applied for a purpose *ultra vires* the company's objects. Has *X* any rights?

10/3 Bank Ltd lent money to *A* Ltd, secured by a floating charge on the whole of the assets, on condition that a fixed charge was not subsequently created. The charge was registered with the Registrar. Lenders Ltd later lent money to *A* Ltd, secured by a fixed charge on the company's factory. What is the position of Bank Ltd?

10/4 Who *must* and who *may* register a charge with the Registrar? What is the effect of *not* registering? What can be done if an omission to register is subsequently discovered?

10/5 What particulars must be registered in respect of an issue of a series of secured debentures?

10/6 Under what circumstances would a Memorandum of Satisfaction be entered in the Register of Charges? May the borrowing company have a copy?

10/7 What charges must be entered in the company's Register of Charges which are not required to appear in the Registrar's Register?

10/8 What remedies are available to a secured debenture-holder upon default by the borrower?

10/9 As regards the appointment of receivers and managers, distinguish between 'debenture-holders' action' and 'appointed out of Court'.

10/10 Give examples of debenture-holders' security being 'in jeopardy'.

10/11 For whom is a receiver an agent? (Compare appointment by the Court and appointment by the debenture-holders.)

10/12 What constraints are there on a receiver appointed by the Court compared with those on one appointed by the debenture-holders?

10/13 There are obviously far-reaching consequences if the debenture-holders have a floating charge on the whole of the undertaking. What additional responsibilities are placed on a receiver in those circumstances?

10/14 What are the consequences for (*a*) the directors and (*b*) the employees if a receiver is appointed? (They are not the same in all cases.)

11/1 Could dividends be paid from the following sources? (*a*) An increase of the balance sheet valuation of property to its market value. (*b*) The writing back of goodwill previously written off. (*c*) Undistributed profits of previous years. (*d*) The Share Premium Account.

11/2 The directors paid a dividend out of capital. What liability accrues to the directors? What would be the position of members who received the dividend? (Both questions require qualified answers.)

11/3 The amount of the final dividend is declared by members in general meeting. How true is this in effect?

11/4 When is a dividend payable if (*a*) it is declared in general meeting, (*b*) it is announced by the directors as an interim dividend, (*c*) it is declared but unpaid when a company is wound up? (The payable date may not be the same date a debt by the company is created.)

12/1 Under what conditions may the end of an accounting reference period be altered after that period has ended?

12/2 What accounting requirements concerning stock valuations were introduced in the 1976 Act?

12/3 Who, in addition to those entitled to vote at general meetings, must receive copies of the accounting records?

12/4 For how long must accounting records be preserved? (Dual answer.)

12/5 What accounting records must be laid before a general meeting and filed, and within what periods? (Private companies; public companies.) What penalties may accrue upon default? (Directors and the company.) What must the directors do before presenting the accounts? (Ss. 155 and 156.)

12/6 Define (*a*) subsidiary company, (*b*) sub-subsidiary company, and (*c*) holding company as set out in the Act. How does the Act specify the circumstances in which a company 'controls the composition of the board of directors'?

12/7 What are group accounts as defined in the Act? What permitted *exceptions* are there to those requirements? (S. 150.) When may the accounts of a subsidiary be *excluded*? (S. 151.)

12/8 The accounts must give particulars of any shares held in another company. How does the 1967 Act distinguish between a subsidiary company and a non-subsidiary for this purpose?

12/9 Directors are required to declare to the company such information as is necessary for the company to give particulars of directors' emoluments in the accounts. What are the two (and, perhaps, three) sets of information to be declared?

12/10 What does the law state concerning loans to *directors* and loans to *officers*? (Refer also to Chapter 8.)

12/11 What disclosures concerning the directors must be made in the Directors' Report?

13/1 Who do the auditors report to and how is the report put?

13/2 What 'qualification' must auditors include in their report in certain circumstances?

13/3 How is an auditor appointed? *A* intends to retire as auditor at the next annual meeting. How would *B* be appointed as the new auditor? Has *A* any rights at that meeting?

13/4 How does an auditor fulfil his duties if the company has subsidiaries?

13/5 Outline the procedure for removing an auditor. What rights has such an auditor?

13/6 *C* resigns his office as auditor because he considers he had insufficient cooperation from the directors. As an exercise, compile a timetable for the complete process from the time the auditor informs the directors.

13/7 An auditor failed to notice irregularities in the accounts and claimed he was deceived by the chief accountant. What factors may decide if the auditor was negligent? As a result of the unqualified report, *A* lent money to the company. The company became insolvent and the loan was irrecoverable. Has *A* any rights against the auditor?

14/1 What is the purpose of the Statutory Meeting and the Statutory Report? What matters may be voted on at the meeting and any adjournment thereof? (Note the special provisions concerning adjourned meetings.)

14/2 Distinguish between 'ordinary business' and 'special business'. Does the former require to be detailed in the notice?

14/3 A company was incorporated on 1st December, 1978. What are the latest dates on which the first and the second annual general meetings may be held?

14/4 A company has four directors and the Articles prescribe the quorum for a board meeting to be three. Two directors resign and no one has taken their place. As a consequence, no annual general meeting has been held. How can the problem be solved?

14/5 Some members require their views on a certain matter to be made known to the body of shareholders. How can they do so in the following circumstances? (*a*) The directors refuse a request to call an extraordinary general meeting to discuss the matter (S. 132). (*b*) The members wish to put a resolution on the matter at the next annual general meeting but the directors refuse to include it in the notice of the meeting (S. 140). (*c*) The item appears in the notice of a forthcoming general meeting.

14/6 State the majority and the length of notice required for each of the following resolutions: (*a*) ordinary; (*b*) extraordinary; (*c*) special.

14/7 Does the Act prescribe minimum lengths of notice of meetings?

14/8 Why is it unlikely that a company (other than a small one) could take advantage of the rule allowing shorter notice of a meeting than that prescribed? Why would the same apply if the notice was invalid? Relate this to the rule for accepting shorter notice for a special resolution.

14/9 Who must receive notice of general meetings? What would be the effect of failure to give notice to a member entitled to receive it?

14/10 What are the rules applicable to Special Notice and under what circumstances must it be given?

14/11 A company has 10,000 ordinary shares in issue, each carrying the right to one vote on a poll. The shares are held by 50 members: 20 members, holding a total of 3,000 shares, attend a general meeting; 2 proxies also attend, representing 2 members holding a total of 400 shares. An ordinary resolution was put to the meeting. (*a*) On a show of hands, 11 members holding a total of 1,100 shares voted in favour. The chairman declared the resolution to be passed and accepted a demand by a proxy for a poll. Was he correct? (*b*) On the poll, the same 11 members voted in favour. The proxies and 6 members holding a total of 600 shares voted against. The remainder abstained. Was the resolution passed?

14/12 The Articles of a company require a special resolution to authorise a certain matter. The resolution was not put as a special resolution because only 14 day's notice of it had been given, but all the members agreed to it. Is there any rule relevant to the filing of the resolution?

14/13 *A* was absent when a poll was demanded on the 1st May. The meeting was adjourned to the 8th May for the poll to be taken. The motion was successful only because *A* attended and voted in favour. The result of the poll was announced on 9th May. Was the resolution effectively passed? What is the effective date of a resolution validly passed in such circumstances?

14/14 To what extent has a member the right to appoint a proxy and how is a member made aware of that right? What notification must be given to the company that a proxy has been appointed? In what ways may a proxy be deprived of the power to vote?

14/15 Can there be a meeting of one?

14/16 Who has the right to inspect minutes?

14/17 At a general meeting requisitioned by the members, the directors refused to attend. The Articles state that general meetings will be chaired by a director. What can the members do?

15/1 Which shareholders are under a requirement to inform the company of their interests in the company's shares? (Type of share; type of company; proportion of class.) What information must be given and within what time?

15/2 How does the above requirement differ from the declaration concerning company securities to be made by a *director*? (See also Chapter 8.)

15/3 What is the company's duty to record interests declared as in question 15/1 above? What can a company do if it suspects that a declaration has not been made when the holder should have made it? (There can be more than one stage in identifying interests.)

15/4 When may the Department of Trade investigate the true ownership of a company? Must it appoint an inspector to do so? What can the Department do if its investigation is made impossible by non-cooperation on the part of certain parties?

16/1 Some shareholders suspect fraud on the part of the directors. How can they demand an investigation of the company's affairs? Must their request be granted? Can any other body demand an investigation?

16/2 Outline the scope of an inspector's powers in investigating a company's affairs. (Related companies; production of documents; examination of persons.) What reports *must* he make and in what circumstances may he make a special report?

16/3 What rights has the Department of Trade to demand production of a company's documents even though no order for investigation has been granted?

16/4 What powers rest with the Department of Trade if it suspects contravention of the law by a director in respect of his share dealings?

16/5 Under what conditions may the Department of Trade petition for a compulsory winding up?

17/1 Outline the Rule in *Foss v. Harbottle*.

17/2 If a company has an apparent right of action against an outside party and the directors (who hold the majority shares) refuse to take that action, what rights (if any) have the minority shareholders? What rights (if any) have they if the action would have been against the directors?

17/3 Does the Act prescribe the proportion of class members who must agree for a variation of rights to be effective?

17/4 The rights of the preference shareholders of *X* Ltd entitle them to payment of a fixed dividend in priority to all other shareholders. No dividend has been paid for the past two years because of losses. The directors now propose to raise a loan which should ultimately make the company profitable, although meanwhile the interest would absorb the trading profit. The preference shareholders maintain (and the directors agree) that without this commitment to pay interest the company would be able to pay the arrears of dividend in the current year. Can the preference shareholders claim that the company must first go through the procedure for variation of their rights?

17/5 The holders of 80 per cent of an issue of preference shares have agreed to a variation of their class rights in a company which has adopted Table A. The holder of the remaining 20 per cent disagrees. Has he the right to protest by action in law?

17/6 Assuming the member in question 17/5 above has the right to object, (*a*) what must the company do following the agreement to vary the rights, (*b*) what action can the member take, (*c*) what must he prove if he is to be successful and (*d*) if the member is unsuccessful, when will the variation be effective?

17/7 Could the minority shareholders complain of oppression in the following circumstances? (*a*) Because of lack of supervision by the majority-holding directors, an executive carried out a fraud which resulted in heavy losses by the company. (*b*) *A* and *B* held 60 per cent of the voting shares, the balance being held by *C*. *C* put more money into the company to save it from insolvency and in return received shares which made him a majority shareholder. In spite of the company's subsequent prosperity, no dividends were paid although *C* drew a very generous salary. (*c*) A private company altered its Articles so as to require any shareholder who is in business in competition with the company to transfer his shares to the other members. *Y* held 10 per cent of the shares and was a competitor. (*d*) *K* was a minority shareholder and a salaried official of the company. All the other shareholders were directors and they passed a resolution to discharge *K*.

17/8 *X*, *Y* and *Z* are the directors and sole shareholders of a company. *X* and *Y* hold 80 per cent of the shares between them. They refuse to consult with *Z* on any matters and make all the decisions without him. They constantly apply pressure on *Z* to sell his holding to them. *Z* suggests that he may have the right to force the company into liquidation on the ground of oppression, but he is advised that if this happened the realisation of the assets would result in loss of some of his share capital. Discuss *Z*'s position and the possible action of the Court.

18/1 What are the powers of the Court under the 1948 Act and the 1976 Act in respect of persons constantly in default in making returns to the Registrar?

18/2 What is contained in the Register of Disqualification Orders and who keeps it?

18/3 Recite the rule in S.9 of the *European Communities Act* concerning the effective date of certain documents filed with the Registrar. What are the documents to which the section refers?

18/4 Summarise the contents of the Annual Return. When must it be made? Who must sign it? What does the Act say about the list of members?

19/1 A company wishes to effect a compromise with its creditors. What special provisions apply if one of the creditors is a director? Who must vote in favour of the scheme to meet the requirements of the law and is there provision for dissenting? Must the Court give its approval if it is requested to do so?

19/2 Under what circumstances may a scheme under S.208 be applicable? What part may be played by the Court in implementing the scheme?

19/3 What are the essential differences between the operation of S.287 and of S.209 where shareholders of a transferor company receive shares in a transferee company? (Consider the different circumstances; who makes the decision.)

19/4 The shareholders approved a S.287 scheme, except *A* who held 5 per cent of the shares. Can *A* be bound by the scheme? Is he bound if he didn't go to the meeting and did nothing subsequently to avoid being bound?

19/5 A company has acquired 95 per cent of the voting shares in another company in a takeover scheme. *A* owns the remaining shares and wishes to retain them. What can he do if the transferee company (*a*) serves and (*b*) does not serve notice of its intention to acquire his shares?

19/6 If a bidding company obtains a Court Order compulsorily to acquire shares under S.209, how is the transfer of the shares and the consideration effected?

19/7 A scheme for company *A* to take over company *B* was agreed between the two boards, a condition of the scheme being that *X* will resign as a director of company *B*. In that event, *X* will receive a cash payment of £5,000 as compensation for loss of office and £10,000 for breach of his service contract. In respect of these proposed payments, what responsibilities devolve upon the directors of company *B* and *X*?

20/1 Outline the procedure for striking off a defunct company.

20/2 Under what circumstances and to what extent would a person be liable to contribute to the assets of a company upon winding up if he had ceased to be a member nine months before winding up?

20/3 What are preferential payments? At the time of winding up, a company is subject to a floating charge to secure a debt of £10,000. Preferential debts amount to £12,000. How would disbursement be made if £11,000 was available after paying the costs of winding up?

20/4 Give examples of 'fraudulent preference'.

20/5 What does it mean if a liquidator 'disclaims onerous property'? Give examples. What can be done by any person interested in disclaimed property?

20/6 Winding up does not terminate the legal entity of a company. How does this fact affect the position of a liquidator as an agent and as a trustee?

21/1 Why is it unlikely that a contributory would petition for a compulsory winding up?

21/2 Why may the Court reject a petition for winding up on the ground of the following circumstances? (*a*) If the Statutory Meeting had not been held. (*b*) Upon failure to commence business within a year of incorporation. (*c*) If the membership had fallen below the statutory minimum. (*d*) If a majority shareholder complains that the directors are deliberately 'running down' the business. (*e*) If a creditor maintains he cannot obtain repayment of £1,000 and the company disputes the 'debt'.

21/3 What alternative actions could the Court take instead of granting a winding-up order following a petition?

21/4 What are the effects of the presentation of a petition for winding up? A company was wound up voluntarily, but subsequently the Court accepted a petition by the Official Receiver for a winding-up order. What circumstances could have led to the petition and from when does the order date?

21/5 When does a winding-up order become operative? What consequences follow its making? (Liquidator; legal actions; employees.)

21/6 Who must submit the Statement of Affairs? What must it contain and within what time must it be submitted?

21/7 Following receipt of the Statement of Affairs, (*a*) what *must* the Official Receiver report to the Court, and (*b*) under what circumstances *may* he make a report?

21/8 How is the liquidator appointed in a winding up by the Court? (Include particulars of the meetings.)

21/9 During a winding up by the Court the liquidator becomes ill and intends to resign. What procedure must follow?

21/10 In a winding up by the Court, has the liquidator power to do any of the following? (*a*) To carry on the business. (*b*) To use the company's seal in order to contract on behalf of the company. (*c*) To defend an action by a creditor concerning a disputed debt. (*d*) To borrow on the security of the company's assets. (Is sanction required?)

21/11 What meetings of creditors and contributories *must* a liquidator in a compulsory winding up call and what meetings *may* he call? Must he carry out any instructions from a meeting of creditors?

21/12 Who nominates members of a Committee of Inspection in a compulsory winding up and who appoints them? Concerning meetings of the committee, what are the rules regarding (*a*) frequency, (*b*) calling, (*c*) quorum, and (*d*) voting?

21/13 The liquidator in a compulsory winding up is unable to obtain certain property of the company but has reason to believe it is in the hands of a particular person. What steps can he take to bring in the property?

22/1 Give examples of circumstances in which (*a*) an ordinary resolution, (*b*) an extraordinary resolution, and (*c*) a special resolution would be passed by a company to wind up voluntarily.

22/2 Summarise the contents of a statutory declaration of solvency. Who must make it? When must it be registered?

22/3 How is the liquidator appointed (*a*) in a members' voluntary winding up, and (*b*) in a creditors' voluntary winding up?

22/4 Six months after being appointed as liquidator in a members' voluntary winding up, *A* is of the opinion that the company is insolvent. What must he do? What consequences may follow for the directors?

22/5 How is the first meeting of creditors in a creditors' voluntary winding up called? What are the directors' responsibilities in respect of the meeting?

22/6 To what meetings, and when, must a liquidator make reports in (*a*) a members' voluntary winding up, and (*b*) a creditors' voluntary winding up?

22/7 In a creditors' voluntary winding up, the creditors appoint a committee of inspection, comprising five members. Can the contributories appoint a similar number?

THE EIGHTH SCHEDULE OF THE *COMPANIES ACT, 1948,* AS AMENDED BY THE *COMPANIES ACTS OF 1967 AND 1976*

ACCOUNTS

PRELIMINARY

1. Paragraphs 2 to 11 of this Schedule apply to the balance sheet and 12 to 14 to the profit and loss account, and are subject to the exceptions and modifications provided for by Part II of this Schedule in the case of a holding or subsidiary company and by Part III thereof in the case of companies of the classes there mentioned; and this Schedule has effect in addition to the provisions of sections one hundred and ninety-six and one hundred and ninety-seven of this Act.

PART I

GENERAL PROVISIONS AS TO BALANCE SHEET AND PROFIT AND LOSS ACCOUNT

Balance Sheet

2. The authorised share capital, issued share capital, liabilities and assets shall be summarised, with such particulars as are necessary to disclose the general nature of the assets and liabilities, and there shall be specified:

(*a*) any part of the issued capital that consists of redeemable preference shares, the earliest and latest dates on which the company has power to redeem those shares, whether those shares must be redeemed in any event or are liable to be redeemed at the option of the company and whether any (and, if so, what) premium is payable on redemption;

(*b*) so far as the information is not given in the profit and loss account, any share capital on which interest has been paid out of capital during the financial year, and the rate at which interest has been so paid;

(*c*) the amount of the share premium account;

(*d*) particulars of any redeemed debentures which the company has power to reissue.

3. There shall be stated under separate headings, so far as they are not written off:

(*a*) the preliminary expenses;

(*b*) any expenses incurred in connection with any issue of share capital or debentures;

(*c*) any sums paid by way of commission in respect of any shares or debentures;

(*d*) any sums allowed by way of discount in respect of any debentures; and

(*e*) the amount of the discount allowed on any issue of shares at a discount.

4.—(1) The reserves, provisions, liabilities and assets shall be classified under headings appropriate to the company's business:

Provided that:

(*a*) where the amount of any class is not material, it may be included under the same heading as some other class; and

(*b*) where any assets of one class are not separable from assets of another class, those assets may be included under the same heading.

(2) Fixed assets, current assets and assets that are neither fixed nor current shall be separately identified.

(3) The method or methods used to arrive at the amount of the fixed assets under each heading shall be stated.

5.—(1) The method of arriving at the amount of any fixed asset shall, subject to the next following sub-paragraph, be to take the difference between:

(*a*) its cost or, if it stands in the company's books at a valuation, the amount of the valuation; and

(*b*) the aggregate amount provided or written off since the date of acquisition or valuation, as the case may be, for depreciation or diminution in value;

and for the purposes of this paragraph the net amount at which any assets stand in the company's books at the commencement of this Act (after deduction of the amounts previously provided or written off for depreciation or diminution in value) shall, if the figures relating to the period before the commencement of this Act cannot be obtained without unreasonable expense or delay, be treated as if it were the amount of a valuation of those assets made at the commencement of this Act and, where any of those assets are sold, the said net amount less the amount of the sales shall be treated as if it were the amount of a valuation so made of the remaining assets.

(2) The foregoing sub-paragraph shall not apply:

(*a*) to assets for which the figures relating to the period beginning with the commencement of this Act cannot be obtained without unreasonable expense or delay; or

(*b*) to assets the replacement of which is provided for wholly or partly:
   (i) by making provision for renewals and charging the cost of replacement against the provision so made; or
   (ii) by charging the cost of replacement direct to revenue; or

(*c*) to any listed investments or to any unlisted, investments of which the value as estimated by the directors is shown either as the amount of the investments or by way of note; or

(*d*) to goodwill, patents or trade marks.

(3) For the assets under each heading whose amount is arrived at in accordance with sub-paragraph (1) of this paragraph, there shall be shown:

(*a*) the aggregate of the amounts referred to in paragraph (*a*) of that sub-paragraph; and

(*b*) the aggregate of the amounts referred to in paragraph (*b*) thereof.

(4) As respects the assets under each heading whose amount is not arrived at in accordance with the said sub-paragraph (1) because their replacement is provided for as mentioned in sub-paragraph (2) (*b*) of this paragraph, there shall be stated:

(*a*) the means by which their replacement is provided for; and

(*b*) the aggregate amount of the provision (if any) made for renewals and not used.

5A. In the case of unlisted investments consisting in equity share capital (as defined by subsection (5) of section 154 of this Act) of other bodies corporate (other than any whose values as estimated by the directors are separately shown, either individually or collectively or as to some individually and as to the rest collectively, and are so shown either as the amount thereof, or by way of note), the matters referred to in the following heads shall, if not otherwise shown, be stated by way of note or in a statement or report annexed:

(*a*) the aggregate amount of the company's income for the financial year that is ascribable to the investments;

(*b*) the amount of the company's share before taxation, and the amount of that share after taxation, of the net aggregate amount of the profits of the bodies in which the investments are held, being profits for the several periods to which accounts sent by them during the financial year to the company related, after deducting those bodies' losses for those periods (or vice versa);

(c) the amount of the company's share of the net aggregate amount of the undistributed profits accumulated by the bodies in which the investments are held since the time when the investments were acquired, after deducting the losses accumulated by them since that time (or vice versa);

(d) the manner in which any losses incurred by the said bodies have been dealt with in the company's accounts.

6. The aggregate amounts respectively of reserves and provisions (other than provisions for depreciation, renewals or diminution in value of assets) shall be stated under separate headings:

Provided that:

(a) this paragraph shall not require a separate statement of either of the said amounts which is not material; and

(b) the Board of Trade may direct that it shall not require a separate statement of the amount of provisions where they are satisfied that that is not required in the public interest and would prejudice the company, but subject to the condition that any heading stating an amount arrived at after taking into account a provision (other than as aforesaid) shall be so framed or marked as to indicate that fact.

7.—(1) There shall also be shown (unless it is shown in the profit and loss account or a statement or report annexed thereto, or the amount involved is not material):

(a) where the amount of the reserves or of the provisions (other than provisions for depreciation, renewals or diminution in value of assets) shows an increase as compared with the amount at the end of the immediately preceding financial year, the source from which the amount of the increase has been derived; and

(b) where

(i) the amount of the reserves shows a decrease as compared with the amount at the end of the immediately preceding financial year; or

(ii) the amount at the end of the immediately preceding financial year of the provisions (other than provisions for depreciation, renewals or diminution in value of assets) exceeded the aggregate of the sums since applied and amounts still retained for the purposes thereof;

the application of the amounts derived from the difference.

(2) Where the heading showing the reserves or any of the provisions aforesaid is divided into sub-headings, this paragraph shall apply to each of the separate amounts shown in the sub-headings instead of applying to the aggregate amount thereof.

7A. If an amount is set aside for the purpose of its being used to prevent undue fluctuations in charges for taxation, it shall be stated.

8.—(1) There shall be shown under separate headings:

(a) the aggregate amounts respectively of the company's listed investments and unlisted investments;

(b) if the amount of the goodwill and of any patents and trade marks or part of that amount is shown as a separate item in or is otherwise ascertainable from the books of the company, or from any contract for the sale or purchase of any property to be acquired by the company, or from any documents in the possession of the company relating to the stamp duty payable in respect of any such contract or the conveyance of any such property, the said amount so shown or ascertained so far as not written off or, as the case may be, the said amount so far as it is so shown or ascertainable and as so shown or ascertained, as the case may be;

(c) the aggregate amount of any outstanding loans made under the authority of provisos (b) and (c) of subsection (1) of section fifty-four of this Act;

(d) the aggregate amount of bank loans and overdrafts and the aggregate amount of loans made to the company which:

(i) are repayable otherwise than by instalments and fall due for repayment after the expiration of the period of five years beginning with the day next following the expiration of the financial year; or

(ii) are repayable by instalments any of which fall due for payment after the expiration of that period;

not being, in either case, bank loans or overdrafts;

(*e*) the aggregate amount (before deduction of income tax) which is recommended for distribution by way of dividend.

(2) Nothing in head (*b*) of the foregoing sub-paragraph shall be taken as requiring the amount of the goodwill, patents and trade marks to be stated otherwise than as a single item.

(3) The heading showing the amount of the listed investments shall be subdivided, where necessary, to distinguish the investments as respects which there has, and those as respects which there has not, been granted a listing on a recognised stock exchange.

(4) In relation to each loan falling within head (*d*) of sub-paragraph (1) of this paragraph (other than a bank loan or overdraft), there shall be stated by way of note (if not otherwise stated) the terms on which it is repayable and the rate at which interest is payable thereon:

Provided that if the number of loans is such that, in the opinion of the directors, compliance with the foregoing requirement would result in a statement of excessive length, it shall be sufficient to give a general indication of the terms on which the loans are repayable and the rates at which interest is payable thereon.

9. Where any liability of the company is secured otherwise than by operation of law on any assets of the company, the fact that that liability is so secured shall be stated, but it shall not be necessary to specify the assets on which the liability is secured.

10. Where any of the company's debentures are held by a nominee of or trustee for the company, the nominal amount of the debentures and the amount at which they are stated in the books of the company shall be stated.

11.—(1) The matters referred to in the following sub-paragraphs shall be stated by way of note, or in a statement or report annexed, if not otherwise shown.

(2) The number, description and amount of any shares in the company which any person has an option to subscribe for, together with the following particulars of the option, that is to say:

(*a*) the period during which it is exercisable;

(*b*) the price to be paid for shares subscribed for under it.

(3) The amount of any arrears of fixed cumulative dividends on the company's shares and the period for which the dividends or, if there is more than one class, each class of them are in arrear, the amount to be stated before deduction of income tax, except that, in the case of tax free dividends, the amount shall be shown free of tax and the fact that it is so shown shall also be stated.

(4) Particulars of any charge on the assets of the company to secure the liabilities of any other person, including, where practicable, the amount secured.

(5) The general nature of any other contingent liabilities not provided for and, where practicable, the aggregate amount or estimated amount of those liabilities, if it is material.

(6) Where practicable the aggregate amount or estimated amount, if it is material, of contracts for capital expenditure, so far as not provided for and, where practicable, the aggregate amount or estimated amount, if it is material, of capital expenditure authorised by the directors which has not been contracted for.

(6A) In the case of fixed assets under any heading whose amount is required to be arrived at in accordance with paragraph 5(1) of this Schedule (other than unlisted investments) and is so arrived at by reference to a valuation, the years (so far as they are known to the directors) in which the assets were severally valued and the several values, and, in the case of assets that have been valued during the financial year, the names of the persons who valued them or particulars of their qualifications for doing so and (whichever is stated) the bases of valuation used by them.

(6B) If there are included amongst fixed assets under any heading (other than investments) assets that have been acquired during the financial year, the aggregate amount of the assets acquired as determined for the purpose of making up the balance sheet, and if during that year any fixed assets included under a heading in the balance sheet made up with respect to the immediately preceding financial year (other than investments) have been disposed of or destroyed, the aggregate amount thereof as determined for the purpose of making up that balance sheet.

(6C) Of the amount of fixed assets consisting of land, how much is ascribable to land of freehold tenure and how much to land of leasehold tenure, and, of the latter, how much is ascribable to land held on long lease and how much to land held on short lease.

(7) If in the opinion of the directors any of the current assets have not a value on realization in the ordinary course of the company's business, at least equal to the amount at which they are stated, the fact that the directors are of that opinion.

(8) The aggregate market value of the company's listed investments where it differs from the amount of the investments as stated, and the stock exchange value of any investments of which the market value is shown (whether separately or not) and is taken as being higher than their stock exchange value.

(8A) If a sum set aside for the purpose of its being used to prevent undue fluctuations in charges for taxation has been used during the financial year for another purpose, the amount thereof and the fact that it has been so used.

(8B) If the amount carried forward for stock-in-trade or work in progress is material for the appreciation by its members of the company's state of affairs of its profit or loss for the financial year, the manner in which that amount has been computed.

(9) The basis on which foreign currencies have been converted into sterling, where the amount of the assets or liabilities affected is material.

(10) The basis on which the amount, if any, set aside for United Kingdom corporation tax is computed.

(11) Except in the case of the first balance sheet laid before the company after the commencement of this Act, the corresponding amounts at the end of the immediately preceding financial year for all items shown in the balance sheet.

Profit and Loss Account

12.—(1) There shall be shown:

(a) the amount charged to revenue by way of provision for depreciation, renewals or diminution in value of fixed assets;

(b) the amount of the interest on loans of the following kinds made to the company (whether on the security of debentures or not), namely, bank loans, overdrafts and loans which, not being bank loans or overdrafts,

  (i) are repayable otherwise than by instalments and fall due for repayment before the expiration of the period of five years beginning with the day next following the expiration of the financial year; or

  (ii) are repayable by instalments the last of which falls due for payment before the expiration of that period;

and the amount of the interest on loans of other kinds so made (whether on the security of debentures or not);

(c) the amount of the charge to revenue for United Kingdom corporation tax and, if that amount would have been greater but for relief from double taxation, the amount which it would have been but for such relief, the amount of the charge for United Kingdom income tax and the amount of the charge for taxation imposed outside the United Kingdom of profits, income and (so far as charged to revenue) capital gains;

(d) the amounts respectively provided for redemption of share capital and for redemption of loans;

(e) the amount, if material, set aside or proposed to be set aside to, or withdrawn from, reserves;

(f) subject to sub-paragraph (2) of this paragraph, the amount, if material, set aside to provisions other than provisions for depreciation, renewals or diminution in value of assets or, as the case may be, the amount, if material, withdrawn from such provisions and not applied for the purposes thereof;

(g) the amounts respectively of income from listed investments and income from unlisted investments;

(ga) if a substantial part of the company's revenue for the financial year consists in rents from land, the amount thereof (after deduction of ground-rents, rates and other out goings);

(gb) the amount, if material, charged to revenue in respect of sums payable in respect of the hire of plant and machinery;

(h) the aggregate amount (before deduction of income tax) of the dividends paid and proposed.

(2) The Board of Trade may direct that a company shall not be obliged to show an amount set aside to provisions in accordance with sub-paragraph (1)(f) of this paragraph, if the Board is satisfied that that is not required in the public interest and would prejudice the company, but subject to the condition that any heading stating an amount arrived at after taking into account the amount set aside as aforesaid shall be so framed or marked as to indicate that fact.

(3) If, in the case of any assets in whose case an amount is charged to revenue by way of provision for depreciation or diminution in value, an amount is also charged by way of provision for renewal thereof, the last-mentioned amount shall be shown separately.

(4) If the amount charged to revenue by way of provision for depreciation or diminution in value of any fixed assets (other than investments) has been determined otherwise than by reference to the amount of those assets as determined for the purpose of making up the balance sheet, that fact shall be stated.

12A. The amount of any charge arising in consequence of the occurrence of an event in a preceding financial year and of any credit so arising shall, if not included in a heading relating to other matters, be stated under a separate heading.

13. The amount of the remuneration of the auditors shall be shown under a separate heading, and for the purposes of this paragraph, any sums paid by the company in respect of the auditors' expenses shall be deemed to be included in the expression 'remuneration'.

13A.—(1) The matters referred to in sub-paragraphs (2) to (4) below shall be stated by way of note; if not otherwise shown.

(2) The turnover for the financial year, except in so far as it is attributable to the business of banking or discounting or to business of such other class as may be prescribed for the purposes of this sub-paragraph.

(3) If some or all of the turnover is omitted by reason of its being attributable as aforesaid, the fact that it is so omitted.

(4) The method by which turnover stated is arrived at.

(5) A company shall not be subject to the requirements of this paragraph if it is neither a holding company nor a subsidiary of another body corporate and the turnover which, apart from this sub-paragraph, would be required to be stated does not exceed £250,0000 (as amended by S.I. 1971 No. 2044).

14.—(1) The matters referred to in the following sub-paragraphs shall be stated by way of note, if not otherwise shown.

(2) If depreciation or replacement of fixed assets is provided for by some method other than a depreciation charge or provision for renewals, or is not provided for, the method by which it is provided for or the fact that it is not provided for, as the case may be.

(3) The basis on which the charge for United Kingdom corporation tax and United Kingdom income tax is computed.

(3 A) Any special circumstances which affect liability in respect of taxation of profits income or capital gains for the financial year or liability in respect of taxation of profits, income or capital gains for succeeding financial years.

(5) Except in the case of the first profit and loss account laid before the company after the commencement of this Act the corresponding amounts for the immediately preceding financial year for all items shown in the profit and loss account.

(6) Any material respects in which any items shown in the profit and loss account are affected:

(*a*) by transactions of a sort not usually undertaken by the company or otherwise by circumstances of an exceptional or non-recurrent nature; or

(*b*) by any change in the basis of accounting.

PART II

SPECIAL PROVISIONS WHERE THE COMPANY IS A HOLDING OR SUBSIDIARY COMPANY

Modifications of and Additions to Requirements as to
Company's own Accounts

15.—(1) This paragraph shall apply where the company is a holding company, whether or not it is itself a subsidiary of another body corporate.

(2) The aggregate amount of assets consisting of shares in, or amounts owing (whether on account of a loan or otherwise) from, the company's subsidiaries, distinguishing shares from indebtedness, shall be set out in the balance sheet separately from all the other assets of the company, and the aggregate amount of indebtedness (whether on account of a loan or otherwise) to the company's subsidiaries shall be so set out separately from all its other liabilities and:

(*a*) the references in Part I of this Schedule to the company's investments (except those in paragraphs 11 (6 B) and 12(4)) shall not include investments in its subsidiaries required by this paragraph to be separately set out; and

(*b*) paragraph 5, sub-paragraph (1)(*a*) of paragraph 12, and sub-paragraph (2) of paragraph 14 of this Schedule shall not apply in relation to fixed assets consisting of interests in the company's subsidiaries.

(3) There shall be shown by way of note on the balance sheet or in a statement or report annexed thereto the number, description and amount of the shares in and debentures of the company held by its subsidiaries or their nominees, but excluding any of those shares or debentures in the case of which the subsidiary is concerned as personal representative or in the case of which it is concerned as trustee and neither the company nor any subsidiary thereof is beneficially interested under the trust,

otherwise than by way of security only for the purposes of a transaction entered into by it in the ordinary course of a business which includes the lending of money.

(4) Where group accounts are not submitted, there shall be annexed to the balance sheet a statement showing:

(*a*) the reasons why subsidiaries are not dealt with in group accounts;

(*b*) the net aggregate amount, so far as it concerns members of the holding company and is not dealt with in the company's accounts, of the subsidiaries' profits after deducting the subsidiaries' losses (or vice versa):

    (i) for the respective financial years of the subsidiaries ending with or during the financial year of the company; and

    (ii) for their previous financial years since they respectively became the holding company's subsidiary;

(*c*) the net aggregate amount of the subsidiaries' profits after deducting the subsidiaries' losses (or vice versa):

    (i) for the respective financial years of the subsidiaries ending with or during the financial year of the company; and

    (ii) for their other financial years since they respectively became the holding company's accounts;

so far as those profits are dealt with, or provision is made for those losses, in the company's accounts;

(*d*) any qualifications contained in the report of the auditors of the subsidiaries on their accounts for their respective financial years ending as aforesaid, and any note or saving contained in those accounts to call attention to a' matter which, apart from the note or saving, would properly have been referred to in such a qualification, in so far as the matter which is the subject of the qualification or note is not covered by the company's own accounts and is material from the point of view of its members;

or, in so far as the information required by this sub-paragraph is not obtainable, a statement that it is not obtainable:

Provided that the Board of Trade may, on the application or with the consent of the company's directors, direct that in relation to any subsidiary this sub-paragraph shall not apply or shall apply only to such extent as may be provided by the direction.

(5) Paragraphs (*b*) and (*c*) of the last foregoing sub-paragraph shall apply only to profits and losses of a subsidiary which may properly be treated in the holding company's accounts as revenue profits or losses, and the profits or losses attributable to any shares in a subsidiary for the time being held by the holding company or any other of its subsidiaries shall not (for that or any other purpose) be treated as aforesaid so far as they are profits or losses for the period before the date on or as from which the shares were acquired by the company or any of its subsidiaries, except that they may in a proper case be so treated where:

(*a*) the company is itself the subsidiary of another body corporate; and

(*b*) the shares were acquired from that body corporate or a subsidiary of it;

and for the purpose of determining whether any profits or losses are to be treated as profits or losses for the said period the profit or loss for any financial year of the subsidiary may, if it is not practicable to apportion it with reasonable accuracy by reference to the facts, be treated as accruing from day to day during that year and be apportioned accordingly.

(6) Where group accounts are not submitted, there shall be annexed to the balance sheet a statement showing in relation to the subsidiaries (if any) whose financial years did not end with that of the company:

(*a*) the reasons why the company's directors consider that the subsidiaries' financial years should not end with that of the company; and

(*b*) the dates on which the subsidiaries' financial years ending last before that of the company respectively ended or the earliest and latest of those dates.

16.—(1) The balance sheet of a company which is a subsidiary of another body corporate, whether or not it is itself a holding company, shall show the aggregate amount of its indebtedness to all bodies corporate of which it is a subsidiary or a fellow subsidiary and the aggregate amount of indebtedness of all such bodies corporate to it, distinguishing in each case between indebtedness in respect of debentures and otherwise, and the aggregate amount of assets consisting of shares in fellow subsidiaries.

(2) For the purposes of this paragraph a company shall be deemed to be a fellow subsidiary of another body corporate if both are subsidiaries of the same body corporate but neither is the other's.

Consolidated Accounts of Holding Company and Subsidiaries

17. Subject to the following paragraphs of this Part of this Schedule, the consolidated balance sheet and profit and loss account shall combine the information contained in the separate balance sheets and profit and loss accounts of the holding company and of the subsidiaries dealt with by the consolidated accounts, but with such adjustments (if any) as the directors of the holding company think necessary.

18. Subject as aforesaid and to Part III of this Schedule, the consolidated accounts shall, in giving the said information, comply so far as practicable, with the requirements of this Act and the *Companies Act, 1967*, as if they were the accounts of an actual company.

19. Sections one hundred and ninety-six and one hundred and ninety-seven of this Act and sections four and six to eight of the *Companies Act, 1967*, shall not, by virtue of the two last foregoing paragraphs, apply for the purpose of the consolidated accounts.

20. Paragraph 7 of this Schedule shall not apply for the purpose of any consolidated accounts laid before a company with the first balance sheet so laid after the commencement of this Act.

21. In relation to any subsidiaries of the holding company not dealt with by the consolidated accounts:
(a) sub-paragraphs (2) and (3) of paragraph 15 of this Schedule shall apply for the purpose of those accounts as if those accounts were the accounts of an actual company of which they were subsidiaries; and
(b) there shall be annexed the like statement as is required by sub-paragraph (4) of that paragraph where there are no group accounts, but as if references therein to the holding company's accounts were references to the consolidated accounts.

22. In relation to any subsidiaries (whether or not dealt with by the consolidated accounts), whose financial years did not end with that of the company, there shall be annexed the like statement as is required by sub-paragraph (6) of paragraph 15 of this Schedule where there are no group accounts.

PART III

EXCEPTIONS FOR SPECIAL CLASSES OF COMPANY

23.—(1) A banking or discount company shall not be subject to the requirements of Part I of this Schedule other than:
(a) as respects its balance sheet, those of paragraphs 2 and 3, paragraph 4 (so far as it relates to assets), paragraph 8 (except sub-paragraphs (1)(d) and (4)), paragraphs 9 and 10 and paragraph 11 (except sub-paragraphs (6A), (6B), (6C), (8) and (8A)); and
(b) as respects its profit and loss account, those of sub-paragraph (1) (ga) and (h) of paragraph 12, paragraphs 12A and 13 and sub-paragraphs (1) and (5) of paragraph 14;

but, where in its balance sheet reserves or provisions (other than provisions for depreciation, renewals or diminution in value of assets) are not stated separately, any heading stating an amount arrived at after taking into account a reserve or such a provision shall be so framed or marked as to indicate that fact, and its profit and loss account shall indicate by appropriate words the manner in which the amount stated for the company's profit or loss has been arrived at.

(2) The accounts of a banking or discount company shall not be deemed, by reason only of the fact that they do not comply with any requirements of the said Part I from which the company is exempt by virtue of this paragraph, not to give the true and fair view required by this Act.

(3) In this paragraph the expression 'banking or discount company' means any company which satisfies the Board of Trade that it ought to be treated for the purposes of this Schedule as a banking company or as a discount company.

24.—(1) An insurance company to which the Insurance Companies Act, 1958, applies shall not be subject to the following requirements of Part I of this Schedule, that is to say:

(*a*) as respects its balance sheet, those of paragraphs 4 to 7 (both inclusive), sub-paragraphs (1)(*a*) and (3) of paragraph 8 and sub-paragraphs (4), (5) and (6A) to (8)(both inclusive) of paragraph 11;

(*b*) as respects its profit and loss account, those of paragraph 12 (except sub-paragraph (1)(*b*), (*c*), (*d*) and (*h*)) and paragraph 14(2);

but, where in its balance sheet reserves or provisions (other than provisions for depreciation, renewals or diminution in value of assets) are not stated separately, any heading stating an amount arrived at after taking into account a reserve or such a provision shall be so framed or marked as to indicate that fact, and its profit and loss account shall indicate by appropriate words the manner in which the amount stated for the company's profit or loss has been arrived at:

Provided that the Board of Trade may direct that any such insurance company whose business includes to a substantial extent business other than insurance business shall comply with all the requirements of the said Part I or such of them as may be specified in the direction and shall comply therewith as respects either the whole of its business or such part thereof as may be so specified.

(2) Where an insurance company is entitled to the benefit of this paragraph, then any wholly owned subsidiary thereof shall also be so entitled if its business consists only of business which is complementary to insurance business of the classes carried on by the insurance company.

(2A) The accounts of a company shall not be deemed, by reason only of the fact that they do not comply with any requirement of Part I of this Schedule from which the company is exempt by virtue of this paragraph, not to give the true and fair view required by this Act.

(3) For the purposes of this paragraph a company shall be deemed to be the wholly owned subsidiary of an insurance company if it has no members except the insurance company and the insurance company's wholly owned subsidiaries and its or their nominees.

25.—(1) A shipping company shall not be subject to the following requirements of Part I of this Schedule, that is to say:

(*a*) as respects its balance sheet, those of paragraph 4 (except so far as it relates to assets), paragraphs 5, 6 and 7 and sub-paragraphs (6A) and (6B) of paragraph 11;

(*b*) as respects its profit and loss account, those of sub-paragraph (1)(*a*), (*e*) and (*f*) and sub-paragraphs (3) and (4) of paragraph 12 and paragraph 13A.

(2) The accounts of a company shall not be deemed, by reason only of the fact that they do not comply with any requirements of Part I of this Schedule from which the

company is exempt by virtue of this paragraph, not to give the true and fair view required by this Act.

(3) In this paragraph the expression 'shipping company' means a company which, or a subsidiary of which, owns ships or includes amongst its activities the management or operation of ships, being a company which satisfies the Board of Trade that, in the national interest, it ought to be treated for the purposes of this paragraph as a shipping company.

26. Where a company entitled to the benefit of any provision contained in this part of this Schedule is a holding company, the reference in Part II of this Schedule to consolidated accounts complying with the requirements of this Act shall, in relation to consolidated accounts of that company, be construed as referring to those requirements in so far only as they apply to the separate accounts of that company.

PART IV
INTERPRETATION OF SCHEDULE

27.—(1) For the purposes of this Schedule, unless the context otherwise requires:
(a) the expression 'provision' shall, subject to sub-paragraph (2) of this paragraph, mean any amount written off or retained by way of providing for depreciation, renewals or diminution in value of assets or retained by way of providing for any known liability of which the amount cannot be determined with substantial accuracy;
(b) the expression 'reserve' shall not, subject as aforesaid, include any amount written off or retained by way of providing for depreciation, renewals or diminution in value of assets or retained by way of providing for any known liability or any sum set aside for the purpose of its being used to prevent undue fluctuations in charges for taxation;
and in this paragraph the expression 'liability' shall include all liabilities in respect of expenditure contracted for and all disputed or contingent liabilities.

(2) Where:
(a) any amount written off or retained by way of providing for depreciation, renewals or diminution in value of assets, not being an amount written off in relation to fixed assets before the commencement of this Act; or
(b) any amount retained by way of providing for any known liability;
is in excess of that which in the opinion of the directors is reasonably necessary for the purpose, the excess shall be treated for the purposes of this Schedule as a reserve and not as a provision.

28. For the purposes aforesaid, the expression 'listed investment' means an investment as respects which there has been granted a listing on a recognised stock exchange, or on any stock exchange of repute outside Great Britain, and the expression 'unlisted investment' shall be construed accordingly.

29. For the purposes aforesaid, the expression 'long lease' means a lease in the case of which the portion of the term for which it was granted remaining unexpired at the end of the financial year is not less than fifty years, the expression 'short lease' means a lease which is not a long lease and the expression 'lease' includes an agreement for a lease.

30. For the purposes aforesaid, a loan shall be deemed to fall due for payment on the earliest date on which the lender could require repayment or, as the case may be, payment if he exercised all options and rights available to him.

31. In the application of this Schedule to Scotland, 'land of freehold tenure' means land in respect of which the company is the proprietor of the *dominium utile* or, in the case of land not held on feudal tenure, is the owner; 'land of leasehold tenure' means land of which the company is the tenant under a lease; and the reference to ground-rents, rates and other outgoings includes a reference to feu-duty and ground annual.

Appendix 3

TABLE OF CASES

Appendix 4

TABLE OF STATUTES

249

Index